ROMAN BRITAIN

In Memoriam
N.M.W. and J.M.C.

ROMAN BRITAIN

JOHN WACHER

WRENS PARK

A Sutton Publishing Book

First published in 1978 by J.M. Dent & Sons, Ltd.
First published in this revised edition in the United Kingdom in 1998 by
Sutton Publishing Limited · Phoenix Mill
Thrupp · Stroud · Gloucestershire · GL5 2BU

This edition published in 2000 by Wrens Park Publishing, an imprint of
W.J. Williams & Son Ltd

British Library Cataloguing in Publication Data
A catalogue record for this book is available from the British Library

ISBN 0-905-778-529

Typeset in 11/14 pt Garamond.
Typesetting and origination by
Sutton Publishing Limited.
Printed in Great Britain by
J.H. Haynes & Co. Ltd, Sparkford.

Contents

List of Illustrations

Preface to the First Edition

This book is an attempt to collect together the great mass of evidence, accumulated down to the end of 1976, relating to the Roman period of British history and to present it in a form which will be of use to the widest possible range of readers. The material has been gathered in an essentially non-historical way, although a broad outline of chronological development has been followed within each topic selected for discussion. Emphasis has been placed on the activities of the population; consequently the core of the book deals with their work and leisure.

I am most grateful to all those people and institutions, mentioned individually below, for their kindness in making available the photographs and other material used for the illustrations. Tony McCormick spent many laborious hours producing the excellent line-drawings, sometimes from indifferent or difficult sources, while Cheryl McCormick lavished great care on the production of an error-free typescript. To both I must record my indebtedness. Marius Cooke was responsible for producing some first-rate photographs and prints. Mark Hassall devoted much time to reading through the whole typescript, as the result of which it has been, in places, greatly improved: my grateful thanks to him. But, as is usual, I must reserve to myself any errors of omission or commission, especially where, owing to my own stubbornness, I have retained arguments with which he disagreed.

John Wacher
Leicester
March 1977

Preface to the Second Edition

Twenty years have elapsed since the first edition was published. In that time many new discoveries have been made in Roman Britain. But since the first edition did not claim to be an exhaustive study of the subject, and moreover dealt more with the factual than the theoretical, most of what was written then is still valid today. However, the text and illustrations have been brought up-to-date where necessary and new expanded captions have been provided for some of the illustrations; otherwise much remains the same. The only major alteration is to the section on Further Reading which has been completely rewritten, not only to introduce new titles, but also to make it more 'reader-friendly'.

I would like to repeat my grateful thanks to all those who helped create the first edition and to add those who have helped to produce the second, notably Adam Sharpe and Jacqueline Nowakowski, who prepared some twenty-five new drawings, and Barbara Kane, who typed the revisions and new captions.

Finally, it is appropriate to record that J.M. Dent & Sons Ltd., the original publishers, were absorbed by Weidenfeld and Nicolson, who declined to undertake a revised edition. I am exceedingly grateful, therefore, to Sutton Publishing for doing so; they have also immeasurably improved the book's appearance.

John Wacher
Hayle
January 1997

Fig. 1. The Roman Empire in the early second century AD (*after A.L.F. Rivet*)

CHAPTER 1

Britain before the Romans

I n 55 BC the first formal intervention by Rome in British affairs took place with the expedition of Julius Caesar. Contacts by traders from Gaul and the Mediterranean had, however, been made before, but it is to Caesar that we owe the first moderately full description of Britain and the Britons. Nevertheless, we must remember that his personal experience was restricted to the south-east, where he described Kent as a thickly populated area and the people as the most civilized, differing little from the Gauls. His information on the interior is more hazy and often at odds with the modern archaeological record.

In Caesar's day much of Britain was culturally in the Iron Age, although a wide and complex variety of developments could then have been detected, owing to the differing backgrounds of many of the original Iron Age migrants and their interaction with the indigenous inhabitants.

Undoubtedly, as Caesar infers, the most advanced cultures, both socially and technologically, lay in the south-east, where the more recent migrants from Gaul had landed and then spread inland to assert their presence in Kent, Surrey, East Anglia, Hertfordshire and Berkshire. In some cases these migrants had been fleeing from Caesar's activities in Gaul. In the main, however, they had crossed to Britain in a succession of waves from about 150 BC onwards, coming mainly from the northern part of Gaul. They are collectively known as the Belgae and represent the third, and last, principal Iron Age cultural group to reach Britain before the final Roman conquest in AD 43. But when the Belgic migrants arrived in Britain they found a country which already possessed a long tradition of earlier Iron Age cultures. Arriving first about the seventh century BC two cultural mainstreams can be detected thereafter, referred to usually as Hallstatt and La Tène.

Fig. 2. Aerial photograph of a prehistoric settlement near Gussage All Saints (Dorset) (*copyright: Committee for Aerial Photography, University of Cambridge*).

1

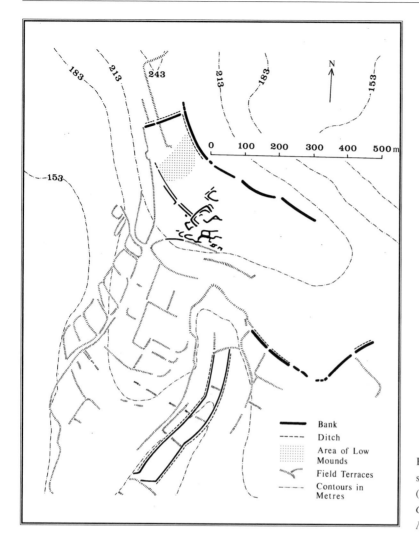

Fig. 3. Pre-Roman village settlement at Cheselbourne (Dorset) (*after the Royal Commission for Historical Monuments for England*).

Hallstatt migrations seem mainly to have affected south and east Britain. It is likely that small parties of migrants, on making a land-fall on the coast, would carry on until they reached a part not yet settled by their fellows, or, similarly, make their way up suitable rivers. In this way they reached Yorkshire in the north-east and the Severn valley in the west, while more isolated parties ventured further up the west coast to Wales and beyond, ultimately reaching Scotland. In time their numbers became great enough to impress their distinctive cultural achievements on the indigenous Bronze Age people of Britain, with whom they ultimately merged. The cultural way of life of these people is named after its principal European site, where excavations first revealed its nature: Hallstatt, in Austria.

To begin with, apart from their use of iron and their ability to fashion better quality pottery, these new immigrants to Britain are scarcely distinguishable from the late Bronze Age inhabitants. Agriculture was their mainstay, being based on individual farms and small communities. However, it is now recognized that the later Bronze Age saw the development of hill fortifications, so that, while most farms and villages (figs 2–4) were still left undefended or at best surrounded by a stockade in the Iron Age, some fortified sites developed along already established lines, and parallel with similar developments on the other side of the Channel. In time, hillforts with a single rampart and ditch became much more frequent, although regional distinctions can be made. In Wessex and areas immediately north and west, hillforts of this type are comparatively common, but in the eastern parts of the country they become rarer and far fewer examples are known.

As yet, no satisfactory explanation of the relationships between hillfort and hillfort, hillfort and village, hillfort and farm, and village and farm, has been put forward, although many views have been canvassed, and we are only now beginning to realize the full complexities of the problems involved. The construction of hillforts must represent a growing sense of insecurity and the start of corporate actions on the part of communities. In turn it is probable that local chieftains emerged to control them, and we can detect the early beginnings of an organized society.

An acceleration in the rate of hillfort construction in the third and fourth centuries BC can probably also be partly ascribed to increasing pressure of migrations from a new source. These groups with their new and different life-styles, are usually referred to as La Tène. One of the most spectacular developments of this culture was the emergence of a highly distinctive, ornamental metalwork, much of it carried out on articles of war, such as sword-scabbards, shields, helmets and horse-harness. This could well point to the existence among the immigrants of an aristocratic warrior class who could commission these weapons from specialist craftsmen. Judging from the appearance in Britain of elaborate horse-harnesses, we may conclude that continental chariot warfare had also been introduced, which may account for the apparent ascendancy gained by these people over the indigenous population. Yet, to start with, the areas they first occupied tended not to be those settled earlier by Hallstatt migrants. But as time went on the La Tène peoples spread, in many places amalgamating their culture with that of Hallstatt to produce a distinctively British product.

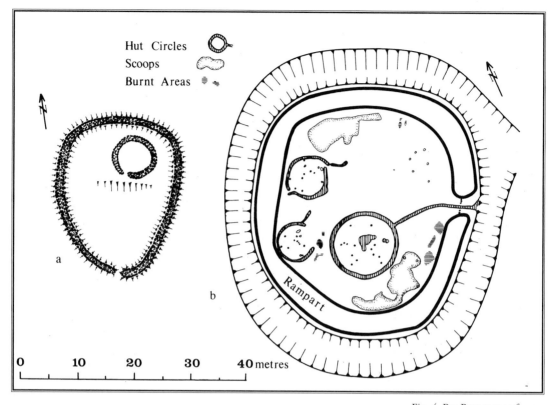

Hut Circles
Scoops
Burnt Areas

a

b

Rampart

0   10   20   30   40 metres

Fig. 4. Pre-Roman type farms at: a) Ells Knowe (Northumb.) (*after G. Jobey*); b) Draughton, (Northants) (*after W.F. Grimes*).

Another development of this period can be seen in the construction of multiple defences for many existing, and some new, hillforts, especially in the west and south-west. There is, however, a tendency for the overall number of hillforts in commission to decline, whereas the size and strength of the remainder are often increased, perhaps pointing to a concentration of local power in fewer hands.

Yet, in many spheres, the way of life of the majority of the inhabitants of Britain can have changed but little in the five hundred or so years of Iron Age migrations that we have been dealing with. It would have depended entirely on agriculture, with individual farms largely based on family units or nucleated communities of varying size sometimes surrounded, at first, by a stockade, by a stone wall, or by a simple bank and ditch (fig. 4). If situated on a suitable hill-top, these rudimentary defences often developed into full hillfort fortifications. The houses themselves were usually circular and constructed of wood with mud-covered walls; the roofs were most likely of thatch or turf (fig. 5). In areas where plentiful stone

Fig. 5. Reconstructed Iron Age
round-house (*P.J. Reynolds,
Butser Ancient Farm Project*).

abounded, such as the south-west, Wales or the northern hill-
country, rough, drystone walls replaced some of the timber and mud.
From time to time, square or rectangular timber-framed buildings
have been identified during excavations, but it is not certain if these
are dwelling houses or granaries for the storage of wheat, barley, rye
or even beans – the main cereal and pulse crops. In some areas,
notably Wessex, grain seems also to have been stored in pits dug in
the ground and probably originally lined with basketwork or skins.
But this method could only be used after the grain had been dried or
roasted over a low fire, to prevent germination and rotting. Recent
experiments in storing grain in this way show that it releases certain
gases which do much to prevent the growth of fungi and insects. It is
probable that, on some occasion, water seeped into such a storage pit
which fortuitously contained certain yeasts and enzymes, so forming
an amber-coloured, slightly frothy alcoholic liquid: ale has been
brewed in Britain ever since. It was apparently the favourite beverage
of the people of north-western Europe.

The fields in which these crops were grown were often squarish, or broad rectangular plots, ranging in size from 0.1 to 0.5 ha., although far more irregular units have been observed in many river valleys (fig. 3). The boundaries were usually marked by a ditch or low bank; the latter, on hillside sites, was emphasized by ploughing. It is possible that hedges and fences were also used between fields, since grazing stock must have been kept from growing crops. Since the first hedge was undoubtedly the result of a farmer using green wood for a fence and so inadvertently striking cuttings, hedges would almost certainly have been a feature of the Iron Age cultivated landscape.

Cows and sheep were the principal domestic animals, although pigs were probably fattened in woods and forests and goats provided not only meat and milk but also a long-staple wool. As in most primitive societies where winter fodder is in short supply, an autumn slaughter of surplus stock would have taken place, leaving only the breeding animals to be fed, and incidentally providing a supply of smoked, dried or salted meat for winter use. Salt was extracted by the evaporation of sea-water on many coastal sites, such as those identified around the Kent and Essex marshes and the Fens. It would have been valuable not only for preserving meat, but also in the curing of skins to make leather.

It is also probable that greater emphasis was placed on cattle and sheep rearing in the hill-country of the north and west, although the existence of certain types of enclosures and linear ridge dykes, in some southern parts, encourages belief in the existence of large-scale grazing areas. Furthermore, these are often found to show little or no trace of cultivation.

As already briefly noted above, a series of new migrations to eastern Britain began about 150 BC; they are normally referred to as late La Tène or the Belgae. Like their earlier La Tène ancestors, they came from much the same areas of northern Gaul between the Seine, the Marne and the Rhine, and they were to affect Britain more radically than any of their predecessors. Culturally and politically they were more advanced, making use of a primitive currency based primarily on gold and silver, later on copper, coins, and possessing a definable tribal structure (fig. 6). However, it must be remembered that their apparent importance in the development of Britain is perhaps mainly due to the fact that we know more about them, either from contemporary classical sources, or from characteristics surviving into the better documented Roman period. If we did not possess such additional information, it is probable that we would compare earlier

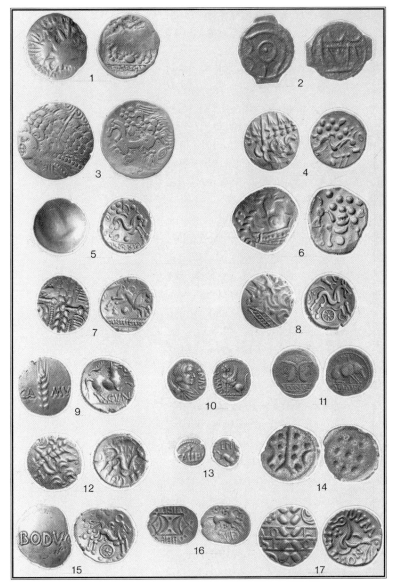

Fig. 6. Iron Age Coins

1. *Gallo-Belgic gold stater, Allen Class B, c. 75 BC.* These are perhaps attributable to the Veliocasses (Dieppe area); their British distribution centres on or near London.

2. *British 'potin' coin, c. 70 BC.* Widely scattered in south-east England from Dorset to Kent, these are best known from concentrations of hoards in the lower Thames valley. Their continental prototypes, appear to be substantially pre-Caesarian.

3. *Gallo-Belgic gold stater, Allen Class A, c. 70 BC.* Attributed to the Ambiani (Amiens area), and widely imported into southern and eastern England. A few worn examples survived to be hoarded with coins of the period of Caesar's Gallic wars. It is generally found within the angle formed by the North Downs and Chilterns.

4. *Gallo-Belgic gold stater, Allen Class C, c. 60 BC.* A coinage of the Ambiani, it is mostly found in Kent though there is a thin scatter to the north of the Thames.

5. *Gallo-Belgic gold stater, Allen Class E, c. 58 BC.* The coinage of the Ambiani during Caesar's Gallic wars. They occur along the line of the Chilterns and North Downs and are numerous along the Sussex coast. Beyond this main concentration is a general scatter extending to Humber and Severn. Only the earlier stages of this coinage are regularly found in Britain.

6. *British gold stater, Allen Class A, c. 60 BC.* The type is found mainly in Surrey, Sussex, Hampshire and east Dorset, with a scatter along and beyond the Thames. Their distribution is complementary to that of Gallo-Belgic, Class C (no. 4) with which they should be broadly contemporary.

7. *British gold stater, Allen Class L, c. 40 BC.* This coinage is largely found north of the Thames, and its distribution seems to centre on the northern end of the Chilterns. There are several varieties, and its issue may have occurred sporadically over many years. It is attributed to the Catuvellauni, and is ancestral to the coinages of Tasciovanus and Cunobelinus.

8. *British gold stater, Allen Class Q, c. 45 BC.* This coinage of the Atrebates is a slightly older contemporary of British L. It is essentially found in Berkshire, Hampshire and West Surrey, though there are numerous others, especially along the Sussex coast.

9. *Gold stater of Cunobelinus, c. AD 25.* Cunobelinus, 'King of the Britons', came to rule most of south-east England from his capital at Camulodunum. He died not long before Claudius' invasion. His coinage shows strongly rationalizing and classicizing tendencies.

10. *Silver coin of Cunobelinus, c. AD 25.*

11. *Bronze coin of Cunobelinus, c. AD 25.* Silver and bronze coins, increasingly frequent in the last half-century of independence, testify to the incipient growth of a monetary economy. Bronze coins in particular, seem to be concentrated on the sites of oppida and temples.

12. *Gold stater of Tincommius, c. 10 BC.* Tincommius, scion of a famous family, ruled the Atrebates. His coins showed a transition from the traditional style to one based on classical concepts.

13. *Gold quarter-stater of Eppillus, c. AD 10.* The brother of Tincommius ruled at Calleva (Silchester). Quarter-staters were particularly characteristic of the Atrebatic kingdom.

14. *Cast bronze stater of the Durotriges, first century AD.* These degenerate descendants of British Class A staters (no. 6) were cast in large numbers towards the end of British independence. They persisted in local currency well into the second century AD.

15. *Gold stater of Bodvoc, c. AD 40.* The gold coins of the Dobunni derived their typology from those of their neighbours, the Atrebates.

16. *Silver coin of Antedius, c. AD 20.* The Iceni struck few gold coins, but a very large series of silver, which is often found hoarded with Roman denarii down to the reign of Nero.

17. *Gold stater of Dumnocoveros, first century AD.* Coins of the Corieltavi are thinly distributed over a large area between south Yorkshire and northern Northamptonshire. They have sometimes been found with Roman coins, and their typology seems to be related to the well-known coinage of Cunobelinus (no. 9).

settlements more favourably with them. Yet, as the main agents in the shaping of Britain immediately before the Roman conquest, they are worthy of greater consideration in the present context.

In the early stages of their migration, the pattern of coastal landings and subsequent dispersals inland is obtained almost entirely from an analysis of the coin distributions. The distributions reflect a complex sequence of movements which primarily affected south-east Britain. The coins themselves, at first imported, later gave rise to British issues, indicating the presence of centralized authorities capable of controlling tribal areas and running the necessary mints, of which a number of examples have been identified, such as those at Verulamium, Colchester and Silchester. It is also probably right to equate these mints with the existence of tribal capitals, and in time several sites appear which are, unlike hillforts, usually situated in plains and valleys and are defended both by natural features and by one, or often more, great dykes enclosing large areas of land (fig. 7). These fortified centres were being modified and extended down to the Roman invasion, a factor which tends to show the insularity of Britain: such dykes, consisting of massive banks and ditches, were probably intended as defences in a mobile form of warfare employing chariots. In 1940, southern Britain was again criss-crossed by similar dykes to counter tanks and motorized infantry carriers. Yet in the first century BC chariot warfare had largely become obsolete in continental Europe, although it appears to have survived in Britain. Indeed, Caesar seems to have been somewhat surprised when he was opposed by chariots on his first landing.

The increase in the number of Belgic settlers in Britain produced more changes than a developing political maturity. Technically they were far more advanced than the indigenous Iron Age people, being able to produce good quality wheel-turned pottery and a much wider range of iron tools. Their leaders also pursued patronage of British bronzesmiths and high quality decorative metalwork continued to be produced. In consequence, farming benefited by the introduction of tools and equipment which enabled more heavily forested land to be cleared and cultivated. Indeed, the growing agricultural prosperity of south-eastern Britain is perhaps best represented by the devices later adopted and imprinted on their coins by two rival tribes: a vine-leaf and an ear of wheat (or barley) (fig. 6.9), each a clear indication of the source of tribal wealth.

The fraternal groups which now existed on both sides of the English Channel also led to greatly increased trade between Britain and Gaul. Wine was imported in large amphoras, together with

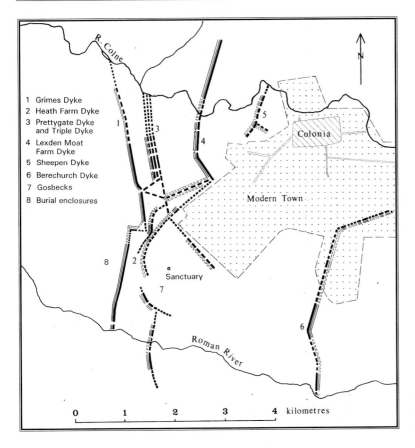

1 Grimes Dyke
2 Heath Farm Dyke
3 Prettygate Dyke
  and Triple Dyke
4 Lexden Moat
  Farm Dyke
5 Sheepen Dyke
6 Berechurch Dyke
7 Gosbecks
8 Burial enclosures

Fig. 7. The Iron Age oppidum at Camulodunum, Colchester (*after P. Crummy*).

glassware, pottery and metalwork, being paid for no doubt by British agricultural produce. This trade reached its peak, as might be expected, in the century or so that elapsed between Caesar's expeditions and the Claudian invasion, and it is to this period that the oft-quoted passage of the contemporary geographer, Strabo, refers; in it, he gives a detailed list of British imports and exports. As in most cases throughout history where a culturally, or technically, more advanced society is trading with a more primitive one, British exports consisted of basic raw materials or agricultural produce, while the imports were largely of manufactured goods.

Different strata in Belgic society can be identified by a study of their burials. In these practices they differed from earlier Iron Age immigrants by cremating their dead and interring them in large cemeteries. Frequent use seems to have been made of square 'barrows', or enclosures, and great clusters of them have now been identified at such places as Verulamium (fig. 8), Stevenage and Welwyn in Hertfordshire and at Burton Fleming, a La Tène 'Arras'

Fig. 8. Iron Age (La Tène III) cremation burial at Verulamium (*photograph by A.L. Pacitto, by courtesy of Ian Stead, Crown Copyright*).

culture cemetery, in east Yorkshire. Each 'barrow' appears to contain a 'master' burial with 'satellite' burials surrounding it; they may represent family groups. A person's position in society was normally indicated by the richness of the grave goods buried with him: fire-dogs, an amphora stand, vessels of pottery or even silver, amphoras of wine, bronze mirrors and personal trinkets. Such burials would represent the aristocratic upper classes. In some places even more elaborate single tombs, often surmounted by a circular barrow, may represent the burial of a member of a royal house. Such a barrow at Lexden, a short distance west of Colchester, contained, beside the usual collection of pottery vessels and pieces of metalwork, a folding stool, a bronze table and a medallion of the emperor Augustus, no doubt presented by a visiting embassy.

The diminishing quality and quantity of grave goods indicates the slide down the social scale, the bottom being reached where the ashes of the cremation are gathered into a single vessel, often handmade in the older traditional manner, or even deposited in the earth without any detectable container at all. It must not be forgotten either that Iron Age society was slave-owning, a practice indicated by the slave-chains and neck-shackles found on a number of sites; slaves would have been a spoil of inter-tribal war. As a class they have probably left less detectable evidence in the form of burials than any other.

Another aspect of the developing society of the Belgic period can be detected by observing the much wider range of 'consumer' goods available. There must have been professional bronzesmiths in the earlier Iron Age, but by now they had been joined by professional blacksmiths and potters and possibly by other craftsmen such as carpenters, together perhaps with shopkeepers and merchants. So, to some extent, the foundation was already being laid for the adoption of an altogether more complex way of life, to which they were shortly to be introduced.

When Caesar arrived in Britain, the Belgic political structure had not fully developed. According to his account, where, for the first time, we learn of British personalities by name, his principal opponent was the tribe of Cassivellaunus, inhabiting modern Hertfordshire, with their main centre possibly at Wheathampstead. He also mentions the Trinovantes of Essex and east Hertfordshire as being one of the strongest tribes in the south-east. Yet, despite their supposed strength, the Trinovantes sought Caesar's help against their western neighbours, and in this apparent paradox lies concealed many of the explanations for what was to come after. It is, in reality, the starting point from which, inevitably, permanent Roman intervention in British affairs ultimately became necessary.

The Britain that Caesar left behind in 54 BC can therefore be described summarily as follows (fig. 9). Except for some remote areas in the hill-country of Wales, Scotland and northern England, it was an Iron Age country with different parts in various stages of cultural development. In the south-west and from there penetrating up the lower Severn valley, along the Jurassic zone of the Cotswolds and into Northamptonshire, Lincolnshire, parts of East Anglia and Yorkshire the culture had a pronounced early La Tène flavour. In some places, this had merged with the underlying Hallstatt culture, while in others it overlay it. Hallstatt itself had survived almost unchanged in many of the areas beyond.

Fig. 9. Physical and political geography of Iron Age Britain.

In the south-east itself, then the most advanced region, both culturally and politically, small tribal groupings seemed to have formed the main stream of development with, as Caesar tells us, no less than four rulers in Kent. The Trinovantes, probably of predominantly Hallstatt stock, seem to have been the most closely knit community, with their territory extending through Essex into much of east Hertfordshire; and already there was the burgeoning power of Cassivellaunus.

The last group of Belgic migrants to reach Britain came after Caesar's expeditions, and they are usually associated with his erstwhile friend, and later foe, Commius, of the Gallic tribe of the Atrebates.

The age of primary Belgic movement to Britain then appears to have ceased, to be replaced, from about 30 BC onwards, by a period of expanding influence among the chief tribal groups, which ultimately reached out to the Severn in the west and the Trent in the north. Then, for the first time also, it is possible to recognize most of the tribal names and territories which ultimately came to be crystalized under the Roman system of local administration. We have already mentioned the tribe of Cassivellaunus, which became the basis for the Catuvellauni, and the Trinovantes. In Gloucestershire and Somerset lay the Dobunni, derived from Commius' Atrebates who themselves inhabited Hampshire, Berkshire and west Sussex; in Dorset there were the Durotriges; in Norfolk and north Suffolk, the Iceni. North-west of the Catuvellauni lay the Corieltavi, and beyond them again the Cornovii and Brigantes (fig. 9).

The emergence of reasonably unified tribal kingdoms did not, however, prevent a power-struggle from taking place, and the principal aggressor was the tribe of the Catuvellauni.

After their defeat by Caesar, the tribe, ruled by Cassivellaunus, was forbidden by the terms of their submission to molest the Trinovantes. Yet a generation or so later, under a new king, Tasciovanus, and with a new tribal capital at Verulamium, these terms were being ignored. We do not know why the site of the capital was changed. Perhaps the old one at Wheathampstead was still tainted by the humiliation inflicted by Caesar, and only the selection of a new site would have helped to erase a memory which could have no part in their growing scheme of aggression.

About AD 10, the Trinovantes were totally submerged beneath Catuvellaunian domination, and moreover, as if to emphasize the completeness of the conquest, a new Catuvellaunian capital was founded adjacent to, and superseding, that of the Trinovantes at Colchester (fig. 7). From this site, the Catuvellaunian king, Cunobelin, proceeded to expand his empire. By then also, Rome itself had undergone major convulsions. Augustus had emerged as the sole effective ruler in 27 BC, and had attempted to place the Roman empire on a sounder footing. In the west the final submissions of Spain and Gaul were secured, and it is said that he even considered taking up the option, left by Caesar, of occupying

Britain. If military action was contemplated by Augustus in Britain, it surely would have been in the years leading up to AD 10, with the shattering of Trinovantian security and with Caesar's treaty in ruins. But by then Augustus had other worries, notably the loss in AD 9 of three legions and their general in Germany. It is perhaps rash, but nevertheless interesting, to acknowledge the ideal timing of Cunobelin's move to Colchester.

If Augustus was embarrassed by Cunobelin's actions, he could take consolation in the alliance he had much earlier formed with the Atrebatic king, Tincommius, Commius' son and successor. Although Tincommius was expelled from his kingdom, perhaps by his brother Eppillus, the Roman alliance held and seems to have played an important part in Augustus' policy towards Britain. So long as there was a pro-Roman power to balance the unfriendly, if not openly hostile, Catuvellauni, Augustus was saved from taking direct action. Yet Cunobelin's moves can hardly have passed without diplomatic protest.

When Tiberius followed Augustus as emperor, he seems to have pursued the latter's policy and allowed British affairs to drift, taking action neither to prevent further Catuvellaunian expansions, nor to strengthen Atrebatic confidence. Consequently Cunobelin's empire extended over most of Kent and also beyond the Thames into northern Atrebatic territory. Moreover, feelers may already have been put out into the upper Thames valley and into the midlands. Only the Iceni appear to have been immune, but whether from lack of interest on the part of the Catuvellauni or from successful resistance is not known, since little more than border encroachments took place.

Despite the indifference shown to Roman aspirations by the Catuvellauni, trade greatly expanded in the decades leading up to the invasion of AD 43, and the number of Italian, Gallic, German or Spanish traders visiting Britain increased with it. As a by-product, knowledge of British geography and lifestyles became more widely disseminated in the Roman world and must increasingly have influenced imperial thinking.

The precedent set by Augustus and followed by Tiberius with regard to Britain seems, during the middle years of the latter's reign, to have been matched by a lull in Catuvellaunian aggression. Cunobelin, perhaps growing older and wiser, and more of a statesman, appeared content with what he held. Perhaps, also, he knew the limits to which he could go before precipitating direct Roman action against him. But in his declining years, especially following the death of Tiberius in AD 37, power was increasingly transferred to his sons. One of these, Adminius, held pro-Roman views; his centre was probably at the old stronghold of Verulamium. Two others, however, Togodumnus and Caratacus, revived the indifference towards Rome. By the time Gaius had succeeded Tiberius as emperor, this pair had sufficient ascendancy over their father to cause Adminius' expulsion; he fled to Gaius for help and the latter mounted his abortive invasion campaign.

About AD 40, Cunobelin died and his two hot-headed sons succeeded to a positon of absolute power, which they proceeded to use in order to expand the Catuvellaunian empire still further. A wedge was driven up the Thames valley into the Cotswolds, so as almost to sever the Dobunni. Here, in newly captured lands a puppet king, Boduoccus, was installed. The pressure which, for many years, had been maintained against the Atrebates was now greatly increased and, apparently without thought of the consequences (for had not Gaius' attempted invasion proved a fiasco?), they captured the last remaining Atrebatic strongholds in southern Sussex and expelled the king, Verica, who like Adminius before him, fled to Rome for help.

Verica was a Roman ally, perhaps even a client king, whose status would have been regulated by treaty. His defeat may well have been judged by the Catuvellauni as a suitable and final revenge for their earlier humiliation by Caesar. For a brief time, Togodumnus and Caratacus must have felt in a commanding position. They ruled all that was worth having in Britain; they were a match even for the Roman empire, which dared not touch them. Indeed, twice in the space of thirty years, Rome had been successfully defied. Catuvellaunian confidence was at its zenith and a demand for the extradition of Verica and his followers went out.

But Gaius had been replaced as emperor by Claudius, and the actions taken by the Roman empire were, more often than not, taken on the varying inclinations of individual emperors. Togodumnus and Caratacus had misjudged their man; Claudius was not Gaius.

The emergence of an entirely hostile power on their north-west frontier presented a new problem to Rome. Necessary retribution had also to be delivered for wrongs done to a Roman ally, for otherwise there would, in future, be little value in such alliances, and Rome then relied on allies to a very great extent to maintain peaceful frontiers.

With the benefit of hindsight, these problems can now be viewed in two ways. It could be argued that when an aggressor, in this case the Roman empire, intends to conquer new territory, a political motive can always be found to justify the necessity of the action. Since Caesar's day, emperors had been periodically contemplating the annexing of Britain. Had the time now come, and was the expulsion of Verica the political expedient for what was in reality a foregone conclusion? Alternatively, the invasion in AD 43 may be seen as the consequence of the coincidence of a number of factors, none of which had all occurred together before and might never have occurred together again. Throughout history, violent events have often been precipitated by just such conjunctions, although one factor alone often acts as the detonator. Roman thinking may have been to some extent conditioned by the first explanation, but it is probable that in the second lies the real reason for the invasion, and we may consider the coincidental factors.

There had been for a long time in Rome the feeling that Caesar had left unfinished business in Britain, to the point where Britain was sometimes even considered as an unoccupied province of the empire. There was the very real political motive afforded by the expulsion of Verica and the need to inflict punishment on his transgressors. In addition, the occupation of Britain would be one further step towards the annihilation of the Druids, who were a source of much anti-Roman feeling in both Gaul and Britain. There was an emperor who sought military triumph and looked upon a British conquest as an easy and not too expensive way of obtaining it. There were the rumours, no doubt carefully fostered by merchants hoping to reap greater benefits after an occupation, of considerable natural wealth in Britain, especially of precious metals.

But probably the overriding reasons were those connected with the military strategy of the north-west empire. If Britain were to be left in the control of an aggressively anti-Roman power, some means would have had to be found for protecting the north-west frontier from attack. Static defences of the type required to keep out small raiding parties – since an all-out assault by the Catuvellauni need not have been contemplated – are notoriously expensive in terms of manpower. It has been claimed that no more men would have been required for a static frontier force along the Channel than were needed for the British invasion – some 40,000. But calculations based on later frontier requirements indicate that at least 85,000 men would have been needed for effective control of the north-west coast of Gaul. The massing of manpower at even the lesser figure along that coast would, moreover, have had undesirable side effects.

In the first place, large quantities of extra food would have had to have been provided by the Gallic provinces, a task which may have been beyond them, since they already had to feed the Rhine garrisons. Secondly, it would have caused a dangerous imbalance of army strengths between the western and eastern empire. Augustus had early realized that the key to his power lay in a loyal army, and that an over-large garrison under the command of an unscrupulous governor could be a threat to the emperor's security. This precept was overlooked several times in later years, with disastrous consequences for the Roman empire. But Augustus had initiated a system whereby the main units of the army were carefully spread between the provinces and already, under Claudius, the Rhine army was overweight, being a legacy of Gaius' futile military operations. To have added a Gallic army on the Channel coast would have been an act of extreme folly on the part of Claudius. However, the surplus army units on the Rhine could be used to advantage, an overall manpower saving could be effected, the commissariat problem could be solved, and the danger of insurrection of an over-large garrison could be avoided, if the invasion of Britain took place, so placing the troops in safety beyond the Channel with an adequate supply of food from fresh sources.

The time was right. The unique conjunction of events had come about. An army consisting of four legions, Legio II, Legio XIV and Legio XX from the Rhine, Legio IX from the upper Danube, together with appropriate auxiliaries and support forces was assembled at Boulogne under the command of Aulus Plautius, recently governor of Pannonia. After a delay caused by a mutiny, the army embarked for Britain.

CHAPTER TWO

Warfare and its Consequences

So far, only one landing place of the Roman army in AD 43 has been positively identified, at Richborough in Kent. There, a fortified beachhead, enclosing about 4 ha within a double ditch, was constructed to protect it. Somewhere, a little further inland, has still to be found the large temporary camp, perhaps as large as 65 ha, where, after coming ashore, the concentration of troops took place. It may be, also, that detachments of the army landed on different parts of the coast, and one attractive theory has suggested that Verica was reinstated directly in west Sussex by a group detailed to retake his kingdom. Contrarily, it has been argued that the splitting of the invasion army into more than one division would have been bad tactics. Yet a force sent to restore Verica need not have been large, since it was landing in basically friendly territory. Politically and strategically a move of this sort, although possibly a risk, would, if successful, have had far-reaching effects on the Britons. It would be the type of action which, if it prospered, would have earned wide acclaim for the commanding general, but equally, if a failure, a wide degree of odium. There seems, however, little doubt that the principal force landed at Richborough and that the main actions thereafter took place in Kent. After some skirmishes in east Kent and a major battle at the River Medway, the Roman army arrived at the Thames and there awaited the emperor Claudius, as they had been instructed to do.

It would probably have taken Claudius at least six weeks to have reached Britain. It seems inconceivable that Aulus Plautius, having already inflicted serious defeats on the enemy, in one of which Togodumnus was killed, would have waited idly beside the Thames for his arrival. Although Plautius could take no official action which would

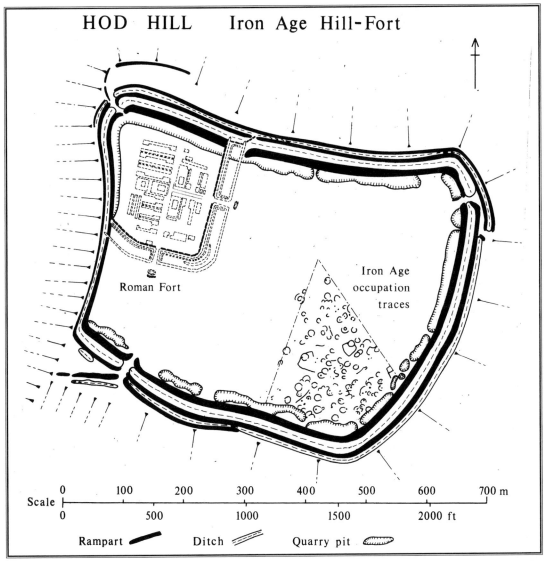

HOD HILL   Iron Age Hill-Fort

Roman Fort

Iron Age
occupation
traces

Scale

| 0 | 100 | 200 | 300 | 400 | 500 | 600 | 700 m |

| 0 | | 500 | | 1000 | | 1500 | | 2000 ft |

Rampart ▬   Ditch ▨   Quarry pit ▱

Fig. 10. Iron Age hillfort at Hod
Hill (Dorset), with a Roman fort
situated in the north-west corner
(*after I.A. Richmond*).

appear to lessen the importance of Claudius' ultimate victory, a wise
commander would have occupied his time in making sure that that
same victory would be inevitable. Claudius remained in Britain for only
sixteen days, but in that time the Catuvellaunian capital at Colchester
was occupied and the surrender of a number of other tribes accepted.

With the departure of Claudius, the campaigns were resumed.
Until then, the army had fought in concert; now it was split into
three battle groups (vexillations), while a fourth remained in reserve
in a newly built fortress at Colchester. Each group had a legion at its

19

core, supported by auxiliary cavalry and infantry, and each was commanded in the field by the legionary legate, who would be assisted as necessary, not only by his legionary staff officers, but also by the prefects or tribunes of the auxiliary units.

The legions themselves, at this stage in imperial history, were organized into ten cohorts, every cohort containing six centuries, each commanded by a centurion. A legion was also expected to be a fully self-contained fighting unit and therefore included in its strength a wide variety of specialists such as armourers, clerks, surveyors, medical orderlies, carpenters, stonemasons, hydraulic engineers, glaziers, even shipwrights and river pilots (see Chapter 6). The total strength was therefore in the region of 6,000 men, although the actual fighting strength was probably nearer 5,300–5,600. All were Roman citizens and in this fact lay the prime distinction between legions and auxiliary regiments.

The Roman army as established in the republican period was composed entirely of citizens. In time, especially after the beginning of the principate, it was realized that the legions were the mainstay of imperial power. Consequently, the number of legions in being was carefully regulated and never exceeded thirty-five in number, seldom enough to guard the ever-widening frontiers. In order, therefore, to supplement the army, it early became the custom to recruit native troops, particularly from the frontier regions. These men did not hold Roman citizenship, although the honour could be conferred on them on discharge, or occasionally on a whole regiment for distinguished service. At first, these regiments were organized in quingeniary units (500 strong), either of cavalry (*ala*), infantry (*cohors peditata*), or of mixed composition (*cohors equitata*). They took their names normally from the region in which they were originally recruited: *cohors VI Thracum equitata* (from Thrace), more rarely from where they were stationed, and occasionally, in the case of *alae*, from the name of their first commander. They were commanded by a Roman officer of the rank of prefect or tribune and were subdivided in the case of infantry units into centuries and in cavalry units into troops.

By the end of the first century, however, larger milliary regiments (1,000 strong) were being recruited, although cavalry units of this strength remained rare because they were expensive to maintain. Other, more irregular units of native troops, such as *numeri* and *cunei*, also existed from the second century onwards, but they did not achieve real importance until the later empire, by which time the whole structure of the Roman army had changed radically.

Of the campaigns which followed the capture of Colchester, most is known about that in the south and south-west of Britain. There, Legio II Augusta, commanded by the future emperor Vespasian, had to wage a vicious war against the Durotriges, and another tribe, who had not surrendered to Claudius. Vespasian's biographer gives some details of his victories: the capture of the Isle of Wight and the reduction of over twenty hillforts. Graphic evidence for some of these battles has come from excavations at the hillforts of Maiden Castle and Hod Hill (fig. 10). At the former, a direct assault on the east gate had to be mounted before it was captured; at the latter, surrender seems to have been more quickly obtained by opening the attack with an artillery bombardment of *ballistae* (spring-guns) on the chieftain's house.

The two other advances, headed by Legio IX Hispana into the north and east midlands and by Legio XIV towards the west

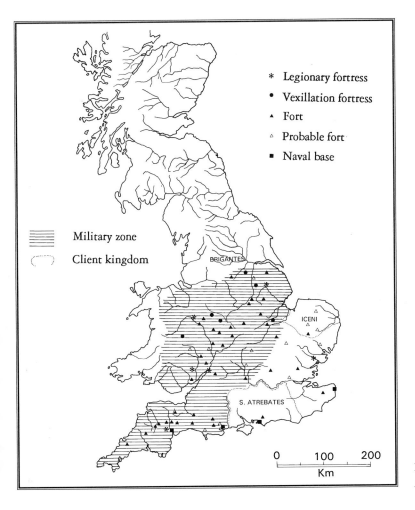

Fig. 11. Britain between AD 43 and 70.

midlands, probably met less opposition as the territory of the Corieltavi in which they were moving had almost certainly surrendered to Claudius at Colchester.

During the advances, the battle groups would have been accommodated in temporary campaign camps, each large enough to contain the whole force. The fortifications were slight, consisting of no more than a low bank surmounted by a palisade and fronted by a small ditch. The leather tents of the men were pitched in the interior. Unfortunately no campaign camps of the invasion period are yet known in south-east Britain, although many have been identified in the midlands, the north and in Wales, where they belong to the activities of later periods.

These initial successes of the army led naturally to a period of consolidation. One of the principal objectives of the invasion, the defeat and occupation of the Catuvellauni and their allies, had been achieved. Tribes friendly to Rome who had suffered from Catuvellaunian aggression, such as the Iceni, Trinovantes, Dobunni and Atrebates, were relieved and refugee princes probably reinstated. It is likely that, at this stage, no further occupation of territory was considered necessary by the Roman high command.

But the newly created province of Britannia had to be protected (fig. 11). It would appear that, in common with practice then in force on other frontiers, the natural boundaries of the rivers Severn and Trent were selected. Behind them was constructed an elaborate system of roads, forts and fortresses to give a deep, fortified zone extending from Devon to Lincolnshire. The main lateral line of communication was the road now known as the Fosse Way, sometimes incorrectly considered the frontier line. The key pivots in this system would have been the three main headquarters of Legio II, Legio XIV and Legio IX, although it is likely that at this stage they were divided into battle groups based on vexillation fortresses. Legio II probably constructed one of its first such bases at Lake Farm, near Wimbourne where a fortress of appropriate size has been partly excavated; another may exist at North Tawton in Devon. The equivalent bases of Legio XIV cannot be identified with certainty; Leicester is a possibility, while a vexillation fortress has been identified at Mancetter on Watling Street but has not been dated. A fortress of 10.9 ha at Longthorpe (fig. 13) near Peterborough most likely served Legio IX, with another at Newton-on-Trent, west of Lincoln.

These early vexillation fortresses, as they are best called, are a comparatively recent discovery in Roman Britain. Apart from those

Fig. 12. Aerial photograph of the vexillation fortress at Longthorpe, near Peterborough (*copyright: Committee for Aerial Photography, University of Cambridge*).

mentioned above, the sites of others, dating to the middle of the first century, are known in outline. Excavations at Lake Farm and more especially at Longthorpe show that they lack the standardized planning of legionary fortresses of the late first and second centuries. They vary in size from 8–12 ha and consequently could not accommodate a complete legion, which would normally require an area of 18–20 ha. It is most likely, therefore, that these fortresses represented a flexible approach on the part of the high command to the problem of British defence, accommodating the regional headquarters, a stores depot and quarters for a mixed force of legionaries and auxiliaries not stationed in minor forts elsewhere, and therefore providing a mobile reserve.

The fortress at Longthorpe (figs 12, 13) was defended by twin parallel ditches and a turf or earth rampart, probably surmounted by a timber breastwork. The four gates were timber-framed; each had two carriageways flanked by projecting towers. The internal buildings, of which the headquarters building at the centre, some granaries, stores buildings and legionary and auxiliary barracks have

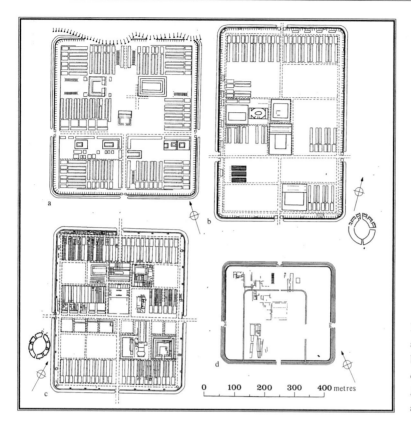

Fig. 13. Legionary fortresses at:
a) Inchtuthil (*after I.A. Richmond*);
b) Chester (*after D.F. Petch*);
c) Caerleon (*after G.C. Boon and R. Brewer*); d) vexillation fortress at Longthorpe (*after S.S. Frere*).

been identified, were likewise constructed round timber frames, with the walling completed with interwoven wattle plastered with mud, or daub. This type of construction was invariably employed by the Roman army in Britain until the end of the first century, and less often later. The system had the advantage of flexibility, since many of the building components could be prepared and, if necessary, transferred from one site to another as the need arose, or stockpiled in a central depot. It does, however, imply the availability of an ample supply of off-site timber, and the implications of this element of Roman army duties are considered in Chapter 5.

Apart from the three main regional bases mentioned above, and in addition to the regular legionary fortress at Colchester, there were numerous auxiliary forts planted in the frontier region. Structurally they were similar to these bases, but were planned to suit the forces in garrison. A degree of nonconformity can therefore be expected according to whether they were constructed for legionary or auxiliary infantry, or cavalry detachments, or combinations of one with another.

One of the best-known forts of this period is that constructed in

Fig. 14. Aerial photograph of
the Roman fort situated in the
north-west corner of the Iron
Age hillfort at Hod Hill
(*copyright: Committee for Aerial
Photography, University of
Cambridge*).

an unusual position in the north-west corner of the Iron Age hillfort
at Hod Hill (figs 10, 14). It contained a headquarters block, houses
for two senior officers commanding, respectively, a legionary cohort
and half a quingeniary cavalry regiment, and the necessary barracks,
stabling and other ancillary buildings. Although the legionary
detachment as a whole, being composed of citizens, would have
taken precedence over the cavalry unit, the prefect of the latter
would have ranked higher than a legionary centurion and would
consequently have commanded the fort. These arrangements are
reflected by the placing of the legionary barracks in the front half of
the fort together with the more spacious house of the cavalry
prefect.

Other forts of this general type are known at Great Casterton, near
Stamford, Waddon Hill, on the Dorset coast near Bridport,
Cirencester, and many other places in the frontier zone. They were
served by a number of coastal supply bases such as Poole, London,
Fishbourne, near Chichester, Fingrinhoe in Essex and Richborough,
where the invasion beachhead was converted for this purpose by the
construction of granaries. In the carriage of supplies inland use
would not only have been made of the developing road system, but
also of suitable rivers.

Within the new British province then set up, most of which was under military government, special administrative arrangements were, however, made in two areas: the client kingdoms of the Iceni and Atrebates, in East Anglia and southern England respectively (fig. 11).

Ever since mid-republican days, Rome had made use of native monarchs both within and outside the boundaries of provinces. Such rulers, in return for protection, were allowed to retain a subordinate 'freedom', the level of which depended much on the strength of the individual kings. They were expected to be friendly allies, who would not treat with Rome's enemies. During Augustus' principate they were also being used to govern territory otherwise too difficult or too inconvenient to administer directly. In essence, their creation and retention was an economy on the part of the imperial government, saving manpower much needed elsewhere. In this respect, it is important to remember that no great army of civil servants moved into Britain in the wake of the invasion. During the first and second centuries the provincial administration was always small and, within closely prescribed limits, the native people were allowed, indeed expected, to run their own affairs (see Chapter 5).

It is probable that agreements made with the rulers, although incorporating certain basic precedents, varied from individual to individual; consequently, in the absence of firm evidence, it is difficult to envisage the arrangements made between the imperial administration and the Iceni and the Atrebates. It is possible to argue that the realm of the Atrebates under Verica's successor, Cogidubnus (fig. 15), became a client kingdom within the province, while that of the Iceni, first under Antedius, later under Prasutagus, and with its extensive coastal boundary on the North Sea, remained outside the provincial boundary. But in both the kings would have been expected to maintain order, to collect tribute and probably to provide a quota of recruits for the Roman army. Had these areas been dealt with in the same way as the rest of the province, extra garrisons would have been required. So, the effect of creating these client kingdoms, in ostensibly reliable territory, was to achieve an economy of manpower and the saving of trouble for the provincial governor and his small staff.

Roman strategy towards Britain began to show signs of weakness in the decades following the invasion. In the first place, Caratacus, sometime joint ruler of the Catuvellauni, had escaped from the campaigns of Aulus Plautius, found new allies in Wales and was clearly intent on carrying on the war. Although the queen of the tribe of the Brigantes in north Britain, Cartimandua, was a professed

Fig. 15. Dedication of a temple to Neptune and Minerva, by the authority of the client king of the Atrebates, Cogidubnus: from Chichester (*Chichester Photographic Services Ltd*).

ally of Rome, she was unable to maintain peace there and was ultimately expelled as the result of civil war.

Although Caratacus was, in the end, captured with the aid of Cartimandua in AD51, hostility continued in Wales and the north throughout that and the following decade. A number of campaigns were mounted, especially in Wales, but they were mostly ineffective, except in purely limited terms. Changes had also been made in military dispositions. The army had evacuated the immediate south-eastern area of Britain, in order to provide the necessary forces to extend the fortified frontier zone up to the Welsh border. This move had, in turn, led to the establishment of a purely civilian administration in the evacuated areas and included the foundation of the first Roman *colonia* at Colchester, a chartered town, for discharged legionary veterans.

Strife inside the province was not unknown and the traumatic experience of the Boudiccan rebellion in AD 60–1 nearly caused its loss. The pressures which erupted in that year had been growing for some time. An abortive rebellion by the Iceni a decade or so earlier had been caused by their compulsory disarmament, when they clearly considered themselves still a free people. The Trinovantes, freed from Catuvellaunian control, found to their surprise that their old capital was not to be returned to them. It was absorbed in the new *colonia* at

Colchester and, instead, they were fobbed off with a new site at Chelmsford which they did not want. It is probable also that a new generation of Catuvellaunians were growing up eager to revenge their earlier defeats. Harsh and unrealistic taxes and compulsory expenditure were being exacted. It only needed an excuse for violence and the rest would follow automatically.

The excuse came with the death of the client king of the Iceni, Prasutagus, and the decision to absorb his tribe into the province. Moreover, Prasutagus, hoping to ensure the succession of his wife Boudicca, unwisely made the emperor Nero co-heir in his will. Nero often considered a half-share of an estate as evidence of ingratitude on the part of the testator and usually ended by taking all. To this mixture was then added the arrogance of the officers sent to secure the inheritance and incorporate the kingdom into the province. No doubt also they were met with equal arrogance from the Icenian royal household. Arrogance and inflexibility led directly to violence. The rebellion had started.

The absence of the governor, Suetonius Paullinus, with a large part of the army in north Wales, meant that at first the rebels were entirely successful. They sacked the new towns of Colchester, London and Verulamium and inflicted a major defeat on the nearest army unit, Legio IX. But the outcome must, to some extent, have been a foregone conclusion. A native rabble, no matter how large, was seldom a match for the ordered discipline of the Roman army, provided the encounter took place in relatively open country. Suetonius Paullinus gathered what forces he could and selected a good site for the battle, variously placed somewhere along Watling Street between Towcester and Atherstone. The rebels were defeated and fled in disorder; it is recorded that Boudicca committed suicide. Then followed a punitive expedition in East Anglia, only stopped when it was feared that future imperial revenue would be seriously depleted.

The consequences were far-reaching. The Iceni, deprived of much of their land, appear never to have fully recovered, always remaining a poor and backward area. The grievances of the Trinovantes seem partly to have been met by a local reorganization which enabled them to renew the use of their old capital as a religious centre. Overall, the Roman attitude to the native Britons was perhaps slightly softened.

A further consequence was the stalemate situation forced upon the Roman army, which lasted to AD 69. No governor, acting either from his own inspiration or from official orders, was prepared to undertake the risk of removing garrisons from areas where open rebellion had

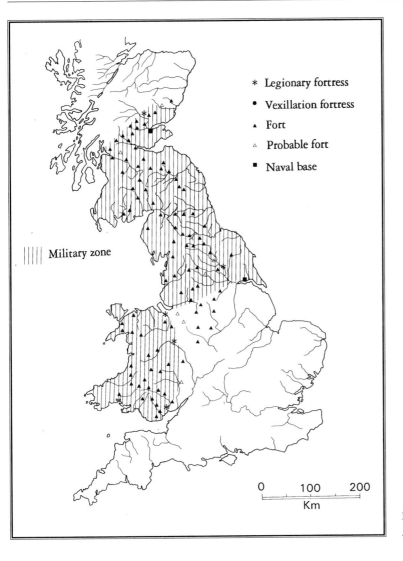

* Legionary fortress
• Vexillation fortress
▲ Fort
△ Probable fort
■ Naval base

||||| Military zone

0   100   200
Km

Fig. 16. Britain between AD 70 and 85.

flared so recently in order to subjugate and occupy Wales. Some must have realized the need to settle the Welsh problem, but were denied the extra army units required for its successful completion. Some had also realized that the original Severn-Trent frontier, facing hostile forces on two fronts, was no longer tenable. The time had come for a radical reassessment of the province's needs.

This reassessment was unfortunately delayed by a serious civil war in the empire, following the suicide of Nero. Within little more than a year three emperors were created in succession, only to be removed with equal rapidity. Finally Vespasian, then commanding an army in Judaea, succeeded where the others had failed.

The principate of Vespasian saw a new and more vigorous policy begin in Britain. In succession three governors, Petillius Cerealis, Julius Frontinus and Julius Agricola, completed the occupation of Wales and advanced the northern frontier to the fringes of the Scottish highlands. Of the three governors, the last, Gnaeus Julius Agricola, is perhaps deservedly the best known, as the result of the biography left by his son-in-law, Tacitus; it was Agricola who placed the seal on the Roman occupation of Britain.

But before the military occupation of Wales and the north could take place, troops in garrison in the midlands had to be released for service. In consequence, this period saw not only the extension of the frontiers in Britain, but also the consolidation, under civilian administration, of what is usually referred to as the civil zone of the province: an area bounded by the Welsh border on the west and the Trent-Dee line approximately on the north (see Chapter 5). Beyond these limits, military government was still firmly ensconced, based on a series of new forts and fortresses (fig. 16).

In the period before Vespasian became emperor, various changes in military dispositions, including the temporary removal of Legio XIV, had led to the foundation of new legionary fortresses at such places as Lincoln, Wroxeter, Gloucester and Exeter. Now, hand in hand with the fresh advances a new generation of fortresses was required in addition to numerous auxiliary forts, and work started at York, Caerleon, Chester and Inchtuthil – the most northerly of all. The logistic problems facing these governors must have been formidable when it is remembered that apart from the fortresses just mentioned, at least eighty new auxiliary forts were constructed as well as over 3,000 km of new roads. The implications of these figures are considered more fully (Chapters 5 and 6).

Although some forts were still being constructed, as in the earlier period, for mixed units or regiments, such as at the recently excavated fort at Strageath, most now became standardized on a basic layout, making use occasionally of innovations to increase the strength of the fortifications. In general, however, the materials of construction – wood, earth, turf, wattle and daub – remained the same; nevertheless, masonry was appearing regularly for building bath-houses. Examples of military construction of this period are the legionary fortress at Inchtuthil on the River Tay, probably built by, and for, Legio XX, and the auxiliary fort at Fendoch at the entrance to the Sma' Glen further south.

The fortress at Inchtuthil (fig. 13) is exceptional in having no modern buildings obscuring any part of it, for it lies in open

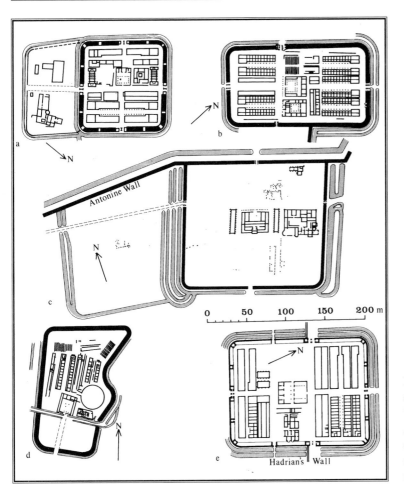

Fig. 17. Auxiliary forts at:
a) Gelligaer (*after V.E. Nash-Williams*); b) Fendoch (*after I.A. Richmond*); c) Mumrills (*after K. Steer*); d) The Lunt (*after B. Hobley*); e) Chesters (*after I.A. Richmond*).

meadow-land beside the river. Moreover, since the fortress was only occupied for a short time, its excavated remains were not confused by later alterations to buildings, and it presents a single-phase plan almost unique in the empire. The defences, consisting of a single ditch and a stone wall backed by a turf rampart, enclosed an almost square area of just over 21 ha. The fortifications were pierced by double-span gates, one to each side. Within the fortress the regular planning of the streets can be observed with the headquarters building in the centre. Other buildings which have been identified are granaries, a large workshop, a hospital, a drill-shed, staff officers' houses, and numerous store sheds. The barracks are arranged in ten groups of six representing the ten cohorts of the legion and their six constituent centuries. It is interesting that the commanding legate's house was never constructed, although the site for it beside the

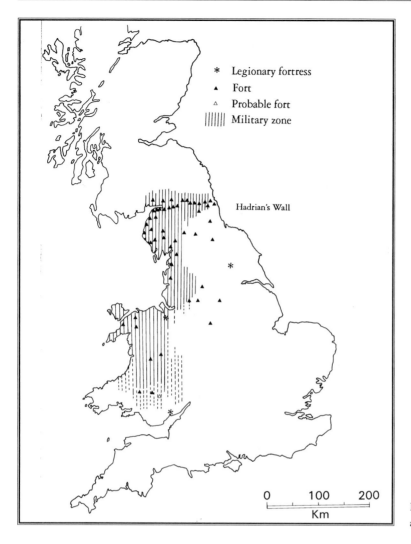

* Legionary fortress
▲ Fort
△ Probable fort
|||||| Military zone

Hadrian's Wall

0   100   200
Km

Fig. 18. Hadrianic frontiers
and military zones.

headquarters block had been levelled and prepared. Internal provisions for the distribution of fresh water had been made, although they had never been connected to an aqueduct; drainage was also taken care of. Outside the fortress to the south-east lay a small bath-house of masonry. There was, in addition, an external stores compound containing a barrack and an office block.

The auxiliary fort at Fendoch (fig. 17), built for a milliary cohort of infantry, presents, as might be expected, many of the features of the legionary fortress but in a miniature and simplified form. The headquarters block, the commandant's house, the hospital, two granaries, stores and workshops and ten barracks, one for each century, can readily be identified within the regular street plan.

Here, provision for piped running water was completed and adequate arrangements for drainage were also made. Cooking ovens, a considerable fire-risk in a fort constructed largely of wood, were placed against the back of the rampart.

The military system of which this fortress and fort were a part (fig. 16) was not destined to last for long without change. Within ten years of Agricola completing his dispositions in Britain, events elsewhere in the empire enforced changes. With no central reserve of troops, Domitian, who was now emperor, could only turn to peaceful provinces for reinforcements. Britain was reasonably peaceful and had to provide one legion, Legio II Adjutrix, which had earlier replaced Legion XIV, and numbers of auxiliaries for campaigns in Dacia and Moesia. Although Wales could still be held, the northern frontier had to be drawn back, first to what came to be only a temporary frontier with a series of signal stations (fig. 25c) along the Gask Ridge, north of Strathearn, then to the Forth-Clyde line and ultimately, by about AD 105, to the Tyne-Solway line, so that all lowland Scotland was abandoned. This last withdrawal may have been caused partly by a renewed call for reinforcements from Britain by the emperor Trajan and partly by enemy action, as some forts, including Corbridge, a fort on the River Tyne, were burnt. For the next decade the northern frontier of Britain must have remained in a state of uneasy peace.

This same decade, however, also saw the consolidation of the three remaining, principal army bases in Britain, – the legionary fortresses at York, Chester and Caerleon (fig. 13) for Legio IX, Legio XX and Legio II Augusta respectively. The defences were made stronger and more permanent by the addition of stout masonry walls, equipped with internal towers, while inside buildings were also gradually reconstructed in masonry. A number of auxiliary forts were treated similarly. The decision to carry out this work must have represented, yet again, a radical reappraisal of the military requirements of the British province. The replacement of easily dismantled, timber-framed buildings by permanent masonry structures can only indicate that the period of mobile welfare, of conquest and advance was considered to be over for the foreseeable future. Static defence increasingly came to replace mobile attack, and these changes are inevitably reflected in military architecture and strategy.

The end of this decade, which coincided with the death of Trajan and the accession of Hadrian as emperor, was marked by a serious war in northern Britain. It was, however, successfully concluded and in AD 122, Hadrian himself visited Britain as part of an extended tour of the provinces. By now, also, the idea of linear fortified frontiers to replace garrisoned zones defending natural barriers was gaining ground, having been tried in Germany and Moesia under Domitian. Probably because of the more hostile and unsettled nature of norther Britain, it was decided to build a much stronger barrier, stronger indeed than anywhere else in the empire.

Hadrian's Wall seems closely to have followed the earlier line of Trajan's frontier along the Stanegate, since some isolated watch-towers of earlier build than the Wall itself have been identified. As first envisaged, the new frontier was to consist of a masonry wall equipped with small fortlets at every mile – milecastles (fig. 21) – with two turrets between each pair, and with the whole work fronted by a large ditch. To the rear were a number of garrison forts connected by the Stanegate. Work started in AD 122, under the governor A. Platorius Nepos, and proceeded westwards from Newcastle. Its construction, however, caused considerable irritation to the tribes it was intended to separate, those to the south being as hostile as those to the north, so much so that, by the time it was finished, many modifications had been incorporated. Chief among them were the removal of the garrisons from the rear to the Wall itself, the reduction in thickness of the barrier west of the North Tyne from 3 m to just under 2.5 m, the extension of the Wall eastwards from Newcastle to Wallsend and ultimately the completion in turf of the section westwards from the River Irthing. In places also the digging of the ditch in front of the Wall proved impossible or unnecessary owing to the hardness of the rock (p. 202) or the presence of cliffs. Moreover, since building work was carried out in short lengths by gangs from the three British legions, II, VI (which had replaced Legio IX) and XX, it proceeded at a somewhat uneven pace from one part to another. Consequently the frontier, when completed in its first stage, must have presented a decidedly patchwork appearance. Travelling from east to west, one would see first a length of narrow wall, 2.5 m wide, from Wallsend to Newcastle, then the wide wall, 3 m wide, as far as the North Tyne. From there to the River Irthing, the narrow wall lay atop the wide foundation (fig. 19), as work on laying the foundations had proceeded faster than the building of the superstructure. From the River Irthing to its termination at Bowness-on-Solway, construction was of turf with, as elsewhere, forts and turrets of masonry, but with the milecastles built of turf and wood instead of stone.

Fig. 19. Hadrian's Wall at Gilsland, showing the narrow wall on the broad foundation.

A number of reasons have been argued for these alterations, notably that a geological fault west of the Irthing caused a complete lack of readily available limestone to burn for mortar. Yet this factor seems only partly to explain the change from masonry to turf and does nothing to account for the narrowing of the masonry wall. Ultimately, the turf wall was replaced by masonry, so the supply of mortar was not an insuperable problem; it would simply have taken longer to complete. The main cause would therefore seem to lie in the need for faster construction; it became increasingly necessary to hasten the work and economies had to be made. It is known that the greatest threat was posed at the west end of the barrier for there was placed the senior officer on the frontier, commanding a milliary ala of cavalry at Stanwix. Such units were rare in the Roman army; only one is known to have served in Britain, so they were placed where need was greatest. Moreover, the frontier itself in this part was strengthened by the placing of three outpost forts at Birrens, Netherby and Bewcastle, to give advanced warning of attacks. In addition the western flank beyond the end of the Wall was protected by a series of mileforts, towers and forts extending along the Cumberland coast as far as Moresby. Between Bowness and Cardurnock the mileforts seem to have been placed between parallel ditches and stockades for extra protection, a system somewhat reminiscent of the German frontier.

Once the garrison forts, fifteen in number, had been sited on the Wall, a military zone was marked out to the rear by means of an earthwork known as the Vallum, a ditch running between two parallel mounds of earth and turf. Hardly defensive in structure, it was probably intended to mark a prohibited area for the local natives. A military road, giving lateral communication between the forts and milecastles, ran within this zone.

The forts of Hadrian's Wall were constructed throughout in masonry, with their size and the nature of their buildings dictated by the type of unit occupying them. In one respect, however, some differed from the normal pattern to be expected for such forts. Those in which cavalry regiments were stationed were so planned that the whole front part of the fort, including three of the gates, projected beyond the line of the barrier (fig. 17e), to enable rapid deployment of the troops in the outfield. Consequently an extra pair of gates had to be introduced in the rear of the fort to accommodate the military way. The milecastles contained at most two small barracks, with gates to front and rear (fig. 21c), while the turrets would have provided shelter for patrols and facilities for signalling.

Fig. 20. Aerial photograph of a campaign camp at Reycross (N. Yorks.) (*copyright: Committee for Aerial Photography, University of Cambridge*).

It is perhaps appropriate to review at this point the strength of the Roman army in Britain, since the garrisons for the new frontier were obtained by withdrawing regiments from south Wales and northern England (fig. 18). In doing this, Hadrian probably took a calculated gamble, removing military control completely from the tribal territories of the Silures, Demetae and Parisi and partly from Brigantia, east of the Pennines. The counterpart of this move, would, as before, have required the setting up of suitable local civilian authorities.

The army in Britain underwent considerable changes in composition between the times of Claudius and Hadrian. Reinforcements of legionaries and ten auxiliary regiments were brought to Britain after the Boudiccan rebellion, but the overall garrison strength was probably temporarily reduced before, and again at the time of, the Civil War in AD 69, when Legio XIV finally departed from Britain. Its place was taken in the early 70s by Legio

II Adjutrix which, however, was withdrawn again, together with auxiliaries, by AD 90. Further temporary withdrawals, or exchanges, of auxiliary units took place towards the end of the first or the beginning of the second century, followed almost immediately by the arrival of reinforcements. By AD 122, or shortly after, Legio VI had arrived in Britain, ultimately to replace Legio IX, and for a long time it was considered that the latter had either been destroyed or disgraced during the war of AD 117. But evidence more recently obtained, although still tenuous, suggests that it was withdrawn from Britain, possibly before that war, to reside for a short time in Holland before probably being sent to an eastern province to perish ultimately in the Jewish rebellion of AD 132. The army in Britain under Hadrian, therefore, consisted of three legions and probably something of the order of fifteen milliary and fifty quingeniary auxiliary regiments, giving a total of about 53,000 men, an overall increase of perhaps 10,000 since the Claudian army landed in Britain. Moreover, it was an increase which had been brought about solely by auxiliaries at the expense of the legions and indicates the changing relative importance accorded to these two fighting arms, a change which, in time, altered the whole structure of the Roman army.

The frontier of Hadrian is generally accorded to have been a tactical success but a strategical and political failure, since, although it could control the troublesome tribes of south-west Scotland and northern England, it was politically divisive and it was too distant from the warlike people of Caledonia. Its initial completion, about AD 130, seems to have been marked by a renewal of serious hostilities, in which the Brigantes were involved, in addition probably to tribes beyond the frontier. Certainly forts in the north-eastern Pennines were reoccupied at this time, and an experienced general, Julius Severus, was sent to govern Britain.

The death of Hadrian and the accession of Antoninus Pius in AD 139 brought with it a review of the British northern frontier, which acknowledged its strategic weakness, and the decision to reoccupy lowland Scotland was taken. Lollius Urbicus, the governor appointed to the task, had won the necessary victory over the Scottish tribes by AD 143 to enable him to establish the new frontier controls on the Forth-Clyde line, the narrowest neck of land in the whole of mainland Britain. Twice before in the first century the northern frontier had rested there. It was not, therefore, unknown country. Yet, when construction took place, a reversion to earlier techniques

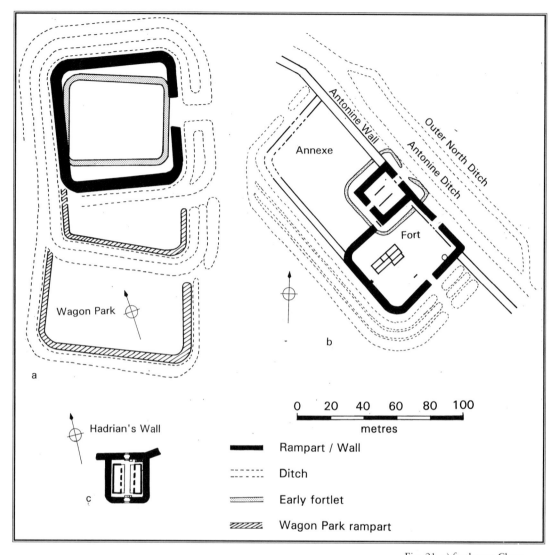

Fig. 21. a) fortlets at Chew Green (*after I.A. Richmond*); b) small fort and fortlet at Duntocher on the Antonine Wall (*after A. Robertson*); c) milecastle at Poltross Burn on Hadrian's Wall (*after I.A. Richmond*).

occurred. The barrier itself was built of turf laid on an unmortared, cobble foundation, with a massive ditch in front of it (fig. 23), while in the forts a combination of structural techniques employed masonry, turf, timber and clay. As with Hadrian's Wall, the work was carried out entirely by detachments of the three legions then present in Britain (fig. 24).

For many years it was thought that the Antonine Wall, unlike Hadrian's Wall, had been built in one operation without any changes in plan. But more recent research has shown that this was not so.

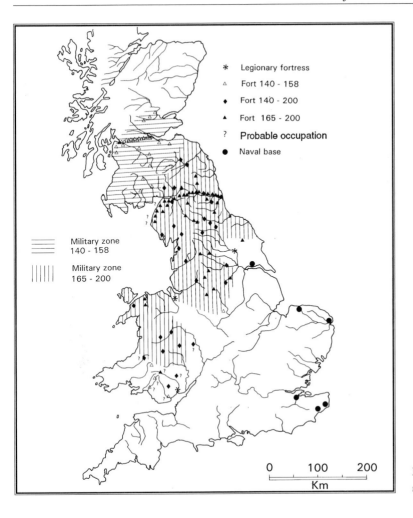

Fig. 22. Antonine frontiers and military zones.

It has long been recognized that the forts on the Antonine Wall represent considerable variations in size and internal planning, split between those large enough to house a complete auxiliary unit and those which could only accommodate part of a unit. Of the former, it has now been shown that at least three, such as Balmuildy, and probably more, were constructed before the Wall, and two of them, including Balmuildy, were the only forts to have been given masonry defences. There is still doubt, however, about Mumrills (fig. 17c) which was the largest fort of all on the frontier. Of the smaller forts only Duntocher (fig. 21b) is demonstrably earlier than the curtain; it superseded a small, free-standing fortlet. The remainder of the forts are now thought to be secondary.

Whether it was intended to build a regular sequence of milecastles, situated between the main forts, as on Hadrian's Wall, is

Fig. 23. The ditch of the Antonine Wall at Watling Lodge (*Hunterian Museum, University of Glasgow*).

still in doubt. But nine fortlets, very similar to the Hadrianic equivalents, have so far been identified; all are either earlier than, or contemporary with the curtain. Another similarity between the two Walls was the construction of a military way for lateral communication, and at least four outpost forts along the main road leading north from the barrier.

The masonry wing walls attached to the northern corners of the fort at Balmuildy might be taken to imply that an all-masonry frontier was originally envisaged, although the idea must have been rapidly jettisoned. The reversion to turf and timber could, therefore, be equated, as on Hadrian's Wall, with the need for speedier construction; alternatively it might imply that the new frontier was to be only a temporary barrier.

For a hundred years now, the Roman army had been attempting to find, often at great cost, a stable northern frontier in Britain, which could be held without too great a drain on manpower. No less than six different positions had been successively tried; none had so far provided the answer. It would not be extraordinary, therefore, if the line of the new Scottish frontier was viewed with some cautious reserve and the greatest economy practised in its construction. Would a further

Fig. 24. Distance slab dedicated by Legio **XX**, from Hutcheson Hill on the Antonine Wall (*Hunterian Museum, University of Glasgow*).

forward movement be possible, or would a withdrawal to the Hadrianic line prove necessary? For the time being, the Hadrianic frontier was freely opened, with new crossing-places being made over the Vallum and with gates removed from milecastles. The forts, however, were kept in good order, perhaps indicating yet another of the uncertainties in the minds of the army staff. But a firm grip was kept on lowland Scotland (fig. 22), although here many of the stations were no more than fortlets, such as that at Chew Green in the Cheviots (fig. 21a).

The new frontier appears to have held until the early 150s, when events within the province and not pressure from outside, compelled its abandonment.

In AD 154, a serious rebellion in Brigantia took place. The effect was immediate and could only be met by a planned withdrawal from Scotland. A new governor, Julius Verus, was sent to Britain with reinforcements for all three legions in Britain; he succeeded in stablizing the situation. His governorship saw the recommissioning

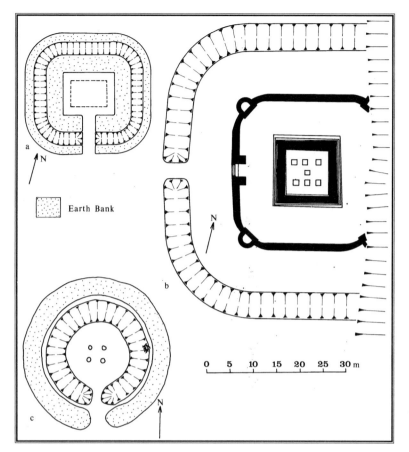

Fig. 25. Signal stations at: a) Roper Castle, part of an arterial chain in the Stainmore Pass (*after I.A. Richmond*); b) Scarborough, a late fourth-century coastal site (*after A. Rowntree*); c) Gask; one of a number along the Gask Ridge (*after I.A. Richmond*).

of Hadrian's Wall and the rebuilding of some forts further south in Brigantia as might be expected (fig. 22).

The rebellion settled and the Brigantes under firmer military control, the return to Scotland was made, probably in AD 159–60. But the reoccupation of Scotland coupled with that of Brigantia placed intolerable strains on the already stretched manpower. By about AD 163 withdrawal from the Antonine Wall had again taken place, and Hadrian's Wall once more became the accepted frontier, served as before by outpost forts which were now increased in number.

The last half of the second century was a turbulent period in Britain. Apart from the events detailed above, there was possibly a revolt in Wales and further assaults on the northern frontier took place, in one of which the Antonine Wall may have been partly reoccupied, and in another Hadrian's Wall itself may have been breached. The century terminated, however, in an altogether more serious disaster.

The emperor Commodus was assassinated in AD 192, and there broke out in the empire another civil war, in which the governor of Britain, Clodius Albinus, was a contestant. By AD 196 he and Septimius Severus were the only survivors in the struggle and Albinus must have realized that he could not succeed to the purple by remaining in Britain. Accordingly he collected together most of the army in Britain and crossed to Gaul where, near Lyon, he was defeated by the superior legionary strength of Severus.

In the meantime, northern Britian had been invaded, the hill-men of Brigantia had again rebelled, in addition probably to some tribes in Wales. They set on the empty forts and burnt them to the ground, and in places even dismantled the Wall itself. Knowing little of imperial politics, they probably considered that the hated invader had departed for good; they could not wait to start removing the most obvious traces of the occupation.

Among the sites which suffered equally were the civilian villages, the *vici*, which had in many cases grown up alongside forts (fig. 26). This process had been a natural one, although regulated by the Roman army. The local population, with an eye to the main chance, early realized that the soldiers were far wealthier than their fellow natives, and hastened to turn this wealth to their own account. They could supply goods and services not normally catered for in the military regime, and to do so built themselves shops, houses and workshops as close to the forts as was permitted by the local commander. So thriving settlements had grown, sometimes to be given a purely local autonomy to run their own affairs. In the south, where military occupation had ceased in the last decades of the first century, many of these villages had been developed to form sizeable towns, capable of independent existence and growth, long after the initial reason for their presence had gone.

In the north and in Wales many of these villages had grown in close juxtaposition to forts. Even during the short occupation of the Antonine Wall properly constituted vici had been established. Their inhabitants were people determined to make the best of things under an alien rule, and even after Scotland had been evacuated, goods from the province continued to circulate, for people there had acquired a taste, in that short time, for Roman-style pottery, metalwork, coinage and other products. But the pacifying effects of trade were not fully to be felt until the fourth century.

During the second century these northern villages were rudimentary affairs with simple, timber-framed buildings providing the necessary accommodation. Neither were they, except in one or two instances, of great extent, usually with the shops and houses lining one or more of the roads leading to the fort. For protection they relied on the neighbouring troops; with those removed, as in AD 197, they suffered the same, if not worse, fate as collaborators as the forts. Yet, with the recovery of Britain in the early third century and, additionally, because of constitutional changes then introduced, these villages were refounded and prospered, being provided with good masonry buildings, proper streets and other amenities, and often grew to considerable size.

Severus restored order in Britain by degrees. It was no easy matter and ultimately required the presence of the new emperor, who set up his headquarters at York in AD 208. By then, most of the wrecked military installations in Britain up to the Wall and its outposts had been restored (fig. 27). There followed a series of ineffective campaigns aimed at punishing the Caledonians. There may have

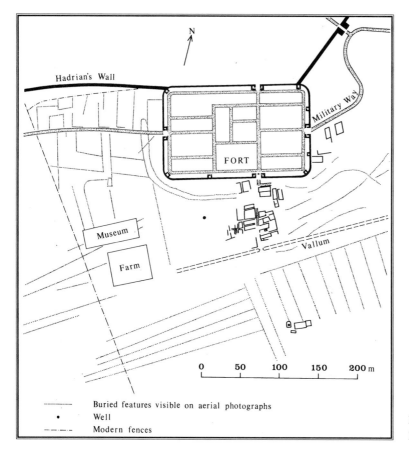

Fig. 26. The fort and vicus at Housesteads, on Hadrian's Wall.

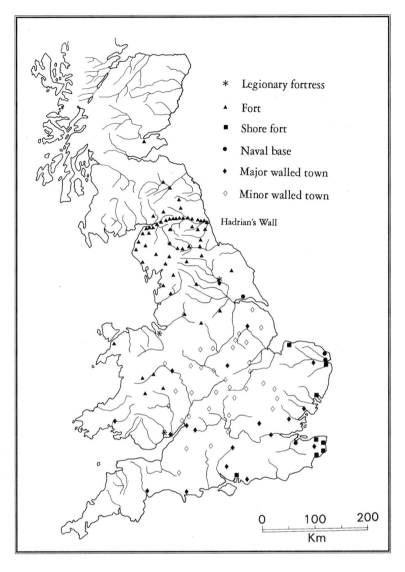

Fig. 27. Third-century Britain.

Legend:

* Legionary fortress
▲ Fort
■ Shore fort
● Naval base
◆ Major walled town
◇ Minor walled town
— Hadrian's Wall

0 100 200 Km

been some intention to reoccupy parts of southern Scotland, and a new fortress, about 13 ha in extent, was built at Carpow on the Tay apparently for a vexillation of Legio VI. Severus was, however, a sick man and he died at York in AD 211, to be succeeded by his elder son, Caracalla, who was with him in Britain. Despite hostile accounts of Caracalla's actions in the province, which may indeed conceal the truth, it was he who brought the Caledonian war to a successful conclusion, imposing terms which were acceptable to both sides. Their effectiveness can be judged by the almost unbroken period of peace on the northern frontier that followed and which lasted until the end of the third century. These actions also effectively stilled the Brigantes. Since their first major defeat at the hands of Petillius Cerealis in the early 70s, almost every new generation that arose made its attempt to throw out the Roman army, resulting, as we have seen, in a series of costly wars throughout the second century.

Other important changes also occurred at this time. In order to prevent a provincial governor, commanding a large army, from being hailed as a pretender, the British province was split in two – Britannia Superior and Britannia Inferior. Superior contained London, Caerleon and Chester, and its governor, ultimately of consular rank, had control of two legions and some auxiliaries in Wales. Inferior included a capital at York, Lincoln and the northern frontier, and its governor, of lower, praetorian rank, commanded only one legion, but many more auxiliaries. Similar divisions were made in Syria and Pannonia.

A further change, of even greater significance for the two new provinces, was the proclamation by Caracalla, in 212, that all free-born men and women should be Roman citizens. This immediately demolished many of the distinctions which had existed between legions and auxiliary regiments and between chartered and non-chartered towns. In many cases it increased the taxes payable to the imperial government, but also conferred privileges. Moreover, serving soldiers were now legally allowed to marry and also to hold land which could be farmed. This last provision exercised the greatest benefit on the northern vici, since soldiers could now buy farms or houses with the prospect of retirement and, in some cases, were even given grants of land. It was only slowly, however, that these constitutional innovations produced any visible effects, but it is probably right to say that they were ultimately responsible for altering the whole character of the empire.

The successful pacification of northern Britain has, nevertheless, to be viewed in conjunction with a growing threat to another part of the province. Seemingly from the late second century, there had been the menace of piratical marauders on the east coast. Coming mostly from northern Germany, they were probably at first only a threat to the considerable volume of coastal shipping plying between the continent and rich centres like York and London. Growing bolder, they may from time to time have landed on the coast and plundered where they could. Hitherto, the British fleet had been stationed at ports on both sides of the Channel, chiefly at Boulogne, Dover and Lympne, although east coast bases at Rochester, Caistor-by-Yarmouth and Brough-on-Humber (fig. 28) were probably also used. With the increasing threat to coastal shipping in the North Sea,

Fig. 28. Aerial photograph showing the relationship of the probable naval base at Brough-on-Humber to the river (*Blackburn and General Aircraft Corporation*).

greater emphasis was placed on the latter sites, and the defences were further strengthened by the provision of forts for auxiliary garrisons at appropriate points, presumably to deal with any raiders who had managed to escape the sea-patrols and make a landing.

A glance at a physical map of Britain (fig. 9) will show that there are three main points of entry on the eastern seaboard: the Thames, the Wash and the Humber. Together they give access to river systems which penetrate the whole of central Britain from the North Downs to the Pennines and stretching almost to the Welsh Border. Here lay the danger points which had to be protected. Accordingly, new masonry forts were constructed at Reculver on the north Kent shore and probably also at Brancaster, on the Norfolk side of the Wash, in the early third century. Furthermore, the naval base at Brough-on-Humber was rationalized in size and provided with fresh defences of turfwork and new internal buildings of masonry.

The forts at Reculver (fig. 29a) and Brancaster represent developments in military architecture introduced to meet changing

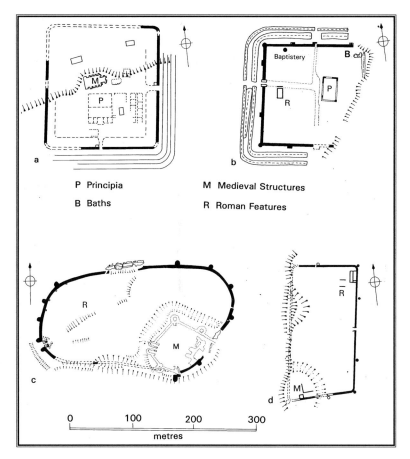

P Principia   M Medieval Structures

B Baths   R Roman Features

Fig. 29. Saxon Shore forts at: a) Reculver (*after S. Johnson*); b) Richborough (*after B. Cunliffe*); c) Pevensey (*after J.P. Bushe-Fox*); d) Burgh Castle (*after S. Johnson*).

conditions. They are larger than the normal auxiliaries' forts of the second century, about 3 ha in area, and therefore probably accommodated naval units as well as the cohorts or alae assigned to them. The gates are smaller, normally containing only one portal (fig. 29).

By the middle of the third century, the whole empire was approaching a state of anarchy. A succession of emperors was put forward by the garrisons of different provinces and the civil war and strife which resulted seriously undermined the structure of society. In addition, a number of barbarian invasions damaged many provinces, including Gaul and Germany, while mounting monetary inflation caused chaos to the economy. Yet, to a great extent, Britain stayed remote from all these convulsions, with the exception of inflation. Outwardly, the resulting loss of confidence in the central government was seemingly expressed in a reluctance to spend money, and little new building work took place. For a time, between AD 259 and 274, Britain, together with Spain, became part of the independent Gallic empire, but this secession can hardly have altered the daily life of the provinces concerned.

Soon after the middle of the century, the earlier threat to the east coast reached more serious proportions, and work was now started on additional forts to combat the menace. For a start, the great triumphal monument (fig. 30), erected at Richborough late in the first century to commemorate the addition of the British province to the empire, was stripped of its ornaments and trophies to become a lookout tower against sea-raiders. It was surrounded by a rampart and triple ditches for protection, but before the work had been completed, the plans were changed and a large rectangular masonry fort was erected on the site (fig. 29b). Other similar forts were started in East Anglia and on the south coast, so that by the time Carausius, a prefect of the British fleet specifically appointed to combat piracy, rebelled and proclaimed himself emperor in Britain, a considerable chain of coastal forts had been established, later to be known as the Saxon Shore defences.

Carausius seems to have received popular support not only in Britain but also in Gaul and Germany. He stemmed the inflationary cycle by a new issue of better quality coins (fig. 83) and apparently reduced the activities of sea-raiders.

But the manpower crisis worsened during the third century. Never easily resolved, it had probably been exacerbated by a number of serious epidemic diseases and by civil war and rebellion. Increasingly, therefore, the Roman army was being strengthened, and at the same time diluted, by troops recruited even more from beyond the frontiers. Particularly in the western provinces they came from free Germany. Their training was undoubtedly poorer and discipline more lax. Today they would be called foreign mercenaries and they probably enlisted more from a desire to obtain as much as they could for themselves, including land settlements, than to protect the empire. Their presence in the Roman army, although necessary due to circumstances beyond imperial control, had a weakening effect.

At about the same time as Carausius took office in Britain, Diocletian had become emperor in Rome and succeeded in reuniting the empire, except for Britain, under his control. He suppressed anarchy, defeated invaders and put down rebellions. His main failure was his inability to defeat Carausius; his chief value was as an administrator. He early realized that the burden of running an increasingly complex empire was too great for one man to carry, so he

Fig. 30. Aerial photograph of the successive Saxon Shore forts at Richborough, together with, in the centre, the foundation of the great monument (*copyright: Committee for Aerial Photography, University of Cambridge*).

appointed Maximianus, a colleague, as co-Augustus with special responsibility for the western provinces, while he, himself, remained in charge in the east. From this act grew the system known as the Tetrarchy, whereby each Augustus appointed a Caesar as heir and after a number of years abdicated in his favour, so hoping to ensure a peaceful and smooth succession instead of civil war.

In the west, Maximianus appointed Constantius Chlorus as Caesar, and it was he who, in the end, retook Britain after Carausius had been murdered. When Constantius Chlorus led the expedition to Britain, he was met by an army taken mainly from the northern garrisons. As in AD 196 when troops had been withdrawn, so in AD 296, an invasion occurred in which the Picts, by which name some Caledonian tribes were now known, inflicted damage to the frontier installations and villages. There followed the usual programme of punitive expeditions and restorations, in which damage from neglect was also made good. With the return of Britain to the empire confidence was restored and prosperity returned.

Among other administrative reforms, introduced by Diocletian to shore up the disintegrating fragments of empire, were many that touched Britain. Civil and military commands were now separated; the governor of a province was no longer commander-in-chief, but only head of a burgeoning civil service, since many of the tasks, once left voluntarily in the hands of responsible classes of society, or carried out by army staff, were now assumed by career civil servants organized in a carefully graded hierarchy.

When Constantius Chlorus, now senior Augustus, died at York in AD 306, his son was hailed emperor in his place. Within six years the Tetrarchy was at an end and Constantine virtually undisputed sole ruler of the whole empire. It was probably then that Britain was again divided, this time into four provinces, each with a governor, but under the unified diocesan control of a *vicarius*, who, in turn, was responsible to the praetorian prefect of Gaul. It is usually assumed that Britannia Superior became Maxima Caesariensis and Britannia Prima, with London and Cirencester as their respective capitals, while Britannia Inferior became Flavia Caesariensis and Britannia Secunda, with capitals at York and Lincoln. Other provinces were similarly subdivided in the early fourth century, a process which must have led to a multiplication of posts in the imperial civil service. Indeed, we might be forgiven for wondering if, as today, some of the multiplication was caused by the necessity of providing an adequate career structure for the growing number of government

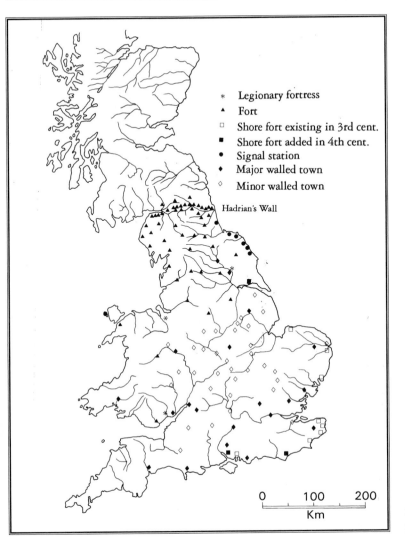

Legend:
* Legionary fortress
▲ Fort
□ Shore fort existing in 3rd cent.
■ Shore fort added in 4th cent.
• Signal station
◆ Major walled town
◇ Minor walled town

Hadrian's Wall

0   100   200
Km

Fig. 31. Fourth-century Britain.

officials, for only in that way would there have been enough senior posts to make promotion possible.

Constantine's reign was a long one, lasting until AD 337, and, as far as Britain was concerned, apparently peaceful (fig. 31). After his death, however, events began to take a graver turn. Renewed attacks seem to have been made on the northern frontier, while increased activity in the Saxon Shore forts, together with the addition of another at Pevensey, suggests that Saxon raiders were again becoming more than just a nuisance; it was probably then that these coastal defences were reorganized under a new office, the Count of the Saxon Shore. It is also possible that units of the mobile field army, a comparatively new introduction, were now in Britain. They were normally billeted in towns and so have left little evidence for their presence, although a unit may for a time have been stationed at Catterick in the late fourth century (figs 32 and 46d).

The fort at Pevensey was the last major addition to the Saxon Shore. These forts, as already indicated above, showed marked differences to earlier auxiliary forts (fig. 29). Most were larger and often, as in the case of Lympne, Dover and Pevensey, irregular in shape. Composite stone walls and earth banks were, in all the later examples, replaced by defences of massive masonry walls up to 4.5 m thick; square angles replaced rounded corners. The gates were narrow and, at some, of unusual design; they were normally protected by massive external towers. Similar towers of varying patterns projected also from the lines of the walls, possibly to provide better deployment of artillery, now used to enfilade the entire length of the fortifications so as to keep an enemy at a distance.

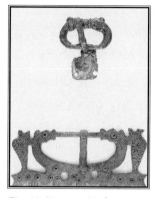

Fig. 32. Zoomorphic bronze buckles from Catterick, which may have come from a military uniform of the Roman army (*by permission of the Trustees of the British Museum*).

It is unfortunate that all too little is known about the internal arrangements of these forts. Possible headquarters buildings and bath-houses have been identified at Richborough and Lympne, but in the main, barracks and other buildings appear to have been constructed with wooden frames, as at Portchester, an interesting return to older methods.

Indeed the Roman army had by now assumed a very different structure from what it had once been. Although some units still retained their old titles, including many of the legions, most were now organized simply in vexillations of cavalry – *equites* – or infantry – *milites*. The legions themselves, despite retaining their original names and titles, were greatly reduced in strength with perhaps no more than 1,000 men, but their number was increased. They no longer held precedence over auxiliaries. Now the distinction lay between the static frontier forces, the *limitanei*, and the mobile field armies of *comitatenses*. The former were not expected to fight at any distance from their bases, which they had to defend. Since their wives and families, homes and farms surrounded the forts they occupied, they had an incentive to do so, but in doing so they took yet another step along the path which ultimately led to their being little better than a local militia. The élite were therefore the mobile field armies, often including heavily armoured cavalry, who were expected to fight in any of the provinces within a given command, according to where the need arose.

These new units, then, may have been serving in Britain by AD 342, when a visit by the emperor Constans in person was considered necessary to restore order. Eight years later Constans was ousted by a usurper Magnentius. Magnentius came of barbarian stock, showing the extent to which such people had penetrated the upper social orders of Rome, often to achieve high office, but he lasted only three years, early suffering defeat by Constans' co-emperor, Constantius II. He appears to have taken what troops he could from Britain, where he had been welcomed, to sustain his cause. For supporting the usurper, people in Britain suffered severe reprisals, and it would seem that the British garrisons remained below strength for some time to come.

Certainly when the next external threat materialized about AD 360, the army in Britain was in no fit state to repel it, and there followed a series of raids by Picts from beyond the Forth, Scots from northern Ireland, Attacotti probably from the western isles, and Saxons. Neither the east nor west coasts, nor the northern frontier were safe, and the raids culminated in the famous barbarian conspiracy of AD 367, when all combined to attack the province.

The effect was disastrous. Hadrian's Wall fell, despite the presence of its garrison, and the commander-in-chief of the northern frontier, the Duke of the Britains, was immobilized and probably besieged at York. The Count of the Saxon Shore was killed in action. The morale of the army seems to have been at a low ebb and many deserted, while the frontier patrol scouts, who should have given the alarm, proved treacherous, so enabling the attack to be a surprise.

This chaotic state lasted almost two years before the emperor Valentinian was able to dispatch Count Theodosius, with four regiments of the field army, to put the provinces in order. Fortunately by then most of the invaders had probably returned home laden with loot and Count Theodosius was only met by small marauding groups. An amnesty for deserters enabled much of the army to be reformed. Then an extensive programme of restoration followed, in which numerous changes in organization can be detected. The frontier forts were reconstructed, probably with the help of labour from civilian areas in the south, and with the standard of masonry showing a marked decline. The numerous villages, sacked at the same time as their parent forts, were not however rebuilt, and the new arrangements inside the forts show that all now lived within their protection.

The failure of the frontier scouts led to their disbanding and to new arrangements, or treaties, being made with tribes beyond the Wall, who may have been given improved status of clients or confederates, and who would be expected to play their part in frontier defence. Count Theodosius also improved the coast defences of Yorkshire and Durham by providing a chain of signal stations at suitable points (fig. 31). This element suggests that part at least of the Pictish attack had been seaborne and descended on the coast south of the eastern extremity of the Wall. The new stations contained a high masonry tower placed within a small fortlet and were sited so as to be able to signal the position of raiders to ships at sea (fig. 25b).

A natural phenomenon was also creating difficulties. A relative rise in sea-level, which seems to have begun at some time in the late third or early fourth century, was influencing coastal sites, among them forts and harbours of the Saxon Shore. Certainly Brough-on-Humber could no longer operate and it is possible that Portchester and Lympne were likewise affected; a new fort at Bitterne on the river Itchen may have been designed to replace Portchester.

In the hinterland of the Wall and on the west coast work was also put in hand with several forts being rebuilt in a more regular manner, together with an additional naval base at Holyhead. The latter, of a new design already in use on the Rhine and the Danube, was walled only on the three landward sides, so providing a protected beach up which ships could be safely drawn.

It is probable also that Theodosius was responsible for stationing regular troops for the first time as permanent garrisons in towns, villages and also some villas (see Chapter 4), but apart from some characteristic items of equipment which possibly bespeak their presence, no evidence has yet been found of specific accommodation; they were most likely billeted among the townspeople.

One further reorganization seems to have been the creation of a fifth British province, Valentia, either in the northern area or in Wales, with Carlisle or Chester as its capital.

Theodosius, when he left Britain, was able to leave behind him a restored, peaceful and ordered diocese, and so matters remained until AD 383, when Magnus Maximus, probably Duke of the Britains at the time, rebelled against the central authority. As had happened so often before, Maximus took a large part of the remaining British garrisons, chiefly from the north-west, and including Legio XX from Chester, to support his claim to be emperor of the west, in which he was successful, until put to death by Theodosius I, son of Count Theodosius, in AD 388. But the regiments taken by him to the continent never returned, and consequently Britain in the next decade was subjected to increased raids, particularly this time by the Irish on the Welsh coast, where they were beginning to form permanent settlements. In the north, however, the confederate tribes beyond the Wall, together with its surviving troops, appear to have held the Picts at bay.

In AD 396, another attempt was made to reorganize the defences of Britain, by the general Stilicho, a Vandal by birth, which seems to have been temporarily successful. But by now, pressure was mounting against the central empire, with Alaric, the Gothic leader, campaigning in Italy and threatening Rome. Yet more regiments were taken from Britain.

The inability of the central government to care for Britain threw up its own solution. The remaining units of the regular army elected in turn three usurper emperors, of whom only the last, Constantine III, survived long enough to take action. But the action he took did not meet with British approval since, in order to protect the Channel coast, he collected together what was left of the army and crossed to Gaul, where serious disturbances were taking place. Despite the fact that he was largely successful, and was recognized by the true emperor, Honorius, he fell into the trap of meddling in central politics and was executed.

Britain was now deprived of any protection by the regular army. In disgust at the activities of Constantine III, the people dismissed his civil servants and, in AD 410, addressed a petition for help to Honorius. Still heavily pressed by the Goths in Italy he was unable to respond, and, in his famous rescript, told the British towns to defend themselves.

We must remember that the Roman army had been withdrawn from Britain before, and there could have been nothing in the circumstances of AD 410 which did not suggest to the inhabitants that, as before, this was but a temporary interruption, to be made good when the situation improved. Indeed there are some authorities who believe that the Roman army did return between AD 416 and 419, but there is no evidence from any British site to support such a view. Destiny ruled otherwise and formal Roman involvement in Britain ceased after 367 years. To view this time-span in perspective, it can be put in modern terms and likened to the period from the defeat of the Spanish Armada until after the First World War!

Complete collapse, however, did not take place immediately, and Roman institutions and way of life continued on a diminishing scale in some areas for several more generations.

We have seen from the preceding description that warfare was largely endemic in Roman Britain. Apart from periods in the third century and again in the first half of the fourth, the frontiers were rarely at peace for more than a decade, and it is not surprising, therefore, that Britain, for its size, contained the largest garrison of any province of the Roman empire. Yet behind the iron curtain of the frontier there developed a civilized and prosperous province, little touched by actual fighting. Moreover, the frontiers in Britain must be viewed in a wider context, for they were also the north-west frontiers of Gaul and Spain. Without them, Gaul certainly would have been at risk, as happened immediately before AD 43. Although more compact, they were therefore as important as the Rhine and Danube frontiers were to other parts of the empire, and warranted the same expenditure of manpower and resources.

What did the native Britons gain? It is probably true to argue that warfare can bring economic benefits to a population, providing the people themselves are not touched by the fighting or embroiled in its political effects. The presence of a large standing army in Britain with its numerous requirements would undoubtedly have been beneficial to many of the inhabitants. It would have put money in peoples' pockets of a value unheard of in the Iron Age. It would have brought foreign traders to Britain in increased numbers, so incidentally introducing the inhabitants to new or improved goods and technology. Even the periodic compulsory supply of grain and food to the army, and taxes to the imperial government, will have acted as a stimulus to increase production and provide work for many hands. It is perhaps no coincidence that the Antonine period in the second century was one of the most prosperous, when that same period saw some of the bitterest and most continuous fighting on the frontiers, with the army probably at its greatest strength.

There was of course a darker side. Arbitrary military rule in the frontier areas cannot always have been pleasant. Recruitment into the army itself was probably not always voluntary. Slaves were bought and sold and exploited with few humanitarian feelings, although in this respect conditions probably differed little from the Iron Age. Life also must have become more burdensome towards the end of the empire, with the growing corruption in public affairs, taxes which did more than shear the sheep and unpleasant jobs made hereditary because there were too few applicants.

On balance, the British province was a success. Once committed to the project, the imperial government maintained it, with only slight faltering, and only yielded when the centre of the empire was itself threatened. Other provinces fared less favourably, being abandoned at an earlier date.

CHAPTER 3

Cities, Towns and Minor Settlements

The geographer Strabo, writing about the turn of the first century BC and first century AD, implied that the backwardness of western Europeans, outside Italy, was derived from their hunting, raiding way of life. Once they were converted to a settled, agricultural existence, urbanism would develop of its own accord.

From this, we might infer that there was nothing in Britain, before the Roman period, which Strabo would have recognized as a town, despite the fact that both he and Caesar respectively refer to fortified woods and forests in Britain as being called *poleis* and *oppida*. But they were presumably employing the nearest Greek and Latin equivalents for whatever Celtic word was used by the Iron Age people. We do not know, nor are we likely to find out, what that Celtic word was, so we cannot say what it was that such sites were called by the people who built and used them. They may have considered them towns, even if they were not to Roman eyes; in the country of the blind the one-eyed man is king. It follows, therefore, that any attempt to ascribe 'towns' to the pre-Roman period in Britain is bound to be subjective and to depend on arguments advanced by modern theoreticians. A hillfort does not become a 'town' just because modern processes of analysis, which are by no means universally agreed, ascribe to it a dominating influence over a purely arbitrary area containing other hillforts of lesser size. Here, as in all things, we must be extremely careful to distinguish between primary evidence and modern inference. We know, from contemporary sources, that towns – even cities – were established in Britain during the Roman period; we have no such basic information for the Iron Age. In this respect it is informative to compare archaeological opinion of some forty years ago with that of today. Then 'village', long used to describe certain types of ill-defined, prehistoric settlement, became a naughty word, used by an archaeologist at his peril. However, within the last years, not only has it again become respectable, but fashion decrees that towns should now also be introduced into Iron Age terminology. Such is the swing of the archaeological pendulum, and it is likely to carry on for many years yet.

This is not to say that some major centres in the Iron Age did not exercise control over lesser ones. We have already seen in an earlier chapter how tribal capitals grew up by reason of developing political, social and economic needs. The argument, therefore, revolves not around their existence, but whether we can justifiably call those sites towns.

Most people nowadays in the so-called developed countries have fairly clear views in their own minds of what constitutes a town. Yet often one person's idea will conflict with another's, and there is probably no universal agreement over borderline cases. It is still possible to insult a resident of a seemingly marginal community by referring to it as a village, when the inhabitants think of it as a town. Indeed this has formed the basis for one of the most realistic definitions of a town: when the people living there think of it as a town, it becomes one. Unfortunately, it is seldom possible to use such an assessment in antiquity, particularly in the prehistoric period. Moreover, such an assessment is just as subjective as those objected to above.

How then are we to define towns in prehistoric and Roman Britain? Some definition is obviously necessary if confusion is to be avoided, and the problem is probably best approached by way of a qualitative, functional analysis. It is desirable to avoid quantitative methods, since there is not sufficient primary evidence available to give them accuracy. In this case, as with computers, if rubbish is put in, rubbish will come out. Locational analyses, for all their apparent scientific appearance, when applied to Roman Britain, too often project in a graphical form only the subjective views of the compiler.

It is generally recognized now that nucleated settlements acquire certain functions, of which some grow with the settlement and others are conferred upon it by virtue of its nature. They can be listed: an economic function connected with trade and industry and its associated shops, factories and markets; an administrative function usually formed when the settlement is selected to act as the centre of some level of local or central government; a communications function often derived from the position of the settlement at an important road or river junction; a religious function represented by a major church or temple; an educational function seen in the provision of schools, colleges and apprenticeship schemes; a protective function generated simply by a concentration of people, but sometimes enhanced by physical fortifications; and a function which provides some degree of amenity and provision for amusements or cultural entertainments, such as theatres, sports stadiums, museums, piped water, sewage disposal systems, good roads and houses, public swimming-baths, etc.

To some extent, and with minor modifications, all these functions, probably together with others – the list is by no means exhaustive – can be applied to the towns and other settlements of antiquity. But if the list is examined more critically it will be seen that some overlap. Communications, for instance, are part of a good road or street system and therefore might be classed under amenities, or alternatively, under the function of trade since they are closely involved with it. Religious devotions can usually be practised anywhere so that the provision of a church or temple might also be seen as an amenity; likewise education.

The original list can therefore be shortened to the four basic functions: administrative, protective, economic and provision of amenities.

We might here usefully invoke the help of the second-century topographer, Pausanias, who in describing the Greek site, Panopeus, says of it: 'A city of the Phocians, if one can give the name of city, to those who possess no government offices, no gymnasium, no theatre, no market-place, no water descending from a fountain, but live in base shelters just like mountain cabins, right on a ravine.' Pausanias clearly had well-established views on what does, or does not, constitute a city and, more helpfully than Strabo, links them to buildings with specific functions, which is useful for our own classification, as will be seen.

Some of these functions can usually be observed in even the smallest hamlet; it may have a shop or pub, or piped water or drains, and it is protective simply by the concentration of people within its boundaries, like a neighbourhood watch scheme. In antiquity, even hillforts may have provided facilities for entertainment or amusement, although any genuine amenities would have appeared pretty primitive to modern or even Roman eyes. But we must be careful not so to judge them. A hillfort might have provided some amenities lacking in an isolated farm of the period. It may also have been the centre of some sort of rudimentary administration.

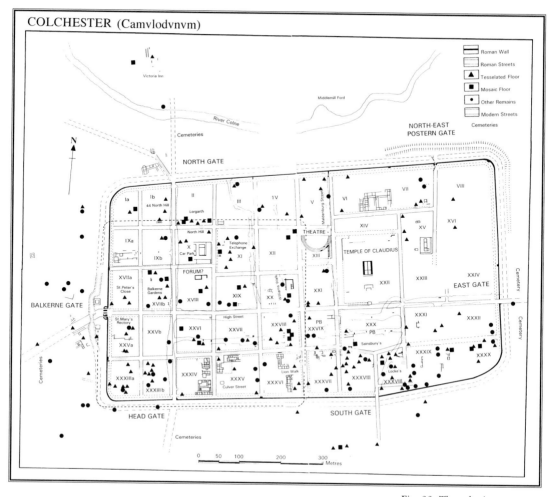

Fig. 33. The colonia at Colchester (*after P. Crummy*).

How then are we to distinguish between a hillfort, an 'oppidum', an Iron Age village, a Romano-British village or a Romano-British city or town? Clearly the assignment of raw functions alone is not enough. In order to refine the method it will become necessary to consider the *level* at which they are applied, and at this point the arguments are bound to become more subjective; one man's village is another man's town. Fortunately, when dealing with Roman Britain, a degree of conformity can be observed within certain classes of towns. There is also an important additional factor to be considered: an element of integrated planning appears in many instances.

However, further difficulties arise involving nomenclature. In the Roman world, as today, there were different classes of town, as well as a variety of Latin words used to describe nucleated settlements:

colonia, municipium, vicus, oppidum, urbs, civitas, and even a Greek word: *polis*. In English also, there used to be a variety of terms: town, city, borough, county town, urban district, county borough, village, hamlet. Most of them had clearly defined legal meanings within the administrative system, although many disappeared during local government reorganization in the early 1970s; but few have exact equivalents with Latin or Greek counterparts. Those which most closely equate are probably city with the chartered colonia and municipium, and vicus with village, although the latter is not as straightforward as it might seem at first sight. Town and oppidum are both so general as to be unhelpful as definitions, and urbs, although it strictly also means city, was largely confined to the City of Rome.

The foundation of towns in Roman Britain followed, to some extent, precedents established elsewhere, especially in Gaul. It is quite clear, from what came after, that the Romans, when they arrived, saw nothing in Britain which even remotely resembled their idea of a town, let alone a city. The provincial government began, therefore, by setting an example to the natives, by the deliberate foundation in AD 49, at Colchester (fig. 33), of a chartered colonia, on the site of the abandoned legionary fortress. Thereby, they partly made use of land which had already been requisitioned and was in imperial ownership. As so often happened, its inhabitants were provided by a discharge of legionaries, probably from Legio XX. Each veteran would have been given a plot of land within the town, on which a house was built, and a somewhat larger plot of arable or pasture, the size commensurate with his rank, in the country surrounding the town. The whole area, the *territorium*, was considered part of the town, was administered from it, and might have been as much as 400 sq km in total extent. It is not entirely surprising that the expropriation of so much land in and around the sometime capital of the Trinovantes, was a principal cause of the rebellion in AD 60.

Later, in the closing decades of the first century, two more similar, chartered coloniae were founded at Lincoln (fig. 37c) and Gloucester, respectively the abandoned sites of legionary fortresses of Legio IX and Legio II Augusta. In both cases, extra land would have been required, and in this instance was probably obtained peacefully from the Corieltavi and Dobunni by the payment of adequate compensation.

Later still, a fourth, well-attested colonia appeared in Britain at York, but by a different process of advancement. It had become the custom, as time went on, to promote existing towns to higher grades.

Normally, the first step was to municipium, of which there were two
types. In Italy and in some of the more central provinces, where most
of the inhabitants would have been Roman citizens, full Roman
rights, in law, would be conferred on the town with its charter. In the
remoter provinces, where few, if any, of the inhabitants possessed the
citizenship, Latin rights were more usually given, with the
magistrates alone being made Roman citizens. The principal
distinction lay in the respective constitutions: a municipium with full
Roman rights would have to abide by Roman law, but, in one with
Latin rights, some native laws could probably still be retained.

When the legionary fortress was founded on the north-east bank of
the Ouse at York in the latter part of the first century, a civilian
settlement began to grow on the opposite bank. Probably at first it
was given the status of vicus; by the later second century it may have

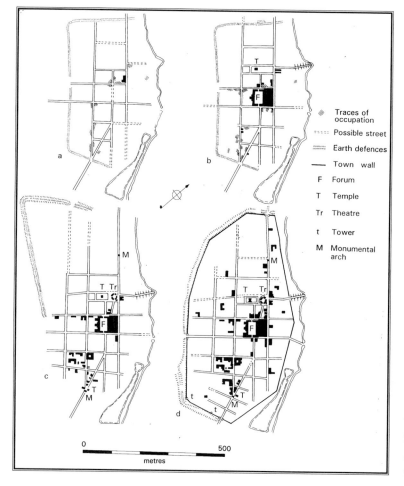

Fig. 34. The development of
Verulamium: a) Claudio-
Neronian; b) Flavian; c) late
Antonine; d) fourth century
(*after S.S. Frere*).

been promoted to the intermediate rank of municipium, and by AD 237 it had become a colonia, by which time also it was the provincial capital of Britannia Inferior.

The evidence for the existence of other coloniae and municipia in Britain is slight. It is likely that London, never part of the local government organization, became a municipium towards the end of the first century, for reasons which are outlined below (Chapter 5) and may even have been promoted to colonia in the early fourth century, when it received the additional honorary title of Augusta. It is difficult to conceive that a town, which was not only the largest in Britain, but also in turn, the provincial capital of Britain, Britannia Superior and Maxima Caesariensis, and the seat of the diocesan vicar, was not so treated.

Verulamium also was probably given a municipal title in the first century (fig. 34). It is sometimes argued, additionally, that certain tribal towns, centres of local government administration, such as Canterbury, Dorchester (Dorset) and Leicester were similarly promoted, but there is no sound evidence to support these claims.

It is not difficult, therefore, to accept the four known British coloniae, the probable municipium at Verulamium, and possibly London, as towns, or even cities, if such a designation is considered more apt. They were chartered; no doubt exists about their status. Below this level, there are some two dozen major settlements which can properly be called towns, together with more numerous other sites, over which general agreement has not yet been reached by archaeologists; it is at this point that a return must be made to a consideration of functions.

The major settlements, which we are about to consider as towns, were those which grew to fulfil the need for centres of local government (fig. 27). The Roman approach to the problems of local administration was extremely flexible. If, in a freshly acquired province, some form of suitable divisions between areas already existed, it was retained and adapted to suit the new conditions. In the three north-western provinces of Gaul and in Britain, the Iron Age tribal structure provided these divisions. Consequently, when the time came for a civilian administration to be formed, it was based, with only minor alterations, on the tribal areas of pre-Roman Britain. Each area was given local autonomy as a *civitas*, a constitution of sorts, and carefully prescribed rights and duties. Each area naturally required an administrative centre, and in response to the need a number of towns appeared, usually referred to now as

Fig. 35. Aerial photograph of the town at Silchester (*copyright: Committee for Aerial Photography, University of Cambridge*).

civitas capitals although such a term had no significance in the Roman period. By the mid-second century, there were in Britain some fifteen such sites. There were also two failures, while, later, local government reorganizations almost certainly created new ones. Not all were founded at the same time, and phases of development can be detected which equate with the pattern of military advance. But no matter how they were founded it must be remembered that, behind the supposed automony of each area, lay the hand of the provincial governor, who could, probably after reference to the emperor, unilaterally revoke or alter the conditions.

The functional level of administration to be observed, therefore, if a settlement is justifiably to be called a town, is that associated, as with the chartered towns, with a self-governing community.

The sites which fall into this category may be considered as follows: Canterbury and Verulamium (fig. 34) probably appeared first, together with Chelmsford, although the Trinovantes were not

attracted by their new capital at the latter site. Caistor-by-Norwich
(fig. 37b), Chichester, Winchester and Silchester (fig. 36) came with
the ultimate absorption of the client kingdoms of the Iceni and
Atrebates into the province between AD 60 and 80. In the 80s also,
and equating with the Flavian advances in the north, Cirencester
(fig. 37a), Dorchester, Exeter, Leicester and Wroxeter (fig. 37d)
appeared, while the Hadrianic troop movements following
the construction of a permanent frontier produced Caerwent,
Carmarthen, Brough-on-Humber and Aldborough.

These towns were essentially native in composition, although
outwardly their appearance would depend on the extent to which
classical architecture was adopted to suit local materials, finance and
needs. But they were built largely by, and for, natives, who paid for
them. Some governors, such as Agricola or Julius Frontinus, gave
encouragement and may have made grants available, probably from
their provincial expense account; some emperors, such as Hadrian,
remitted taxes. Initially, also, help may have been given by military
architects and builders, for the constructional methods then
introduced would have been strange to most natives; alternatively,
there was probably no lack of civil architects from neighbouring
provinces.

If the plans of most of the towns are studied, it will be seen that
there is some degree of conformity between them. In the early stages
of their development, fortifications were seldom provided, or needed,
since the protective function was exercised largely by the Roman
army on the frontiers and by the concentration of people in one place.
Only at Verulamium, Silchester and Winchester, and probably
Chichester, have fortifications dating to the first century so far been
found and there are probably special reasons for their construction.
The remainder were open towns, and almost every one shows evidence
of integrated planning, with a regular grid of streets laid out at right
angles to one another. Planning on this scale could only have been
carried out by a competent authority on a virgin site owned by the
tribal rulers on behalf of the tribe, since there were no powers of
compulsory purchase. The existence of a planned town therefore
implies the existence of a self-governing community which, in the
cases at present being considered, would be the tribal civitates. It will
be noted, also, that quite a number of these towns overlay the sites of
earlier forts or fortresses: Verulamium, Exeter, Cirencester, Wroxeter,
Leicester and possibly Aldborough. The forts would have been
originally sited on land requisitioned with, or more likely without,

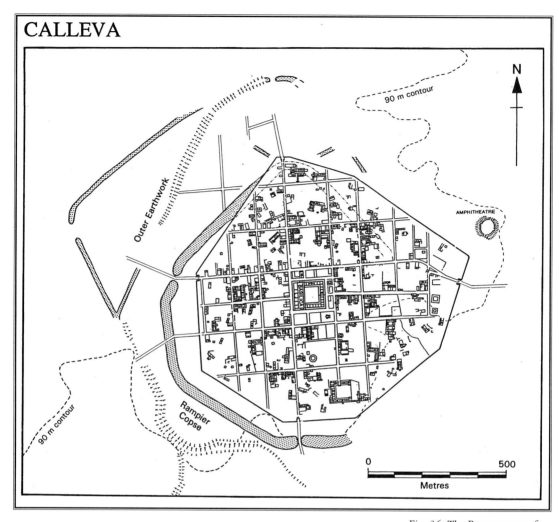

CALLEVA

90 m contour

N

Outer Earthwork

AMPHITHEATRE

BASILICA

Rampier Copse

90 m contour

0   500

Metres

Fig. 36. The Roman town of Silchester lying within the dykes of the Iron Age oppidum (*after M. Fulford*).

compensation for the evicted owners. With the evacuation of the forts and the constitution of a civil authority, the land was presumably made over *en bloc* to the latter and not returned to the original holders.

One major question to be answered involves the choice of sites. Why, for instance, did a civitas capital appear at Dorchester or Cirencester and not at Ham Hill, Badbury or Bourton-on-the-Water, all important sites in the pre-Roman period which gave rise to Romano-British settlements? The answer can best be obtained by considering a specific example of the mechanics involved.

At Cirencester, a fort was established within a year or two of the invasion. Its siting was dictated by the overall strategic requirements of the first frontier of Roman Britain and by the tactical needs of the local position (fig. 99). The fort itself was established at an important junction of roads from Silchester, Verulamium, Leicester and Bath, at a point where a river had to be crossed. Fords have always been favourite places for ambushes, consequently the military needs of the position are readily explained. The positioning of other forts in Dobunnian territory will have been governed by similar reasoning, but at Cirencester an additional factor was the existence, some three miles to the north, of the native oppidum at Bagendon the seat probably of the restored Dobunnian ruler and his court.

While military administration lasted in the country of the Dobunni, any instructions relating to the natives would have been relayed from the governor to the local army commander, or directly

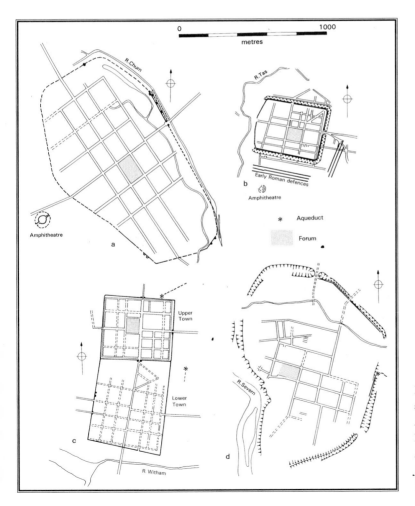

Fig. 37. Outline plans of towns at: a) Cirencester (*after A.D. McWhirr*); b) Caistor-by-Norwich (*after Norwich Castle Museum*); c) Lincoln (*after M. Jones*); d) Wroxeter (*after G. Webster*).

through the procurator's men (see Chapter 5), who would have been required, as far as was possible, to maintain workable relations with the native rulers. In turn, the natives would have been allowed considerable freedom in managing their own affairs providing they behaved themselves.

Any body of troops, especially when stationed in a foreign country, has always acted as a magnet for local traders. Those at Cirencester were no exception, and it is probable that, to begin with, local traders made daily journeys with their wares to and from Bagendon and from other nearby sites. The inconvenience of such an arrangement soon seems to have been realized and, within a decade or so, many had actually removed, and a thriving trading centre was growing up on land immediately north-west of the fort. The reflection of this movement can be seen at Bagendon, where from the late 50s the population markedly declined before dwindling away altogether. The new settlement would have been encouraged and regulated by the Roman army and before long would probably have had the formal status of a vicus conferred upon it.

When the time came for the removal of garrisons from Dobunnian territory, for reasons already outlined in the preceding chapter, local government would have been handed over to the newly constituted *civitas Dobunnorum*. The vicus at Cirencester was thereupon chosen, with the governor's approval, to become the civitas capital, presumably for no other reason than that the principal tribal leaders, who would now be expected to run it, already lived there. The new capital was then developed in the normal manner, not only on the area of the vicus, but also on that of the abandoned fort. The trade provided by the soldiers was replaced by the sale and purchase of merchandise produced not only in the town but also in the surrounding countryside. In this respect Cirencester would have acted like a country market town and would, moreover, have attracted traders from further afield hoping to capture new markets. These traders, if from other provinces, would have brought with them more than goods for sale; they would have brought new ideas relating to improved technology and agriculture, to the standard of living, cultural advancements, religious beliefs and to more sophisticated amusements. They were to play an important part in the romanization of Britain. It is probable also that, among the native population, the more go-ahead members of society will have been attracted to the newly created towns, avid for the opportunities they offered and eagerly embracing the new way of life.

The process of urbanization just described for Cirencester was repeated elsewhere. At Dorchester, the tribal aristocracy living in the hillfort of Maiden Castle caused the civitas capital of the Durotriges to be set up at Dorchester nearby. Sometimes, as at Canterbury, Verulamium or Leicester, little or no movement of people was required, since the relevant fortifications of the army were sited close to the existing native centre. Sometimes, also, where the tribe exhibited little or no centralized organization, a legionary fortress with its greater number of better paid soldiers provided the extra attraction for the tribal leaders, as at Exeter and Wroxeter.

In all cases, it is probably true to say that the foundation of these towns was a voluntary process, carried out with the encouragement and approval of the provincial administration, but not by compulsion. Even given their conformity of planning, there is too much variation from town to town for them to have been the product of a rigorous enforcement. While it is possible, as it was from time to time in Roman Britain, to compel people to do many things and push them around to a great extent, one thing that cannot be done is to force them to spend their own money on goods, buildings and services they do not want. To be effective in the face of opposition, the money has first to be taken from people in taxes and the revenue then used by government agencies, in which case a 'standard pattern Romano-British town' would probably have emerged to grace the province. It did not, and probably the only example of a site for a capital being foisted by the provincial administration upon a civitas was Chelmsford for the Trinovantes; it failed. Moreover, the Roman administration simply did not have the personnel for general enforcement of this nature. So few were they that it is likely that a very large number of the inhabitants of Britain would not have seen a Roman soldier or provincial administrator from one year's end to another. It was the native Britons, perhaps joined in some cases by other provincials, who built towns and maintained them, and this fact cannot be emphasised enough. The Roman administration did little more than provide the initial models, approve the sites and give some spasmodic help.

So far, we have considered three classes of town, and we have still to justify fully the use of the term to describe the civitas capitals.

Their planned nature, as already observed, is a prerequisite. Although irregularities in the street systems sometimes occur, in the main, the streets were laid out at right angles to one another forming rectangular blocks of land – *insulae* – between them. Two main streets, usually carrying through flows of traffic, intersect at the centre and were referred to as the *cardo maximus* and *decumanus maximus*. In one of the four insulae beside this crossroads was normally to be found the forum and basilica, the principal public buildings; Cirencester (fig. 37a) and Silchester (fig. 36) are both good examples of such planning. Occasionally, when a town enlarged its boundaries, a fresh alignment was adopted for the new streets, as can be seen at Wroxeter (fig. 37d). Occasionally, also, some elements of an earlier, unplanned street system were preserved when a new grid was laid out, as at Silchester and Caistor-by-Norwich (fig. 37b). In most chartered towns in the Roman world it was an offence to encroach on or interrupt any public right-of-way, so special interest attaches to the few examples where a house had been built over a street, as at Gloucester. As time passed, subsidiary roads, often providing additional access to a particular building, were constructed, so effectively reducing the size of some insulae, as at Leicester and Canterbury.

The streets themselves were constructed of local materials; gravel and limestone brash were perhaps the commonest as both tend, when compacted, to cement themselves together by natural processes. The surface was frequently cambered and side drains were provided to carry away water. Whenever a surface became worn or pot-holed, as must frequently have happened, a new layer of aggregate was put down. Extensive wear also caused formidable quantities of dust, or mud if it was wet, to accumulate, and this, combined with repeated resurfacing, must have been a grave nuisance to house- and shop-holders, as it resulted in a gradual overall rise in the level of the streets. Consequently, when a town street is excavated today, it is often found that the level has risen by as much as 3 m over 330 years, a rate of about 1 cm per year. Over a lifetime therefore, a householder might have found that instead of walking out onto a surface level with his front door, he was having to negotiate a considerable step up. In many cases this led to floors being raised in houses and in extreme cases to complete rebuilding after the site had been relevelled. This one factor, more than any other, probably accounts for the great depths of deposits to be found in most Romano-British towns.

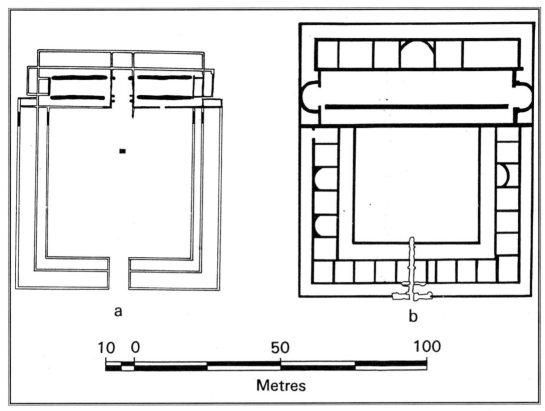

a b

10 0   50   100

Metres

Fig. 38. Successive forums and basilicas at Silchester. The first (a) dates to the late first century and was built of timber. It was succeeded by a masonry building (b), dating to the early second century (*after M. Fulford*).

Foremost among the functions of these towns was the need to act as adminstrative centres for the civitas. In the chartered towns, the administration was in the hands of two, or sometimes three, pairs of magistrates, who were responsible to an 'elected' council of up to a hundred members. Although we have only a little evidence from Britain, it is probable that the civitates were similaly governed. In the chartered towns, the basilica or more correctly the council chamber provides the physical evidence for the existence of the council and magistrates. Likewise, the civitas capitals were provided with basilicas and we may deduce, therefore, a similar level of administration. However, a degree of caution must be exercised, as the development of the monumental, unified, forum-and-basilica complex, like those at Cirencester, Silchester (figs 38 and 39a) or Leicester, did not occur in the western provinces much before the end of the first century. Before, less easily recognized buildings may have served the same purpose, so that, although we may argue that their presence represents a certain level of local government, an absence, especially in the years soon after

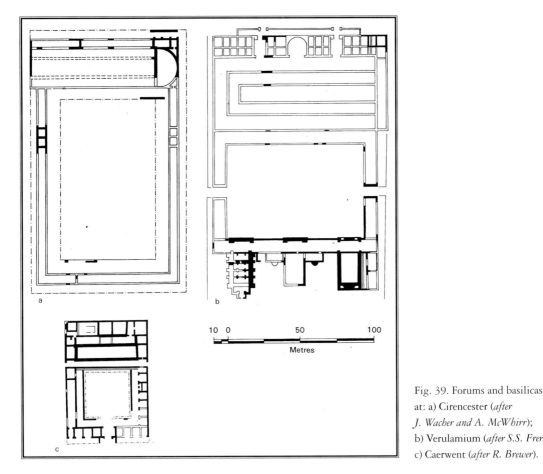

Fig. 39. Forums and basilicas
at: a) Cirencester (*after
J. Wacher and A. McWhirr*);
b) Verulamium (*after S.S. Frere*);
c) Caerwent (*after R. Brewer*).

the invasion or in the fourth century, does not necessarily imply that
such government was non-existent. For instance, the three early towns
of Colchester, Verulamium and Canterbury have yet to produce
evidence for commensurately early basilicas.

The forum and basilica of a town usually consisted of a large open
space surrounded on three sides by porticoes, perhaps fronting rows
of shops and offices, and with the basilica occupying the whole of the
fourth side. An elaborate entrance was usually sited in the middle of
the range facing the basilica, and in some cases, as at Silchester
(fig. 38), an external portico surrounded the whole, or part of, the
building.

The basilica was a long, two-aisled hall with at one, or more
usually at both ends of the nave, raised platforms, or tribunals, used
by the magistrates for conducting judicial and official business. A
range of rooms was attached to the hall on the side away from the

forum; they were used as offices and for meetings of the council, while one room, centrally placed in the range, probably served as a shrine for statues of the emperors or local protective deities. Occasionally for reasons of economy, one of the aisles of the hall was dispensed with, as at Silchester (fig. 38), Caerwent (fig. 39c) and Caistor-by-Norwich.

The forum, as already described, consisted primarily of an open space which could be used not only for gatherings of a political or administrative nature, but also as a place in which, on market days, stalls could be set up. If rooms were additionally provided around this area, they could be rented out as shops, or used as offices by the administration.

The plans of most of the forums and basilicas in Britain strongly resemble those of military headquarters buildings, and is one reason for supposing that army architects were seconded to towns to help in their construction. There are some exceptions, notably at Verulamium (fig. 39b), where the plan owes more to central Italian designs, and the council chamber and tribunals are centrally placed in the range opposing the basilica and were later flanked by temples.

A settlement, therefore, which had been provided with a basilica and forum, possessed the requisite level of local administration for it to be called a town and if chartered, a city. This is the main reason for supposing that London became a chartered town as, at the end of the first century, these buildings were constructed.

Another of the principal functions which enable us to distinguish between a town and a lesser settlement was that associated with the provision of amenities (see Chapter 8). As with the administration, these can often be linked with certain specific structures. In addition to the provision of well-paved, spacious streets and covered porticoes, we may number among them running water from an aqueduct, good sewage and surface water disposal, provision for public lavatories and bath-houses, a reasonable standard of comfort in private dwellings and the availability of entertainments, amusements and educational facilities.

It can be shown that every chartered town and civitas capital in Britain was supplied with fresh water from an aqueduct, and distributed by means of wood, lead, stone or ceramic pipes or channels. Drinking basins were often provided at street corners and fed from this supply, as at York and Gloucester, but most of the water would have been channelled to the public baths, which consumed large quantities. Waste water from the baths was used to

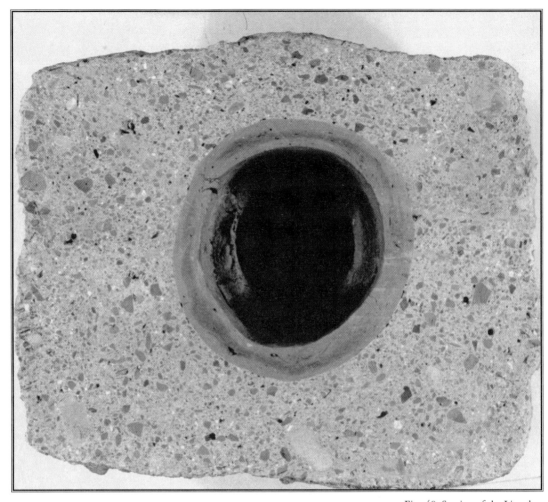

Fig. 40. Section of the Lincoln aqueduct pipe, showing the spigot end of one of the ceramic pipes within the concrete jacket (*photo: F.M.B. Cooke*).

flush lavatories and the main sewers. Some private supplies were also arranged, for which the user would pay a water rate; examples can be seen of shops so served at Wroxeter and Verulamium.

The aqueduct channels which brought water to the towns of Britain were, like their military counterparts, of simple construction. The comparatively gentle undulations of the British countryside did not call for grandiose structures like those often to be seen in parts of Gaul and Spain, where steep, narrow gorges had to be crossed. The nearest sufficiently high source of water was chosen for the supply, either by damming a stream or diverting a spring, and the flow conducted by gravity in carefully contoured channels dug in the ground, as at Dorchester and Wroxeter. Only at the hill-top town of Lincoln is there seemingly a more sophisticated arrangement where, owing to valleys having to be crossed along the route, the water was carried in ceramic pipes, jacketed in concrete (fig. 40) to withstand the pressure. An aqueduct of the former type was capable of carrying several million litres of water a day.

Fig. 41. The main sewer of the bath-house on the Jewry Wall site, Leicester.

The counterpart to an aqueduct was an adequate sewer. Once an aqueduct was working, its flow could only be controlled with difficulty – there was no turning off at the main. Provisions had therefore to be made for carrying away, not only effluent, but also any surplus capacity. Major sewerage systems constructed of masonry are well illustrated by examples at Lincoln, Leicester (fig. 41) and Verulamium, where they ran under or beside main streets, but sometimes, as at Cirencester or Caistor-by-Norwich, they were only lined and covered with wooden planks.

Public lavatories were occasionally provided by enterprising shopkeepers, but more normally were to be found connected to the public bath-house, where they were flushed by waste water from the baths. In Britain they seem to have consisted of wooden seats placed either directly above the main sewer, or over an inclined shoot connected to it. A shallow gutter in the floor in front of the seat carried water for rinsing the sponges or moss tied to sticks, which were used in place of lavatory paper. Multiple capacity was the norm and no sex discrimination was apparently observed. The alternative was probably a backyard earth-closet or the jars placed at street corners by the fullers for the convenience of passers-by; fullers used stale urine for the treatment of cloth.

The principal amenity in the Roman world was undoubtedly the bath-house (fig. 42). Although some rich members of society had bath-wings attached to their town houses, they were rare, and in the main, people of all classes made use of the public baths. The buildings became, therefore, more than just places for ablutions, and people gathered to exchange news and gossip, or take exercise, even to buy and sell goods, since many public baths were equipped with shops or had itinerant merchants displaying their wares.

Most public bath-houses were based on one of two standard plans. Those in Britain, as with forums and basilicas, owed much to military prototypes, and the commonest basic form consisted of a suite of rooms arranged in series with each maintained at a different temperature, so resembling the modern Turkish bath, which is, after all, derived from Roman models. Minimally there was a dressing-room, with a latrine leading from it, an unheated room, a warm room and a hot room. Each might be provided with a small plunge

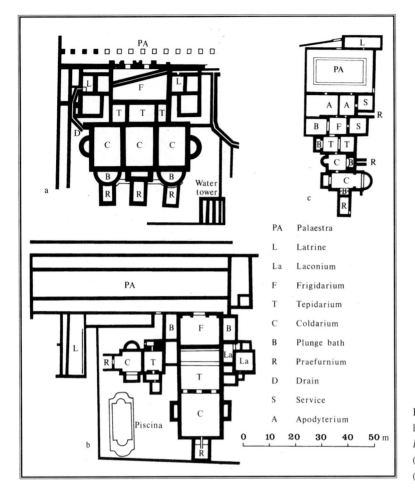

PA   Palaestra

L   Latrine

La   Laconium

F   Frigidarium

T   Tepidarium

C   Coldarium

B   Plunge bath

R   Praefurnium

D   Drain

S   Service

A   Apodyterium

Fig. 42. Plans of town bath-houses at: a) Leicester (*after K.M. Kenyon*); b) Wroxeter (*after G. Webster*); c) Silchester (*after G.C. Boon*).

bath maintained at an equivalent temperature, and sometimes one or more of the rooms or the plunges would be duplicated. The heated rooms were kept moist by injections of steam but there might be, additionally, one or more small rooms kept with an intense dry heat, as in the modern sauna. Most bath-houses also had either an open area, perhaps surrounded by porticoes, or a covered hall, attached to them, where the bathers could exercise or play games.

The hot rooms were kept at their required temperatures by conducting heat from external fires through stokeholes, under the floors and up ducts built in the walls and sometimes in the roofs also; the latter were normally vaulted, sometimes with a cavity construction to conserve heat. A boiler made of copper or lead sheets was placed over the stokehole to provide steam and hot water for the plunges.

Fig. 43. Surviving remains of the bath-house at Wroxeter. The largest fragment of wall marks the doorways between the exercise hall and the bath-house. In the foreground are shops lining Watling Street.

The normal bathing process employed the hot rooms to open the pores of the skin and create a good sweat, after which the dirt was scraped off by means of a curved iron or bronze blade – a *strigil*. If the bather were fortunate a slave or friend did it for him; otherwise he managed as best he could by himself. Soap was known, but seems rarely to have been used. A retreat through the unheated room, and possibly a dip in the cold plunge, closed the pores, and, after drying, the oils lost from the skin in the process were replaced by anointing with suitable animal or vegetable substitutes.

The site occupied by a bath-house obviously had to be related to the provision and removal of water. No standard place in the town, unlike that occupied by the forum and basilica, can therefore be expected, although where possible they were situated near the centre.

As towns developed, so the standards of living of their inhabitants improved. By the early second century, this rise is demonstrated by the appearance of comfortable, well-appointed houses. At first, most townspeople were probably concerned with trade and lived over or in their shops. But as wealth accumulated, so separate living accommodation tended to be provided by the richer merchants for themselves, inferring that either their businesses had been sold at a profit or were being managed by tenants or slaves.

The earliest houses were frequently simple in plan, usually having no more than five or six rooms connected by an external covered portico. Often, in areas where there was little good building stone, they were constructed with wooden frames, with the walls made of wattle and daub, and the roofs of tiles. This did not, however, prevent the walls from being plastered and painted with frescoes: one second-century example from Verulamium was decorated with imitation columns. Neither did it prevent the householder from having glazed windows or a mosaic floor laid in his dining-room, nor good concrete or wooden floors in other rooms. It meant, however, that underfloor heating on the hypocaust principle could not be employed and rooms were no doubt warmed by braziers, while lighting was provided by oil-lamps or candles. Sometimes these houses contained a further wing, usually set at right angles to the main residence and reached by an extension of the covered portico. Markedly plainer in design and execution, it probably contained the domestic offices and quarters for slaves or servants.

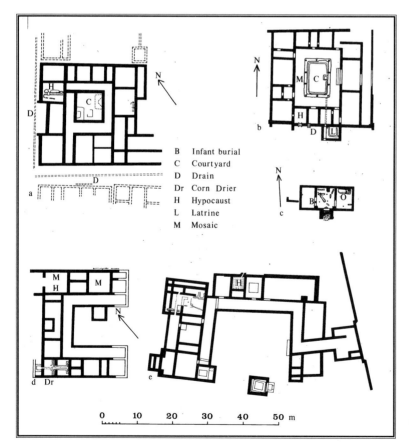

B	Infant burial
C	Courtyard
D	Drain
Dr	Corn Drier
H	Hypocaust
L	Latrine
M	Mosaic

Fig. 44. Town houses at:
a) Gloucester (*after H. Hurst*);
b) Caerwent (*after V.E. Nash-Williams*); c) Dorchester (Dorset) (*after Royal Commission on Historical Monuments for England*); d) Verulamium (*after S.S. Frere*); e) Silchester (*after G.C. Boon*).

The standard of upper-class housing increased rapidly, sometimes as the result of extending existing buildings, sometimes by complete reconstruction. When reconstruction occurred, wooden frames were frequently replaced by masonry walls, or by a combination of masonry and cob, or half-timbering, so enabling hypocausts to be incorporated for heating. As then planned, the houses often formed two or more wings around an enclosed courtyard, which may have been laid out as a garden (fig. 44). Such houses, although owing something to Mediterranean styles, were usually less compact. Land was still abundant and cheap, except in the very centre of a town, where most shops lay, and so there was no need to practise economy in layout. Such planning also provided the owner with maximum privacy and security from thieves, a very necessary precaution in the absence of a police force to apprehend criminals. The best rooms in the house would be decorated with mosaics, painted ceilings and frescoes, often of an elaborate character. One house in Leicester, obviously the residence of an important and wealthy inhabitant, had the whole of the inside wall of the portico round his courtyard painted with continuous frieze incorporating flowers, animals, birds, human figures and architectural perspectives executed in the Pompeian manner (fig. 127). Another at Verulamium had a mosaic in the dining-room – the most important room in the house – illustrating a lifelike portrait of a lion carrying a stag's head in its mouth, with realistic drops of blood falling to the ground (fig. 45).

The use of decorative features such as these, originating in the centre of the empire, imply the presence in Britain either of copybooks containing the designs or of travelling artists employed on contract. It indicates, also, the extent to which native Britons had wholeheartedly adopted the new way of life. But the rooms in these houses would, to modern eyes, appear sparsely furnished. An assortment of couches, basket chairs, low tables, often circular with three legs, and some cupboards or presses were all that the householder required. Occasionally a small domestic shrine was included, as in a shop at Verulamium.

Less evidence, somewhat naturally, survives to represent the other end of the social scale. It is sometimes claimed that apparently vacant areas within a town were taken up by small huts, forming shanty towns. To what extent this would have been allowed by the authorities is not known, for, since the land presumably belonged to someone, any occupants would have been tenants or squatters. Indeed, we might doubt their existence, for such people, if they were

Fig. 45. Mosaic depicting a lion holding a stag's head in its mouth from a house in Verulamium (*St Alban's Museum Service*).

not retainers or slaves and so accommodated in their masters' premises, are unlikely to have gravitated to towns. A peasant class, whether free or bound to the land, would almost certainly have remained in the country, where some sort of living could be more easily scratched. It is probable, however, that every town had its quota of beggars and itinerant pedlars, living rough and snatching sleep in porticoes and alleys if they could not afford the price of a night's lodging. Moreover, if the patronage system of Roman society extended at all to Britain, as seems probable, particularly in towns, there would have been few people in a really penurious state.

Other amenities (see Chapter 8) provided in towns were entertainments or amusements, catered for by amphitheatres and theatres. The former were relatively common features in Britain, the latter are less seldom seen and when they existed were more often than not connected with temples. A third place of entertainment, the circus, where chariot- and horse-racing were carried on, has yet to be positively identified in Britain, although there is evidence of an interest in the sport.

Amphitheatres were large, elliptical structures, built so that the maximum number of people could view the entertainment, normally of a vulgar nature. The seating in most British amphitheatres was raised in tiers on earth banks, retained by wooden or masonry walls, and surrounding a central arena. Access to the arena was obtained by entrances at each end of the long axis, while the seats were approached from round the circumference. Probably the best surviving urban, as opposed to military, examples are those at Cirencester and Dorchester (p. 288 and fig. 126a, c).

There is some evidence for gladiatorial shows. But they were expensive and since most spectacles were put on and paid for by influential townspeople, it is likely that wild-beast shows were more commonly promoted, in which various types of animal were matched against each other as in bear-baiting and cock-fighting. Executions for high treason were also carried out in the arena and were usually considered excellent entertainment. Estimates of the seating capacities of amphitheatres have shown that they could accommodate a town's inhabitants and visitors from the countryside as well. Special boxes were provided for distinguished people, and one or more shrines, usually dedicated to Nemesis, were incorporated by the arena entrances.

The few theatres attested in Britain were intended for a very different kind of entertainment, since almost all were connected with temples, usually of the Romano-Celtic form. The development of the Gallo-Roman theatre from the classical norm, for example at Verulamium, may be due therefore to the ceremonial requirements of the cult, rather than to the intention, as is sometimes claimed, that they should act also as amphitheatres (p. 286 and fig. 125c). One of the largest near-classical examples is that at Canterbury which was built in the early third century to replace one of very different plan (fig. 125a). But even here it was situated adjacent to a large temple enclosure, so a religious connexion is almost certain. The building covered an area slightly greater than a semicircle; the stage was set along the chord of the circle, and the seating rose in tiers around the circumference. Immediately fronting the stage below the seats, a nearly semicircular area at ground level – the orchestra – provided seating spaces for distinguished members of the audience. Even though the prime function of the theatre may

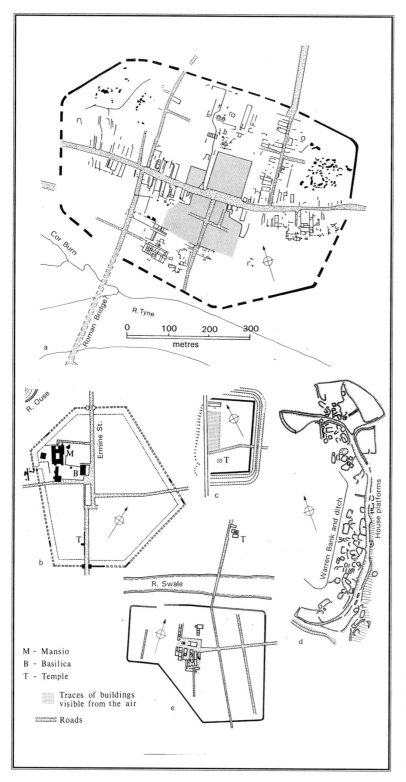

Fig. 46. Minor towns and villages at: a) Corbridge (*after P. Salway, M.C. Bishop and J.N. Dore*); b) Godmanchester (*after M. Green*); c) Thorpe-by-Newark; d) Chisenbury Warren (*after Royal Commission on Historical Monuments for England*); e) Catterick in the fourth century.

M – Mansio
B – Basilica
T – Temple

Traces of buildings visible from the air
Roads

have been associated with religious or semi-religious ceremonials and festivals, there seems no good reason why purely secular entertainment, consisting of recitations, mimes, pantomimes, tragedies and farces should not have been staged; many shows of this nature were often highly topical, and satyrical, in their content.

Education may also be considered an amenity. Certainly, Latin and civilized manners are known to have been imparted to the youth of Britain, and Tacitus records that they made excellent pupils. Schools, however, were informal affairs, and most rich parents probably employed private tutors to teach grammar and rhetoric. Plutarch records that he had conversations with a schoolmaster, Demetrius of Tarsus, 'recently returned from Britain'; it is possible that this same Demetrius was the one who dedicated to the gods of the governor's residence at York (p. 214).

The remaining functions of towns, economic and protective, tend to be shared by settlements of a lesser nature. It is as well, therefore, that some consideration should now be given to the latter.

Apart from the urban sites already described, there were in Britain a large number of nucleated settlements showing considerable variation in size and composition. Some were fortified, others were not. Some became primarily trading centres, the result, once they had been founded for one reason or another, of spontaneous economic growth to meet local requirements; others developed as mining, industrial or religious settlements, providing for the needs of the relative communities in the surrounding areas. Those which became fortified have been referred to by archaeologists as 'small towns', but the term proved inadequate, since some were little smaller than genuine towns, while it is now recognized that many of the sites which were apparently never fortified often covered very considerable areas. For the same reason, the term village is hardly applicable in all cases, although it might suitably be applied to some. An attempt has also been made to call them 'native' towns, but it should be resisted, since it is difficult to justify its use. Moreover, to be so claimed these sites should only exhibit archaic forms of architecture current in the native Iron Age; they frequently do not, and employ largely Roman styles, if in a simplified manner. Consequently, they are only separated from towns proper by degree and, when all is said and done, civitas capitals were as much native towns as these sites. The use of the word 'native' in this context is as meaningless as 'small town'.

Many of them, however, began in the same way as most civitas
capitals, as vici attached to forts or else as existing pre-Roman, native
settlements. Thereafter, the processes of development were very
different. Sometimes, the fort was replaced by a *mansio*, an inn
provided for members of the imperial post, a building found in most
civitas capitals as well. With the lesser sites, the presence of a mansio
often acted in a similar way to a fort and attracted local natives, as at
Catterick or Wanborough. The sites themselves seldom exhibit any
trace of deliberate planning in their layouts, usually starting as ribbon
developments of shops and houses alongside main roads. Then, as
need arose, side streets or lanes were constructed in a haphazard
manner to give access to more distant houses or land. Frequently,
many grew to cover large areas, perhaps as much as 40–50 ha in
extent (fig. 47a). But if fortifications were later erected, they equally
frequently enclosed only a small proportion of the whole.

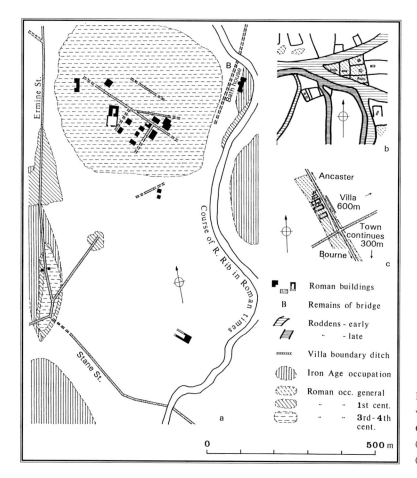

Fig. 47. Minor towns and
villages at: a) Braughing (*after
C. Partridge*); b) Hacconby
(*after B. Simmons*); c) Sapperton
(*after B. Simmons*).

As a group, therefore, these sites defy easy classification, and it is likely that no one word or phrase will ever do to describe all. It is possible that some possessed the Roman legal status of vicus, but even if they did, apart from Water Newton (fig. 48), we do not know which, and it would not serve as a meaningful distinction, since most civitas capitals ranked so. It may be that we should follow the practice of some archaeologists and call them lesser, or minor towns. But if we are to use town to describe them, albeit in a qualified form, we must firmly remember the distinctions which separate them from towns – or cities – proper. Even so, it seems unsuitable to dignify some of these sites as towns, for by no stretch of the imagination were they any such thing. The whole subject of 'small' towns bristles with difficulties and contradictions caused by, as much as anything, a lack of sound evidence about them.

The principal distinction between these sites, whatever they are to be called, and our defined towns is their complete lack of any but the most superficial planning, their association with only the lowest grades of local administration and the lack of all but the most primitive amenities. Even if an element of planning seems to be involved, as at Alchester, Catterick, Corbridge or Godmanchester (fig. 46), evidence for public baths, aqueducts, theatres, amphitheatres or high-standard housing is almost entirely absent. Nevertheless, it would be a mistake to apply this prescription too rigidly, since some exceptions do exist. Catterick possessed a working aqueduct, admittedly inherited from an earlier fort, and might also have had a small bath-house, had the construction work been completed; in addition, a small theatre may have been part of a religious complex in an extramural suburb. The mining settlement at Charterhouse-in-Mendip appears to have had an amphitheatre but its origins again might be military; Wanborough (Wilts.) had at least one dwelling-house with mosaics; Braughing (Herts.) had a small bath-house, but perhaps not of a public nature (fig. 47a); Wycomb (Glos.) seems to have had a theatre, although probably connected with a religious establishment. Despite these exceptions, it is probably true to say that no site of this type contains a preponderance of structures related to amenities, as are to be found in our defined towns.

Moreover, none has yet produced evidence for a forum and basilica, although a further caution has to be exercised in this respect, since, by the third and fourth centuries, when many of these minor sites reached their maximum development, the provision of a forum or basilica was no longer considered essential for the good ordering of local government. So later promotions to the rank of civitas capital cannot be detected by this means, and sites such as Ilchester, Water Newton, Bath, Towcester and Carlisle – all strong candidates – cannot readily be distinguished.

But all these sites, whatever their size or reason for existence, share two of the main functions of the higher forms of urban settlement: trade and protection.

In all sites, large and small, of high and low status, buildings early appeared which can be identified as shops or workshops, the two words being largely synonymous in the present context. They can be identified soon after the establishment of great towns such as Colchester, Verulamium and Cirencester. They are to be found in the minor towns such as Water Newton, Margidunum and Catterick, in the military villages of the north, such as Housesteads, and in the less well-defined settlements such as Camerton and Wycomb. Normally, they occupy the frontages of main roads or principal streets in town centres, which were the most desirable commercial sites. As today, land values were probably higher in town centres, with the length of frontage frequently governing the cost. Consequently, most shops of Roman Britain had narrow frontages and jostled one another in close profusion. Enlargement of a successful business could, therefore, only take place either by buying up neighbouring premises or by extending the building to the rear, a process which can frequently be seen to have taken place, as at Caerwent, or at Verulamium in the second century, and at Cirencester over an extended period of time.

Most shops appear as narrow strip-like buildings with the long axis at right angles to the frontage (fig. 49). The front probably contained a single wide entrance, extending across most of the width of the building, to be closed, when necessary, by wooden shutters, the emplacements for which can be admirably seen in one at Catterick (fig. 50). The entrance would give on to the business section, while behind it would be either storerooms and workshops or the living-quarters of the shopkeeper. There is good reason to suppose that many shops had an upper storey, in which case the positions of stores and residence could be interchanged according to need. Frequently also in the better class towns, shops were provided with covered porticoes at the front to protect goods on open display and provide shelter for shoppers.

Fig. 48. Aerial photograph of the minor town at Water Newton, near Peterborough. The haphazard layout of streets can be clearly seen (*copyright: Committee for Aerial Photography, University of Cambridge*).

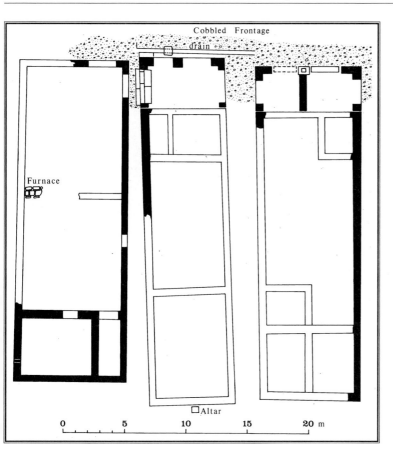

Cobbled Frontage
drain
Furnace
Altar

0   5   10   15   20 m

Fig. 49. Shops lining one of the
main streets at Caerwent. In
this instance narrow alleys
between shops provided access
to the rear and also served to
catch water draining from the
eaves (*after V.E. Nash-Williams*).

There is some evidence to show, occasionally, that blocks of shops
were built as an investment, either for sale or letting, as at Verulamium
and Cirencester. At the former it is difficult to say precisely which, but
at the latter piecemeal redevelopment, shop by shop, with masonry
gradually replacing timber-framed buildings, implies that each shop
had been sold separately. Market forces were being applied, as at least
two shopkeepers had bought up their respective neighbours.

These same forces also affected the quality and size of the
buildings. At first, most shops were constructed with timber-frames
and wattle-and-daub, or cob, walls. The floors, if not of planks raised
on joists, would have been of puddled clay or chalk, gravel or
sometimes concrete. Such structural methods did not always preclude
refinements and an early shop at Cirencester had good quality frescoes
on the walls of the living quarters. As capital accumulated in the
hands of the successful, so their premises were enlarged or improved,
and as noted above, masonry replaced wood, neighbouring shops were

amalgamated, standards improved. But there would always have remained, at the lower end of the scale, humbler buildings of a commercial nature. Consequently we can envisage several types of contemporary operation. Shops may have belonged to resident freeholders; they may have been let to tenants; or they may have been managed on behalf of the owner by a retainer or slave.

Apart from shops, however, there were other buildings in towns which possessed commercial functions, although they are normally to be found only in the major settlements. First among them, as briefly indicated above, was the forum. There would be provided not only shops let out by the local authority, but also covered porticoes and a large open space for temporary market stalls, best demonstrated by evidence from Wroxeter, as, when the forum was burnt down in the later second century, stalls erected in the external portico were upset in the panic and deposited their contents of pottery and knife-sharpening stones in the nearby gutter.

But an open space, without porticoes or permanent shops, could function just as adequately as a market. When the forum at Wroxeter was burnt down a second time at the end of the third century, it was never rebuilt. Yet the levelled space seems to have remained in use and may have continued to serve a similar purpose. In the same way, open gravelled areas in the centres of the minor towns at Catterick and Godmanchester (fig. 46) probably provided market-places since forums were not to be expected.

In some more prosperous towns, such as Wroxeter, Leicester, Cirencester and Verulamium, the need was felt for additional, formal market space, so extra buildings were provided, often modelled on the forums. They usually appear as open areas enclosed by one or more ranges of shops and sometimes also possessing external and internal porticoes. At Leicester, a large, basilica-style covered hall was also added; it can be distinguished from the main basilica by its lack of tribunals.

The goods and services provided by these premises covered the whole range of commercial activities, but it is not always easy to identify the trade of a particular shop, for two reasons. Shops which traded in organic materials such as bread, fruit or vegetables are unlikely to provide evidence because of the perishable nature of the goods when buried under normal soil conditions in Britain. Also, most shops, unless destroyed in a catastrophe like a volcanic eruption or a fire, will have been cleared of their goods before being rebuilt or left unoccupied. Despite these restrictions there is, nevertheless, a growing body of material related to their commercial activities being

Fig. 50. Slotted stone emplacement at the front of a shop at Catterick. It served not only to support a wooden door shutter, but also as a base for one of four posts holding up the frontage of the shop. The aqueduct channel runs beyond (*Crown Copyright*).

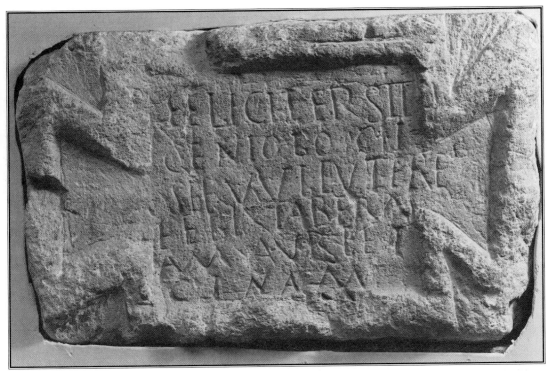

Fig. 51. Inscription from a goldsmith's shop at Norton (E. Yorks.). It wishes good luck to the spirit of the shop and to a young slave, who was presumably the manager (*Yorkshire Museum*).

put together by modern methods of research. Almost every trade can now be represented by one form of evidence or another.

Pottery and glassware shops are known at Colchester having been burnt in the Boudiccan rebellion, so sealing the stock below a level of ash and building debris. Wine shops are known in Verulamium; oysters were sold in the forum at Caerwent, while a slave managed a goldsmith's at Norton in east Yorkshire (fig. 51); other goldsmiths worked at Verulamium, Cirencester and London, where some interesting remains were found below the governor's palace (see Chapter 5). Coppersmiths' workshops have been identified at Catterick and Verulamium, while individual coppersmiths are known by name at Colchester, Lincoln and in Suffolk. A silversmith operated a large establishment at Silchester, while a glassworker at Leicester (fig. 52) indulged, as a sideline, in the illegal smelting of base, late silver coinage to recover the valuable metal. Blacksmiths, more than any other craft, must have been ubiquitous, with few towns or villages lacking a resident practitioner. Silchester, Verulamium and Great Chesterford have all produced caches of ironwork, so implying their presence, while an anonymous tombstone from York depicts a blacksmith with the tools of his trade. Dedications on altars indicate the activities of sculptors and stonemasons from other provinces in the Bath–Cirencester region. Glassware, mainly window glass and simple vessels, was manufactured at Caistor-by-Norwich, Mancetter and Wilderspool, as well as at Leicester.

Tanners and dyers seem to have operated at Silchester and Alcester, while breadmaking on a commercial, rather than on the more normal domestic, scale is indicated at Canterbury, London and Lincoln. At Cirencester, a row of shops may have provided cooked meats, while opposite them lay a butchers' market. Another butcher's shop has been claimed at Verulamium.

From other provinces come also an interesting series of monumental reliefs depicting commercial activities: a wine shop, a butcher's, a cutler's, a cobbler's, tailors' and possibly a moneylender, among others. Painted frescoes at Pompeii depict cupids dyeing and preparing cloth. All these trades were no doubt represented in the main urban centres, while many would also have been found in the minor towns and villages.

In societies which are largely based on agriculture the specialist tradesman, whether in town or village, provides a key service to the rural communities. Only the largest country estates in Roman Britain could have maintained their own technical workforces. All other farmers would have depended on town or village craftsmen for the supply of new equipment and the repair of old. It was probably by this process, more than any other, that information about new technology became disseminated.

In addition to the manufacturing and distributive trades carried on in towns and other minor settlements, there were some (p. 216) which not only required the presence of industrial raw materials but which, if carried out in normal settlements, would have caused considerable inconvenience. The mining of metal ores and coal, charcoal-burning, quarrying stone, sand, gravel and clay, lime-burning, brick, tile and pottery manufacture, salt extraction from seawater or saline springs: all were activities which could be most easily carried out at source, and frequently, therefore, they gave rise to their own specialized communities.

Of metals occurring naturally in Britain, gold, silver, lead, copper, iron and tin were the only ones in which interest was shown in the Roman period, and the most valuable, gold and silver, were mostly worked under direct imperial control, or under licence, for they were needed to augment supplies of coinage.

Fig. 52. Glass-furnace in a shop in the market-hall at Leicester. The owner was also illegally melting down base silver coinage to recover the precious metal.

Gold, as far as we yet know, was only mined at Dolaucothi in Carmarthenshire, mainly during the second century. The scale of the workings there, together with obvious signs of well-ordered control, strongly suggests operations under imperial licence, with protection and oversight possibly being provided by an adjacent fort. The mines were large, using both open-cast and underground methods of extraction. An extensive settlement grew up to supply the needs of the community, although it is probable that here, as in other mines, much of the labour would have been provided by convicts or slaves. Unfortunately little is known in detail about the settlement, but manufacturing goldsmiths seem to have been present, so some of the produce at least must have been sold, probably by auction, on the open market.

The ores of silver and lead occur naturally together. In the Roman period, the chief areas of mining activity were the Mendips, developed within a few years of the invasion, the Peak District of Derbyshire, and the area around Shropshire and the north Welsh border, both developed by about AD 80; other districts in the north Pennines may have later provided a quota. Down to the end of the second century, many of the mines were supervised by military detachments, notably from Legio II and Legio XX, but increasingly they were transferred to concessionary hands and the names of local authorities, private individuals and at least two companies are known, from dies cast on ingots of lead, to have been involved. Little is known, however, of the settlements connected with the mines. At Charterhouse, in the Mendips, a sizeable centre has been identified with an amphitheatre, although the latter may have been associated more with a military detachment in the area than with the settlement. One of the main companies was the *Societas Lutudarensis* in Derbyshire; somewhere, perhaps close to the fort at Brough-on-Noe, must lie its headquarters.

Iron was probably the most important metal to native Britons. The ores are found widely distributed throughout the Weald of Kent, the Forest of Dean, and in a band following the oolitic ironstone from Northamptonshire through to Lincolnshire. Outlying areas occur in Yorkshire, Norfolk, Cheshire and Northumberland. Indeed, the metal occurs so commonly in Britain, that is is unlikely that any formal control was exercised over its extraction, except for certain areas run by military or naval detachments for their own use. Some rather sprawling settlements of no great size grew in Northamptonshire, east Leicestershire, Lincolnshire and Norfolk, although it is not always easy to differentiate between small settlements of this type and those where production apparently centred on a villa. Not much is known of their equivalents in Kent, Sussex or Gloucestershire, although it is probable that the wealth of the two minor towns at Kenchester and Weston-under-Penyard (Herefs. and Worcs.) depended largely on the ironworkers of the Forest of Dean.

The primary extraction of tin and copper does not seem to have spawned any great settlements, most of the work being carried out on an extremely local basis. Tin was found in Cornwall, where it was both mined on the surface and recovered from stream beds. Surprisingly, official interest only seems to have been shown in the late first and again in the fourth centuries; in between times, the British source could not compete with the rich Spanish mines, and only when the latter were exhausted did interest revive in Britain. Secondary working of pewter, an alloy of tin and lead, took place at Camerton and at Lansdown, outside Bath, presumably using Mendips' lead. Some copper may also have been produced in Cornwall and a workshop for the manufacture of bronze (an alloy of tin and copper) brooches may have been set up at N'or Nour in the Isles of Scilly. Elsewhere, copper was found in Shropshire, north Wales and Anglesey. Again, quantities produced do not seem to have warranted official intervention and most was produced on an extremely local basis, especially in Anglesey. Nevertheless, as with tin, so with copper, British sources came into their own in the fourth century, when a shortage of the metal for coinage arose.

By comparison, some considerable settlements arose around the pottery industry, of which the best known is probably at Water Newton (fig. 48). There, a fortified nucleus of 17 ha was surrounded by extensive areas of kilns, workshops and the houses of potters. Much of the pottery produced is of a type known to archaeologists as Castor ware, a colour-coated pottery, imitated at a number of other sites and common in many parts of Britain in the third and fourth centuries. Other major pottery-producing centres are known at Mancetter, Nuneaton, Norton (Yorks.), Farnham and in the region round Oxford. Some production areas, however, seem only to have given rise to the most primitive settlements, as in the New Forest. Many of the chief potteries grew up around acknowledged towns, where they were not only assured of a local market but were also in a position to take advantage of wider connexions. At Colchester, pottery was produced which reached many distant markets, including military sites in the north, and an attempt was even made to manufacture samian ware in the last part of the second century, but it failed owing to the lack of suitable clay. Lincoln was another such site and, indeed, it is probable that most towns produced their own pottery in suburban areas. Similarly, brick and tile was normally produced close to where it was needed. Municipal brickworks existed at Gloucester and private companies operated around Cirencester.

The manufacture of pottery, brick and tile has four requirements: clay, wood, water and transport facilities. All sites in Britain possessed the first three; the fourth was not so easily come by, since the most suitable form of transport for pottery is by water, the goods being bulky, heavy and fragile. Consequently, it is often found that the most successful centres, with the widest markets, were situated close to suitable rivers, or within easy reach of them.

Little is known about settlements specifically associated with quarrying, coal-mining or salt production. As with the production of brick and tile, most quarrying operations will have been carried out in the neighbourhood of existing settlements to meet local needs. Huge quantities of stone, sand and gravel must have been extracted for construction work. Certain types of stone, used for specific purposes, were carried long distances: Bath stone appears as tombstones at Colchester, Barnack stone from Northamptonshire at Verulamium, Lincolnshire limestone and Kentish ragstone in London. Moreover, exotic stones from abroad such as porphyry and various marbles were imported to decorate public and private buildings.

Coal was employed extensively as a fuel in Britain. It seems to have been mined from outcrop formations in a number of areas, including Northumberland, Yorkshire, Nottinghamshire and Somerset. It was carried widely and used for industrial and domestic purposes.

Salt, an important item in the diet and also necessary for preserving food and skins, was obtained by the evaporation of seawater on coastal sites around the Wash, the Essex marshes and the Thames and Severn estuaries. The evaporation was carried out in ceramic pans supported over open fires and their situation on bleak coastal marshes did not encourage the growth of associated permanent settlements. Nevertheless, there is some indication of Fenland sites acting as collecting and marketing points. Two inland centres, given the name of Salinae in contemporary sources, at Droitwich and Middlewich respectively, may have grown to meet the requirements of salt manufacturers evaporating brine from mineral springs.

There were also a number of settlements which grew up connected with religious sites, of which probably Bath, and Buxton, both associated with hot springs, are the best known. Other lesser sites have been identified at several places, including Springhead, near Dartford, Wycomb, near Cheltenham, Frilford, near Oxford and possibly Gosbecks, near Colchester (fig. 7). Such sites certainly attracted numerous pilgrims, whose needs had to be catered for, and who also provided a ready source of income for tradespeople. It is interesting to note that theatres were built at Gosbecks (fig. 125b) and possibly at Wycomb, in addition to an amphitheatre at Frilford, so that large crowds could be accommodated.

Apart from the distinctive central temple or temples, the settlements related to them varied little from the norm, although they might be expected to contain a rather higher proportion of buildings providing accommodation. Bath is probably the best example to consider (p. 253), where a great classical temple stood in the centre dedicated jointly to the local deity Sul (fig. 105) and the Roman goddess Minerva. The hot spring rose from the ground within the temple courtyard and the water was channelled into an elaborate bathing establishment (fig. 104). A number of military tombstones are known from the area and, although there was possibly an early fort, it may have been used by the army in Britain as a curative or convalescent centre of a type known in some other provinces. In all these settlements, commerce must have provided a strong motivation for their existence.

The last main function of towns and other settlements that we have to consider is protective, and all, no matter their size or status, exercised it to a greater or lesser extent. Even the smallest nucleated centre offered some mutual protection to its members by virtue of their being gathered together in one place, so deterring bands of robbers or perhaps even the attentions of rapacious landowners. Later, as the nature of the threat to communities, or to essential services accommodated within them, changed and became more menacing, the protecive function was, in many cases, supplemented by the provision of physical fortifications of ramparts, ditches and walls. Not all settlements were so treated, while there is also a time factor to be considered. Moreover, additional complications arise, since there was probably a strong element of official policy involved, as the central government had to protect its regional administrative and supply centres. It may be, however, that the provision of fortifications for certain sites, but not for others, will enable us in time to refine our classification of settlement types.

The erection of urban fortifications in the early empire seems to have been generally forbidden except under licence from the emperor. This was presumably the counterpart of the law which prohibited the carriage of arms by citizens except for hunting or personal defence on a journey; protection was expected to be provided by the Roman army on the frontiers. Consequently, when urban fortifications were erected, we have to look behind the act in order to seek some reason for the exercise of the imperial licence. Consequently, also, such fortifications are going to reflect imperial attitudes and policy and will only rarely be constructed for purely local reasons.

These provisions seem generally to have been observed in Britain; most towns and other settlements started as undefended sites and remained so until the end of the second century. There were, however, some exceptions. At an early date, the new town of Verulamium was fortified with an earth bank and single ditch. Similarly, the new town of Silchester may have been accommodated within the existing defences of the Inner Earthwork (fig. 36), so in effect providing fortifications and doing away with the need for a new circuit. Why they should have been defended and not Colchester, London and Canterbury is difficult to explain with our present knowledge. Verulamium, if not yet a municipium, must have been acting as a civitas capital, while Silchester almost certainly lay within the kingdom of Cogidubnus. Yet a common reason may explain both cases, since both lay uncomfortably close to the new frontier beyond which, in the late 40s, Caratacus was still freely operating. Even after his capture, warfare continued in south Wales, so that, with no linear barrier, small raiding bands could easily have slipped between the forts and their patrols and caused havoc in the province. Celtic tribes were adept at this form of guerrilla warfare. Physical protection for the nearest towns might, therefore, have seemed essential, although it was only a temporary measure; within a decade or so, both towns had expanded beyond these limits.

The next main scare, which prompted urban fortifications, seems to have been during the civil war of AD 69–70, although it has been argued that Colchester was provided with walls in the interim period during the aftermath of the Boudiccan rebellion (fig. 53). Attention has already been drawn in the previous chapter (p. 26) to the part which Cogidubnus may have played in the affair. Whether or not he was given legatine authority, as was sometimes thought, rests on the

Fig. 53. The surviving remains of the Balkerne Gate at Colchester, beside the aptly-named pub The Hole in the Wall, which occupies much of the area of the gate. The southern foot passage and the adjacent quadrant bastion can be seen to the right of the pub. The northern bastion overlaps its left-hand side.

interpretation of a damaged area of the Chichester inscription, which was dedicated under his authority (fig. 15); it is now generally supposed that he was not so dignified. Nevertheless, there can be little doubt that, as an acquaintance if not a friend of the successful emperor Vespasian, it may have been to him that the latter appealed for support when he found himself unable to cope immediately with British affairs, and when he was faced with a governor of uncertain loyalty and an army on the verge of mutiny. It would make sense in the circumstances if Cogidubnus, in order to protect his kingdom, most likely from that same army, fortified Winchester and Chichester, and possibly also the three minor road stations in Sussex at Hardham, Alfoldean and Iping. It was once thought that Silchester was included in the scheme, with the Outer Earthwork providing fortifications for the expanded town. But it is now known that the Outer Earthwork was part of the Iron Age oppidum, and was also never completed on its eastern side.

Between AD 70 and the second century, when the next phase of major fortification occurred, some individual towns were provided with defences. It would seem that the two coloniae at Lincoln and

Gloucester inherited the ramparts of the legionary fortresses which they had supplanted. By then, however, the ramparts would have been standing for a considerable time; timber lacing and breastwork would have rotted and all would have been in a state of disrepair. Consequently, they were rapidly strengthened by the addition of masonry walls. It is probable that both cities took advantage of their senior status in Britain and their semi-military origins to petition the emperor for the rights of enclosure, as had happened in Gallia Narbonensis under Augustus. An element of pride may have influenced the applications, since there was no obvious defensive reason for fortifications at that time.

The sequence of events which surrounded the usurping of imperial power by the governor of Britain, Clodius Albinus, in AD 193 has been described in the previous chapter. One of the by-products of his actions may have been the initiation of a programme of urban fortification greater than ever before. Alternatively, it has been variously argued that either no single date can be ascribed to them all and that they were consequently the result of a piecemeal approach, or they were the concerted reaction to an earlier invasion of the northern frontier, probably in 180–4, when the governor was killed. Be that as it may, the available evidence still allows Albinus to have been the originator and, in many ways, better explains the sequence of events. After he was proclaimed emperor, he no doubt soon realized that, to contest his claim successfully against other usurpers, he would have to remove the larger part of the army from Britain, leaving the province virtually defenceless. Permission or orders, therefore, seem to have been given for most major towns and some minor settlements to erect fortifications. It is probable, also, that Albinus misjudged the time which he had at his disposal before having to force the issue. At any rate, work appears to have begun in a number of towns and, unlike earlier attempts at fortification, was started in masonry. At Cirencester, Exeter, Verulamium and possibly also at Caerwent and Silchester, the construction of gates and internal towers commenced, while at Dorchester the foundations of part of the curtain wall were laid. The whole project was immense and would probably have involved the placing in position of over half a million cubic metres of masonry, with all that meant in terms of stone-quarrying and dressing, lime-burning, sand-quarrying, mortar-mixing, employment of skilled masons and, above all, transport. It is not surprising that time ran out before the task had hardly started. Consequently, the work had to be completed in a hurry with a return to earlier methods of earth banks and ditches, and in some places timber gates. Only London, the provincial capital, appears to have had its defences completed in masonry, while among all the civitas capitals, Leicester and Canterbury, for some as yet unexplained reason, seem to have stayed aloof from the turmoil.

Somewhat naturally the area enclosed by the new fortifications was kept to a minimum so as to reduce the overall length of rampart to be erected. Consequently, isolated buildings on the perimeter were often omitted, such as houses at Cirencester, Dorchester and Leicester. This policy usually resulted in the amphitheatre being left outside, since the large area of ground it demanded was only normally available well away from the centre.

Some minor sites, also, such as Kenchester, Bath, Dorchester-on-Thames and Irchester, were then fortified. While it is possible to account for such activities in major cities and towns, it is not so easy to explain why some lesser sites were involved, especially when a large number were not.

In view of the participation of the provincial government in the programme of work, it is likely that the minor sites affected contained some key installation which had to be protected. What it was we can only guess, and a number of possibilities arise. The minor towns in Britain had probably, by the end of the second century, become important in the second level of local administration, acting as centres for country districts – *pagi* – within the frameworks of the civitates. It is likely that they contained buildings, either associated with local records and tax-collection, or the imperial post, and would, therefore, require protection. This may explain why, at some very large settlements, only a small area at the centre was fortified. Unfortunately such buildings are not always easy to identify, even when they have been excavated, and still too little is known altogether about the internal buildings of minor towns.

Certainly the end of the second and the beginning of the third century was a period when the central administration was extending its tentacles more and more into the countryside, often by the secondment of army officers to individual regions. There lies at the centre of Godmanchester an early third-century building, not unlike a military headquarters block, which has been claimed to be a 'town hall' for a newly constituted civitas. A more likely explanation, which may also give us a clue to the functions of these minor towns, is probably provided by a contemporary inscription from a building at Combe Downe, outside Bath (fig. 54). It refers to the restoration

Fig. 54. Inscription from a building at Combe Down, just outside Bath. It records the restoration from ground level of a derelict *principia* by an imperial freedman, Naevius, who was also a procurators' assistant (*Bath City Council*).

by a procurators' assistant of a building called a *principia*, or headquarters, either of an imperial estate or of a tax-collection area. The structure at Godmanchester is probably best viewed in the same way, and would provide a reason for the fortifications erected round the site.

One further point is worth making in connexion with the late second-century programme of urban fortifications. No physical barrier is effective unless it is properly manned. In the absence of the army from Britain, this could only have been managed by a local militia. There must, therefore, have been a degree of relaxation in the law relating to the carriage of arms if the fortifications were to be fully effective.

For reasons not yet completely understood, the urban defences erected in the late second century seem to have been retained after Severus retook Britain. Indeed, by the end of the first decade of the following century, work had been resumed on the erection of masonry fortifications. This time, though, all major towns including Leicester and Canterbury, as well as some additional minor towns, were incorporated in the scheme, which by the early fourth century had been expanded yet again to take in such sites as Catterick and Thorpe-by-Newark. The scale of the work was so great that it is not surprising that it took over a hundred years to complete. This may have been due to two causes: shortage of skilled masons, or shortage of cash, or possibly both. Taking the construction of Hadrian's Wall as an analogy, which is not entirely reliable when translated to a civilian context, a force of some 10,000 masons would have been required, if the work had proceeded on all fortified towns at once and if a reasonable completion date was to be achieved. Did Britain possess so many? Moreover, there is evidence from other provinces that the cost of all this work would most likely have fallen on the civitates or other municipal authorities, and would have been financed out of annual revenues. Problems of cash flow undoubtedly affected progress, leading to interruptions at such places as Chichester and Winchester and to economies being introduced during construction, as at Cirencester. Indeed, it can be envisaged that once masonry fortifications were started, what with repairs or alterations to parts already completed, almost continuous work would have been required thereafter, well into the fourth century, when new fashions in military architecture, then being introduced, caused yet further changes.

However, there are some structural distinctions which can be drawn between the earliest and latest attempts at urban fortification. For instance the first gateways to be erected, as at Colchester, Lincoln, Cirencester and Verulamium were built in the monumental manner with double portals and sometimes with additional foot passages. They were also provided with massive, external towers. Later, the size of gates was drastically reduced, often to a single portal surmounted by a tower, as with gates at Canterbury and Caerwent. In general, the fortifications consisted of a masonry curtain wall up to 3m thick (fig. 55), backed by an earth bank which normally, but not always, incorporated the remnants of earlier ramparts. In front lay one, or at most two, ditches. Occasionally, internal masonry towers formed an integral part of the defences, but their placing was, in many cases, seemingly haphazard.

The last major structural alterations to urban fortifications were the addition of external towers; since these often overlapped the lip of the inner ditch, it was customary to fill it and cut a new wider, but often shallower, ditch beyond. Orthodox opinion would ascribe these towers to the work of Count Theodosius, following the barbarian invasions of *c.* 369, when he was responsible for the reorganization of Britain's defences. But not all fit such a tight chronology, some appearing to be earlier; moreover, their provision

Fig. 55. The south wall of Caerwent looking west from the south gate. An added polygonal, exterior tower shows on the far left.

is not only uneven from town to town, but also within individual towns. Thus Cirencester seems to have a complete sequence encompassing the entire curtain wall, whereas Silchester has none, Verulamium has only two so far identified, while Caerwent is provided with them along north and south walls (fig. 55) but not along east or west sides. It might be best, therefore, to consider their addition as part of the almost continuous process of construction, repair and upgrading which had been going on for some time in most towns. If towns were not so, or only partly, equipped it is probably more a reflection of the state of municipal finances than anything else. It also used to be thought that they were built for the more effective use of artillery. But artillery required trained army personnel, for which there is no evidence in the towns with towers; a more recent proposition sees them as providing vertical concentrations of defenders using more conventional weapons.

Certainly though by the late fourth century, a number of towns, as well as some other sites, including villas, contained detachments of the regular Roman army, who left characteristic items of equipment behind them, such as belt buckles with animal-head decorations. We do not know in most cases if they were units of the field army, but at Catterick, about AD 370, a major reorganization took place to allow the billeting of troops within the town, in which many of the residents appear to have been evicted from their houses and shops.

We have considered the principal functions of cities, towns and other settlements, their distinctions and their foundations, and it remains to review their subsequent developments.

No matter what dictates governed the choice of site or the reasons for the establishment of a town or village, it would, once founded, have been almost entirely at the mercy of economic forces. Consequently, although many may have shared a common purpose at first, their subsequent developments were by no means always comparable. In some instances there is clear evidence for the foundation date of a civitas capital, such as Canterbury, Caistor-by-Norwich, Wroxeter or Leicester, although the most important public buildings were often not functional until some little time later. Following the famous passage in Tacitus' *Agricola*, it used to be thought that most of these were constructed through the inspiration of this governor. That may have been so, but if it was, few were advanced far during the first century and a good many date to even later. Only at Verulamium is there incontravertible evidence for his participation, and even then it is likely that the forum had been started before his arrival as governor. A further complication has now been introduced by the discovery of some timber-framed forums, such as those at Silchester (fig. 38a) and Exeter, which may represent cheap and quickly-erected alternatives to masonry buildings. It is possible that the time lag was due to apathy, but it is far more likely that, as in the case of town defences described above, this tardiness was caused by cash flow problems. Delays in the construction of public buildings of up to ten years were not uncommon in some Mediterranean provinces, while they appear to increase, in Africa at least, towards the end of the second century. Public works, where evidence exists, seem to have been financed chiefly from the fees and gifts obtained from office-holders on their appointments. Occasionally, personal intervention by an emperor is attested, but fiscal means were usually employed, such as the remission or lightening of taxes. Hadrian is recorded as having cancelled a debt of billions of sesterces owed to the treasury by impoverished municipalities. It is not impossible, therefore, that his visit to Britain saw the remission of taxes on a liberal scale, which allowed public building programmes, in something of a decline during the early second century, to be resumed. Admittedly Silchester possessed a public bath-house before the end of the first century (fig. 42c), but at Leicester, Wroxeter (figs 42b and 43) and Caistor-by-Norwich they were not built before the middle of the second. At Cirencester (fig. 126a) the amphitheatre was not constructed until the early second century and only completed in masonry by the middle, whereas Canterbury and Chichester were provided with buildings for public entertainment before the end of the first. The theatre at Verulamium was not built until the middle of the second century, at about the same time as one was being constructed at out-of-the-way Brough-on-Humber. Moreover, the growing need to accommodate larger numbers of spectators is evident at Canterbury, where the theatre was completely rebuilt on a more generous scale in the early third century, and at Verulamium, where an enlargement took place in the early fourth (fig. 125). A considerable disparity between towns often exists, therefore, in the rate at which public buildings were provided reflecting, as with forums and basilicas, the contrasting needs and the variable availability of the necessary finance.

The rate of expansion in commercial enterprise is likewise indicated by the provision of extra public markets. For instance, Verulamium was provided with one in the late first century. Cirencester and Wroxeter were catered for by the middle second century and Leicester by the early third.

The development of private housing and shops is more difficult to summarize since, with them, we are dealing with a much greater variety of personal circumstances and not with reasonably predictable, corporate communities. Something has already been said about the standard of housing and shops earlier in this chapter, but we can usefully add the example of private-housing developments in the colonia at Gloucester. At first the legionary veterans were accommodated in terraced houses which, in blocks, much resembled a legionary barrack. Partial demolition and rebuilding of separate houses within a block rapidly occurred and by the second or third decades of the second century a block had been replaced by a number of small, detached houses. Further, by the middle of the century, a number of these small house properties had become amalgamated, incidentally extinguishing a public right of way, and a single house with a compact, Italianate plan had been constructed (fig. 44a). As already indicated earlier, such houses are rare in Britain, although others have been identified at Colchester and Caerwent (fig. 44b). Their existence may point to a soldier, or trader from another province, settling permanently in Britain.

If it is true to say that the middle of the second century saw a period of maximum development in cities and towns, the same cannot be said for minor towns and other lesser settlements. In many, development lagged behind that in major towns, and it was often not until the third or even fourth century that they began to show signs of possessing less ephemeral buildings. This is particularly true of the military vici in the north where the peaceful conditions, brought about by Caracalla's settlement of the frontier problem, ushered in a new era of prosperity. Here, as elsewhere, alterations were also brought about by changing legal and social conditions. Caracalla's award of citizenship to all free-born members of the empire tended to erase the earlier distinctions between cities, towns and other settlements, and in so doing presumably removed some of the gloss from the former, possibly making it not so unfashionable to live in a minor town of village.

Despite the rising prosperity of many settlements, the third century was, nevertheless, a time of recession for most of the empire. Britain seems to have suffered less than other provinces, but must, like all, have been affected by the appalling inflation. But it should not be forgotten that, for certain classes, inflation can in the short term be a benefit. One of the causes of the inflation was the continually increasing need to give higher pay to the army. Britain had a large garrison, so that it may be that more and more of the money supply, but of ever decreasing value, was ultimately finding its way into the pockets of British shopkeepers and merchants. Large fortunes were undoubtedly made, if the size of some late third-century coin hoards are taken as indicators, even if inflation rendered them almost valueless. In the major towns, however, the third century was marked by a decline in the construction and maintenance of public buildings, shops and houses. But it was a decline perhaps more apparent than real, since it may have been enhanced to some extent by the need to concentrate labour and money on the expanding programme of town defences (see p. 100 above). The volume of masonry erected round a town, as its fortifications, probably exceeded, by a sizeable amount, the sum of all the masonry in its public buildings.

late 3rd

With the return of Britain to the central government in the early fourth century, confidence was restored; moreover, most of the town walls had been completed. This was demonstrated outwardly by a spate of building activity. Once more, attention was turned to the construction of amenities, with the restoration and enlargement of the Verulamium theatre and the erection outside it of a new triumphal arch across Watling Street. In Cirencester, considerable alterations were made to the forum and basilica, prompted perhaps by the town becoming a provincial capital; extensions were made to the market, and at least one other major building was erected where, earlier, there had been private houses. Many dwellings were enlarged and refurbished to include mosaics then being produced by a local firm of craftsmen. Comparable activity was reflected in most other towns.

Typical of the period was the formal doubling of the size of the colonia at Lincoln (fig. 37c). A very large number of towns had generated prosperous suburbs, which sometimes tended to be abandoned when fortifications were erected. But, at Lincoln, a large suburb on the slope of the hill below the colonia was of sufficient importance to be enclosed, first apparently on at least part of the circuit by a bank surmounted by a fence and then by a wall, although it is not easy to ascribe a date to the latter, since several phases of construction have been observed; it probably belongs to the fourth century. Unlike most suburbs, however, this area had been laid out in a regular manner with a grid of streets, and many amenities and important buildings.

Minor towns and settlements are also eloquent of the new confidence. Military vici in the north flourished as never before and some, such as Carlisle, Corbridge and Catterick (fig. 46), were enclosed within defences. In the centre of Corbridge lay two separate, third-century, enclosed compounds devoted to the manufacture of arms and equipment for the army. But civilian buildings, notably a group of temples, clustered round them. At Catterick, despite the fortified enclosure on the south bank of the River Swale, inside which work had also started on a small bath-house, confidence was such that a suburb developed on the north bank. Carlisle prospered equally, its importance probably being enhanced when it became the capital of a newly constituted northern civitas. In many other minor towns, such as Water Newton, Ancaster, Margidunum, Thorpe-by-Newark, Alcester and Wanborough, the picture is the same, often with masonry buildings replacing timber-framed ones.

There were, however, some exceptions. At Brough-on-Humber, local opinion seems to have opted for continuing country life and it seems likely that the town, even though a civitas capital, failed to prosper. Certainly by the fourth century its theatre was in ruins and being robbed of its masonry. Chelmsford too, although given earthwork fortifications in the late second century, suffered a disastrous fire at about the same time, from which, seemingly, it never fully recovered, for it never warranted the construction of masonry defences.

The early fourth-century influence continued for some time, but began to falter by the middle of the century. From then on it gradually but fitfully declined. First-class houses were still being constructed at Verulamium and Cirencester in the last decades of the century, but they tended to be exceptional. The public baths at Wroxeter had for some time been rendered unusable; no attempt was made to rehabilitate them. Instead a series of quite substantial timber-framed buildings replaced its carefully dismantled exercise hall; the earliest dated from *c.* 367, but the latest almost certainly extended into the fifth century. Towards the end of the fourth century, a major fire destroyed the forum and basilica, the market-hall and many shops in the centre of Leicester; they were left in ruins. The overall impression gained is of a slow running-down process. If a major building was destroyed accidentally it was not replaced; if parts wore out they were seldom repaired. In contrast, there is evidence to show that, in a large number of towns and minor settlements, daily life continued much unchanged, even beyond the official rescript of AD 410. At Cirencester, for instance, the forum continued in use until at least 440, although the floor of the piazza had worn out, while the defences were kept in good order. At Verulamium, masonry buildings were being constructed well into the fifth century, while the flow from the aqueduct was still maintained and distributed in the town.

The active survival of towns and other settlements, after 410, was due in part to the bands of federate soldiers recruited from Germanic peoples and used as urban garrisons. This was a practice that had started earlier elsewhere in the empire, when such people, in return for military service, were given land in payment. Some at least of these soldiers were left behind after the formal withdrawal of the Roman army, or were at any rate quickly replaced by others. The presence of detachments has been shown at a number of places, such as Dorchester-on-Thames and Canterbury. At the former, a rapid degeneration of accommodation took place from good quality masonry buildings to wattle-and-daub houses with sunken floors. At the latter, a number of sunken houses, dating from the fifth to the seventh centuries, have been found, largely concentrated in a central insula; in one place a number roughly lined a street. This might suggest that a complete insula had been given over to these federate soldiers and that at first a degree of order and discipline was being enforced on them, even though they continued to live in their ancestral manner.

All nucleated settlements were, however, under pressure. The general insecurity of the countryside and disrepair of the roads had severed them from their main sources of supply. Yet they managed to survive on crops grown in their own surrounding fields, even if they were now administered by 'strong men' in place of the magistrates and council.

But the new garrisons were both treacherous and unreliable. It must also be remembered that they had been engaged partly to fight against their own kin, since the number of Anglo-Saxon raiders and settlers was increasing. Before long, probably about 440, there was a mutiny and parts of eastern Britain then became permanently Saxon. It seems likely, although as yet there is no firm proof, that the Saxons were aided in their efforts by an outbreak of a serious epidemic disease which inflicted severe mortality on the remaining inhabitants of the towns and lesser settlements. Only thus is it possible to account for the apparent abandonment of the walled town at Cirencester, with bodies left lying in ditches beside the streets, in favour of the nearby amphitheatre, which seems to have been put in a defensive state.

The evidence for what happened in the fifth century is tantalizingly slight, but it appears that after the initial Saxon successes around 450, the surviving British rallied. It is the age to which Arthur properly belongs, and the myth has probably grown around some major war leader of the late fifth century. At the battle of Mount Badon, usually put at that time, the British inflicted a defeat on the Saxons and there ensued a period of peace and prosperity, coupled with a maintained balance between the warring factions. It is probable that the dykes around Silchester were constructed during this period to act as boundaries between the surviving Romano-British town and its land on the one hand and a neighbouring Saxon enclave on the other. In other places there was a reversion to hillforts as strongholds, probably because, with a falling population, they were more easily defended than the long circuits of town walls.

In the end, towns and minor settlements slid into a slow decay, partly as their inhabitants died, were killed, or deserted them, partly as the economic system, in which they had played a central part, crumbled. It is doubtful if any became fully deserted, but they had long ceased to possess the institutions or amenities by which they could be called towns.

Finally, it is interesting to record that, as the major centres of urban civilization collapsed, they approached the condition of their humbler cousins which, perhaps, altered little. Therein lies the principal distinction which enables us to distinguish the former, but not the latter, as *towns*.

CHAPTER 4

Farms and Gardens

Roman Britain, as with all countries before the Industrial Revolution, was first and foremost an agricultural community. Farming was the basic provider of wealth, and although many inhabitants might have come in time to accept town life, the larger part of the population remained in the countryside, practising husbandry in a variety of ways and at different levels.

The basic methods of farming in Roman Britain differed little from those used in the Iron Age. Consequently, any improvements, of which there were many, came about by an extension of familiar ways and by better facilities for the marketing of produce.

Farming in the Iron Age was largely a matter of subsistence agriculture. Since most people farmed and had their own produce, there was no market in which to dispose of a surplus, and therefore farmers grew only for their immediate needs. But the ability to produce a saleable surplus was probably there, waiting for the right economic climate. To some extent this came about with the expansion of the Roman empire to the Channel coast. The army consumed enormous amounts of grain and other materials which they were unable to produce themselves. It is likely that Caesar's forcible requisitions of corn, while in Britain, perhaps gave the local inhabitants the idea of selling corn to the army once he had returned to Gaul, and, by the beginning of the first century AD, Strabo lists corn as a British export. Consequently, by then, a surplus was being produced and the ear of corn, or barley, adopted as a symbol by Cunobelin on his coins is eloquent proof of where extra cultivation was being carried out.

With the arrival of the Roman army in Britain in AD 43, a large, permanent consumer of agricultural produce became established. Their basic rations were obtained by compulsory requisitions of grain and other goods from the farmers, a tax known as the *annona militaris*, for which a token payment may have been made. The amount was calculated as a percentage of the crop, so that a farmer, working only at subsistence level, had to produce that much more if he was not himself to starve. Once he was growing that increase, he probably realized that, by extending his production still further, he would have a profitable asset, in which he would have been helped by three other new factors.

The development of cities, towns and, to a lesser extent, minor settlements promoted classes of society which were no longer agriculturally self-supporting. They now had to be supplied with food. The extension of the road system, coupled with increased use of river transport, beyond the original military needs for arterial routes, linked town and countryside, enabling the goods to be more easily brought to the new consumers. Once there, the ready availability of a good currency, with ample small change for even the smallest transaction, will have smoothed the passage of goods from one hand to another.

The increase in production was brought about mainly by the cultivation of larger areas of land, since yields did not greatly alter. But the introduction of more and better quality implements such as ploughs, iron-shod spades, scythes (fig. 56) and even 'mechanical' reaping machines will have greatly aided this expansion.

It is all too easy at this point to enter into a circular argument: towns could not have developed satisfactorily without an agricultural surplus to feed them, yet at the same time they were largely responsible for enabling a surplus to be produced. So it is difficult to say precisely where the process started.

A simple, light plough which cut, but did not turn, a furrow was known in Iron Age Britain, and undoubtedly continued in use in many places, and probably in far greater numbers, throughout the Roman period. But there were several improvements. A heavier plough, of similar type, or with the share fitted with ears or ground-wrests, could be used to turn a furrow to one side or another, and its use could also allow denser soils to be cultivated. A further development was the plough with a heavy knife-coulter fitted to the beam to cut a vertical slice into the soil. If accompanied by an asymmetric share, there was a manifest intention to turn the furrow to one side only. Such a plough would also have possessed a wooden mould-board to complete the turning (fig. 56a). Both coulters and shares of this type are known from Britain in the Roman period, although they are rare and we cannot say how frequent was their use.

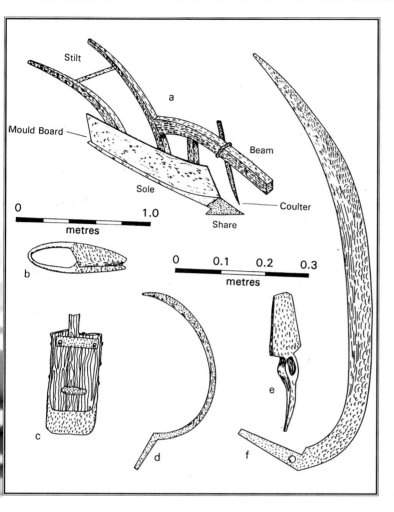

Fig. 56. Romano-British farm implements: a) a heavy plough with mould board, coulter and asymmetric share (*after C. Bowen*); b) sprung sheers, of a type still made today; c) wooden spade with iron-tipped blade and sheathing; d) balanced sickle; e) mattock head; f) scythe blade.

But it is worth remembering that even modern steel plough-shares wear out with great rapidity; shares and coulters of the Roman period would probably have been worn out almost beyond recognition before being discarded and returned to the blacksmith for reuse. Only seldom will they have been lost in the field. Consequently the number found cannot truly reflect the number then in use, since they will only turn up in blacksmith's stocks, or as 'spares' kept in a farmyard — both rarely found occurrences. But an increase in the overall number of more primitive ploughs would also have led to a great improvement. Not only could land, cultivated slowly and laboriously before with spade or hoe, now be ploughed more quickly, but the time saved also allowed more to be brought into production.

The introduction of the iron-shod spade (fig. 56c) would have greatly facilitated the digging of drainage ditches, so improving the quality of both pasture and arable, and causing fens and marshes to be turned to agricultural production. Better quality iron axes, saws and mattocks meant that scrubland, and even heavier forest, could be cleared efficiently for cropping. The introduction of the two-handed scythe (fig. 56f), with portable sharpening anvil on which notches in the blade could be beaten out, allowed a much greater quantity of hay to be cut for winter forage; moreover, since it speeded the work there was less chance of loss due to summer storms. Similarly, a properly balanced sickle (fig. 56d) ensured a quicker and less arduous grain harvest, while spring-handled shears eased the clipping of fleeces (fig. 56b). These implements were the principal benefits conferred on British agriculture by Roman technology. Many others, such as improved stonemasons', carpenters', wheelwrights', coopers' and blacksmiths' tools added to the general betterment of husbandry.

Improvements, however, were not only confined to equipment. Spelt, a form of wheat suitable for a damp climate, had been introduced in the Iron Age as an addition to barley and emmer, and enabled winter crops to be grown as well as the normal spring sowing (fig. 57). In the Roman period its use seems to have increased, together with rye, oats and flax. Root crops, such as turnips, carrots and parsnips not only provided vegetables for human consumption, but were also welcomed, in addition to rape, as winter feed for stock.

The cereals which were grown still needed to be parched before storing and the simple Iron Age process was elaborated by the construction of well-designed corn-drying ovens or kilns (fig. 58). They were normally built of brick or stone with one or more flues, carrying hot air from an outside furnace, running beneath the floor. It is probable that the grain was spread to dry on an upper floor of wood and the whole would have been made weatherproof by a wooden shed. Considerable variations in size and shape are known.

There is also good evidence that careful breeding and the better supplies of winter fodder improved the strains of cows, sheep and horses. Goats were still raised for their hair and two British products of woven goat hair achieved a considerable fame in the empire. Pigs continued to be fattened in increasing numbers, and geese and fowl were raised for eggs, meat and their feathers. Good timber in increasing amounts for construction must have been a valuable crop, even if regeneration took a long time. In the Diocletianic price code, a 23 m fir tree, 60 cm in diameter was listed at a price of 50,000 denarii,

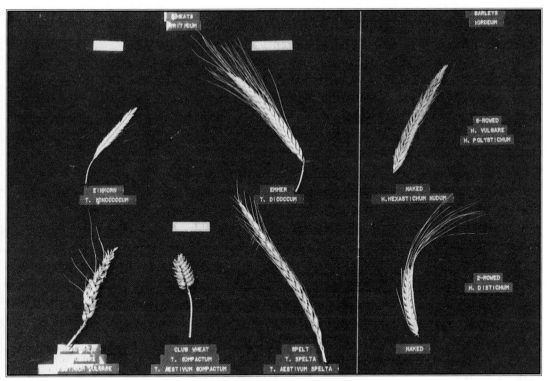

Fig. 57. Iron Age and Romano-British cereal crops: wheats on the left of the line, barleys to the right (*P.J. Reynolds, Butser Ancient Farm Project*).

whereas the same sum could only be earned by selling the wheat from about 5 ha of ploughed field. Felling of mature trees in an estate could therefore provide a very useful capital sum for an owner if he wished to develop. In between felling and regeneration, some annual income could have been obtained by coppicing for fuel and charcoal.

Fields (fig. 59), however, remained much as before, but there is evidence that the number of 'Celtic' fields in use on southern downlands greatly increased in number during the Roman period. In places, however, some fields appear to be overlaid by others with less square proportions and of undoubted Roman date, and such changes to 'long' fields may have been brought about by greater use of heavier ploughs, but there is, as yet, no general agreement. In some areas, also, 'open' fields may have been employed, but are difficult to prove in the absence of visible boundaries. A form of crop rotation was employed, allowing for a fallow period, and, since most farms would have had a mixture of pasture and arable, stock could have been run in the fallow fields to feed off the stubble and weed growth, while at the same time manuring the soil. Consequently hedges or fences, or in some places drystone walls, along boundaries would have been a necessity. Manure was also collected in farmyards and spread on the land, so accounting for the widespread scatter of heavily weathered pot sherds to be found on such fields, for broken pots from the farm buildings were no doubt thrown on the manure heap. Marling of light soils and liming of heavier ones was also practised.

In many areas it is possible to associate fields with settlements or farms, and we find that even villas continued to use the old type of 'Celtic' field (fig. 59). Contemporary agriculturalists recommended that a field should be of a size which could be conveniently ploughed by one man in a day, and, although there were variations, perhaps brought about by the larger and more efficient ploughs, this seems to have remained the basic factor governing their size throughout the Roman period. In some areas, stock enclosures replaced or were added to fields, being used no doubt for annual round-ups, for

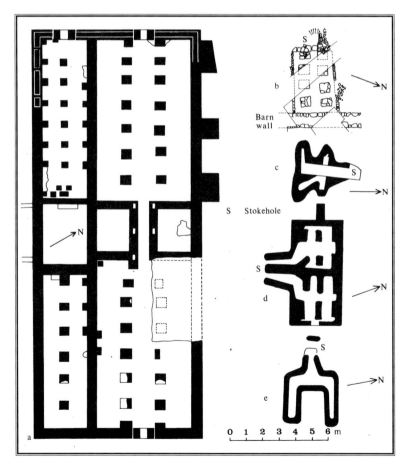

Fig. 58. a) A barn with raised floor at the Lullingstone (Kent) villa (*after G.W. Meates*); corn-driers at: b) Great Casterton (Rutland) villa (*after P. Corder*); c–e) Hambledon (Bucks) villa (*after A.H. Cocks*).

wintering cattle and sheep and possibly for lambing and calving. These frequently go hand in hand with large open spaces on moor, down, or fen, containing no fields; they are usually interpreted as ranches which, in some cases, may have continued to be delimited by Iron Age dykes, or in others by new boundaries. At Rockbourne Down (Hants.) there was not only extensive evidence of large-scale grain production, but also a ditched and hedged enclosure of nearly 40 ha for sheep or cattle.

Increased surplus brought increased profits to the farmers, which in turn brought further improvements to the farms. These can be most easily demonstrated by a study of the domestic farmhouses, which, when sufficiently romanized, are called villas.

It has been often repeated that villa, in Latin, means a farm, and so it does. But it implies the *whole* farm and not simply the residential building at the centre. Unfortunately, although in Roman law there was a narrow definition restricting use of the word to country buildings related to farming, in practice the Romans themselves were much more lax and sometimes used it to describe country-based industrial centres. In provinces like Britain, there is also the additional difficulty caused by native farmsteads continuing to exist side by side with their romanized counterparts. At what point, therefore, does a farm become a villa?

Many attempts have been made to define the term in a Romano-British context, some more successful than others. In essence it would seem that a villa is a building with an agricultural basis, displaying some degree of romanization in its structure and plan and belonging to the social and economic system of the province; moreover it should be in the countryside. But the latter restriction poses an immediate problem. There is a good deal of evidence for the existence of farms, and farmhouses, in towns. Are they to be called villas? Opinion is still divided and no easy solution is likely to present itself. Furthermore, it is strictly incorrect, according to our definition, to describe as villas the houses of master potters situated around Water Newton; yet they are so called. Again there is no ready answer.

The growth of villas in Britain was somewhat naturally a slow process: Iron Age roundhouses first gave way to simple rectangular cottages, often of cob or half-timbered construction, which in turn were rebuilt in more elaborate ways (fig. 60). There were, nevertheless, some anomalies to which exceptional circumstances can usually be ascribed. Few villas with any degree of sophistication

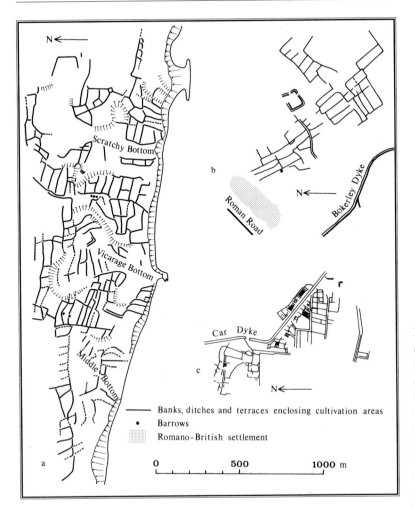

Fig. 59. Field systems at:
a) Chaldon Herring (Dorset);
b) Martin Down (Hants). Some squarish Celtic fields have been converted to longer fields to accommodate heavier ploughs (*both after Royal Commission on Historical Monuments for England*); c) Cottenham (Cambs). See also fig. 71 (*after P. Salway*).

developed before the second century in Britain, although the area around Verulamium seems to have seen some growth after the Boudiccan rebellion. It is probable that these early farmhouses represent the dwellings of Catuvellaunian gentry, who continued to reside on their country estates centred round villas such as Park Street, Gorhambury, Hemel Hempstead and Boxmoor. Mostly, they consisted of a single range of some half a dozen rooms, sometimes with a cellar, and with the rooms connected by an external portico.

At Boxmoor, an additional room had been included at each end of the range to provide symmetrical wings, while the whole building would have been readily recognized by any British colonial administrator in India or Africa during the early twentieth century, but in the Roman period the type of planning is more characteristic

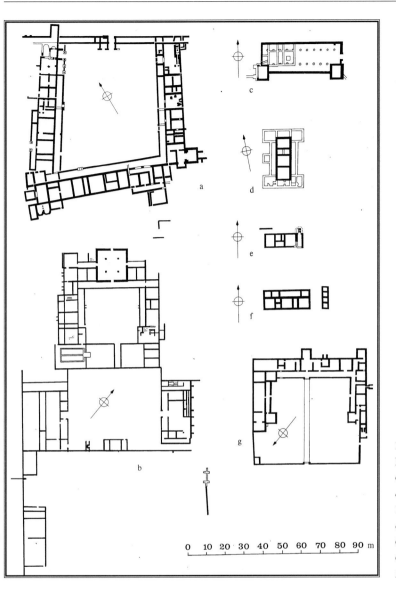

Fig. 60. Villas at: a) North Leigh (Oxon.); b) Woodchester (Glos.); c) Stroud (Glos.); d) Hambledon (Bucks.); e) Park Street (Herts.) in the first century; f) Little Milton (Oxon.); g) Spoonley Wood (Glos.) (*a, c–g after I.A. Richmond; b after G. Clarke*).

of later villas in Britain, and owes much to Gallic examples. We need have no doubt, therefore, that, in the late first century, when it was being erected, it represented the most up-to-date design in Britain, and that its owner was in touch, probably through being a decurion or having business contacts at Verulamium, with continental architects and craftsmen. Mainly, however, villas at this time lacked the refinements, such as mosaics and bath-suites, of later examples.

In another area, a villa at Eccles, near Dartford, was more luxurious with mosaics, a bath building and a garden courtyard containing an ornamental basin. It may have belonged to an influential nobleman of the Cantiaci, or equally it could have been the residence of an emigré from another province, investing his wealth in British land, or even that of a Roman official.

In the same class as Eccles is a villa at Angmering on the Sussex coastal plain below the Downs, while some miles further west, near Chichester, was an altogether more exceptional building at Fishbourne. Here was built, in the last decades of the first century, a villa of a size and with a magnificence to remain unsurpassed in Britain. The building was constructed on a terrace of some 33,500 sq m. In the middle there was a large courtyard laid out as a garden. A central walk, flanked by ornamental arbours, or parterres, crossed the garden from east to west (fig. 61). Water was furnished by ceramic pipes for irrigation and probably to supply fountains and pools.

Fig. 61. Garden bedding-trenches flanking the north side of the main walk across the central garden at Fishbourne. They are arranged to form alternate semi-circular and rectangular parterres (*Fishbourne Roman Palace*).

The garden was surrounded on all four sides by porticoes and ranges of buildings. In the centre of the east range an entrance hall with external portico and ornamental pool afforded access to the long walk. In the centre of the opposing range, placed at a higher level, was an apsidal room, interpreted as an audience chamber, and approached through the portico from the garden walk. The north range was made up of suites of rooms with their own private courtyards and terminated at the east end by an aisled hall.

The south range, owing to the presence of modern structures, cannot be fully excavated, but appears to contain the main residential quarters of the owner, with a bath-suite at its east end. To the south again there was probably a private garden commanding a wide view over the Fishbourne inlet, whose waters in Roman times came close to the building with a quay situated on the shoreline.

The whole structure was furnished in a most sumptuous manner. Mosaics (fig. 62) and frescoes of a very high quality were used to decorate principal rooms, some of which were heated by hypocausts. But in addition to these modes of decoration, neither of which is uncommon in Britain, use was also made of ornamental stucco work and thin, coloured stone veneers to embellish the walls and floors, the stones including several different kinds of imported marbles.

We have, then, a building laid out and constructed in the very latest fashion by an owner who must have commanded a considerable personal fortune. It has been estimated that to build such a place today would cost the equivalent of several million pounds. Who possessed such money in Roman Britain?

Fig. 62. Mosaic with a cupid
riding a dolphin at Fishbourne
(*Fishbourne Roman Palace*).

It could have been built for some important official, but it is difficult to visualize anyone below the rank of governor owning such a villa. Neither is there any specific evidence by which it might be so related. Also, it was constructed at a time when governors were still actively campaigning in Britain and they would, therefore, have had little time for leisurely country life away from the army or the capital.

Consequently, it is best seen as the work of some British prince, and in view of its position, the name that immediately springs to mind is the client king Cogidubnus. If he had successfully aided Vespasian in AD 69–71, it is likely that he received a handsome reward, sufficient probably to finance the palace, for so it should be called. Certainly the date of its construction can be closely tied to these events. It would have served, in turn, as a family residence for his dynasty and centre for administration of his kingdom and, in his declining years, a place of retirement away from the crowds of nearby Chichester.

Palace possibly, probably still a villa, at the centre of a great estate and managed in a more elaborate way, but nevertheless at heart linked with agriculture. Not perhaps a villa of the kind more normally to be met in Britain, where the construction, development and upkeep had largely to be financed by the sale of agricultural produce.

It is interesting to speculate further on the dozen or so villas which grew in the Verulamium region in the decades following the Boudiccan rebellion. In some cases, such as Park Street (fig. 60e), they replaced native farmsteads which had been burnt during the revolt, and there would seem to be some link between the development and the events of AD 60. It is hardly likely that a native farmer, who had just lost all, would have been in an financial position to start replacing his burnt house with a dwelling of much more expensive design. Two possibilities arise: either the farmer himself was killed with all his family, leaving the land without an owner or heir, or, alternatively, the farm was burnt and the farmer evicted in reprisals after the rebellion. Either way, the land belonging to a number of farms became vacant, and may have been taken by, or given as compensation to, loyal survivors among the Catuvellauni. So the changes which occurred to these villas are best assigned to new owners and not simply to improving circumstances.

By the middle of the second century, increasing capital resources enabled more and more farmers to demolish existing, native-style farms and rebuild in a modern manner, while those who already possessed villas were able to enlarge them. Ditchley (Oxon.) (fig. 63) is one such example where a winged villa was built in the middle of the century, while Park Street and Lockleys (Welwyn, Herts.) had wings attached to the earlier single range of rooms. But even now these villas lacked the refinements possessed by many contemporary town houses. Few had mosaics, and, although bath-suites were becoming commoner, they were by no means always provided. It would appear that social as well as economic changes were occurring, which can be explained in a number of ways.

We have already seen in the preceding chapter that towns in the middle of the second century were at a peak of development, which must be equated with a large investment of money. Comfortable town houses appear in considerable numbers and can only imply that, to some extent, the upper classes had now, if not before, forsaken the countryside for life in the town. There were laws in force compelling decurions to live in towns or within a short

Fig. 63. Aerial photograph of the villa at Ditchley (Oxon.). It lies within an enclosure containing other buildings (*Ashmolean Museum*).

distance of them. The rising standards of town life, coupled with the discomforts of commuting, may have led many, therefore, to take up residence where previously they had dwelt on their estates. The later first and early second centuries had also seen large financial commitments to public buildings, all supported by private funds, but with the programmes of public building largely completed, more cash was available for private developments.

To whom then did these early villas belong and who lived in them? It is often said that the modest villas of the first and second centuries are the residences of farm managers, running farms on behalf of landed gentry who were themselves forced to live in towns because of the duties there required of them. That may be so, but it would imply a fairly high standard of living for the managers, who might be no better than slaves. Alternatively, we may see the houses as country retreats of the landowners, with deliberately modest facilities since they seldom spent much time in them.

There is a further explanation. They could be deemed to be the houses of a growing number of 'middle-class' farmers, either tenants or freeholders, who did not at first possess the property qualifications which virtually required them to become decurions, although following generations might have aspired to such wealth. Distinct from the big landowners, they would not have been attracted by the opportunities provided by the towns, and would not have been expected to subscribe to public buildings or festivities. Instead they opted for continuing country life, putting their profits back into the land they farmed and its buildings, so that as they prospered by slow and gradual degrees, they may have become the owners or tenants of quite respectable farms. Certainly, the probabilities are that such men existed, and it is not necessarily correct always to associate the best, or even the second best, villas with the curial classes.

One last possibility exists: that these villas were the result of other provincials, from Gaul, or Spain or Germany, investing in the new province once it was safe to do so. There is, unfortunately, no more evidence in favour of this than in the preceding explanations; all remains as supposition.

The developments outlined above continued unabated throughout the second century. Then came the upheavals at the end of the century, followed by the Severan victory over the British contender, Clodius Albinus. There can be no doubt that many landowners in Britain supported Albinus; they would have had difficulty not to. In the aftermath, it is likely that many estates were sequestered by the new emperor, as happened extensively in Spain, either for retention as imperial estates, or for sale to his supporters. In consequence, a number of villas, such as Ditchley and Lullingstone, show evidence for abandonment, although it need not be suggested that the farms ceased to be worked; only the residential quarters were empty.

The economic recession of the third century also affected many, although perhaps less severely in Britain than was once thought. But, as in the towns, there was less real money about, less confidence, and less incentive to undertake new developments. Some, however, perhaps avoided the difficulties.

The villas may also have begun to feel the effects of changes which were happening in other parts of Britain. There is considerable evidence to show that increasing amounts of arable land were becoming available in the north, particularly in Wharfedale and around certain forts. Consequently, there will have been growing competition between the villas and these new sources of grain, in which the latter had the advantage, as far as military contracts were concerned, of being nearer the consumers. In a time of recession and inflation, such competition could have been serious.

However, with the recovery of Britain in the late third century, marked social and economic changes occur in the countryside. The early fourth century saw a massive increase in the number, the size, and the standards of comfort of villas. The phenomenon cannot solely be accounted for by improved conditions and restored confidence, and there were clearly new factors playing a part, which must be considered.

Something of the general changes which took place then have been catalogued in preceding chapters. It is important to remember, in this context, two in particular: the greatly increased level of taxation and the new laws which not only prevented certain men from changing their jobs, but also made the jobs hereditary. Furthermore, there was also a provision whereby decurions, who had always been responsible for collecting and forwarding taxes, now became personally liable for the taxes of some defaulters, such as their tenants.

There can be little doubt that a man residing in the country, farming his own land, living largely on the produce and spending both his capital and his income, not on investments to bring further wealth, but on luxuries and consumer goods, has a distinct advantage over his town-based counterpart when it comes to tax avoidance, or even evasion. It is likely that many of the curial class, who, until now, had probably also been the main landowners, found the new obligations especially heavy. Some must have faced bankruptcy, in which case, if they possessed country estates, they would have been forced to sell. Some may have been more fortunate and were able to bribe or buy themselves into a higher social class, when they were relieved of some of the burdens. Their residence, or frequent attendance, was then no longer required in town, so they could retire from close proximity to the tax collectors. Perchance, also, one or more neighbouring estates might have been up for sale, so leading to a consolidation of landholdings in fewer hands and to amalgamations totalling several thousand acres. Yet, this reason, for long thought a principal one for many of the changes, and still undoubtedly valid, has perhaps been over-emphasized.

Parts of Gaul had, in the second part of the third century, suffered grievously from enemy action, rendering much of the countryside unsafe for habitation, whereas Britain had not suffered to anywhere

Fig. 64. The situation of the villa at Chedworth, in a small east-facing combe opening on to the valley of the River Colne. The modern house stands in the centre of the villa and still draws water from a spring emerging behind and to its right. The wood behind is comparatively recent.

near the same extent. It has been suggested that, when affairs returned to normal in the late third or early fourth century, there was a flight of capital from Gaul on the part of wealthy landowners who had been shaken by their recent experiences. Certainly one of the phenomena of the period is the emergence of a hundred or so villas which can happily be ranked with continental examples, and which are generally far superior in standard to the native product. This suggestion of a Gallic migration, although largely surmised, is to some extent supported by a coincidence of designs between British and Gallic mosaic pavements and by the presence in parts of Britain of dedications to specific deities otherwise only known in Gaul.

Unfortunately, there are so many imponderables when dealing with villas that any conclusions drawn are bound to be tentative. It is as well to remember that there were about a thousand or so country buildings in Britain which could be loosely classified as villas. Each one reflects a different set of circumstances, governed only by the whims of successive owners. To try to create general patterns, therefore, is an almost insuperable task, given our present evidence. Moreover, the situation must have been changing all the time. Villas could be bought and sold, rented or managed, sequestered or bankrupted; they could prosper or decline. A miserly millionaire

Fig. 65. A mosaic from the villa at Low Ham (Somerset) depicting scenes from the story of Dido and Aeneas. Venus, flanked by cupids, occupies the central panel (*Somerset County Museum*).

owner could live in a humble building at the centre of a great estate, while around him his tenants or lesser neighbours enjoyed the most palatial villas. Consequently, although it is usually argued that a large villa corresponds to a large estate, it might not always be safe to do so.

Yet the fourth century was the golden age of the villa in Britain, whatever its causes. It may be apt to compare it with the spate of country house building in eighteenth- and nineteenth-century England. It is not improbable, therefore, that fashion may have to be considered as a supplementary cause; an element in which the lesser man aped his peers and kept up with the Julii next door. At the very least, it can probably be said with some confidence that the villas represent a very considerable injection of capital into the countryside, while also signifying some social and economic changes which are less well understood.

A considerable number of the largest and most sumptuous villas are to be found in Gloucestershire and Somerset: Woodchester (fig. 60b), Chedworth (fig. 64), Witcombe and Low Ham (fig. 65) may be singled out. More occur in the Darenth valley of west Kent and include Lullingstone, while others are scattered over Hampshire, Wiltshire, Oxfordshire and Sussex, of which that at Bignor, near Chichester, is perhaps the most significant. A further group lies in Dorset and yet another ranges through Northamptonshire into Lincolnshire and east Yorkshire.

These buildings were a direct development of earlier villa types. We have already seen how the earliest single-range house was enlarged by the addition of wings at each end. In the buildings presently under discussion, the wings, when further extended, became ranges in their own right so completing three sides of a square, or rectangle, surrounding a central courtyard. The enclosure of the latter could then be completed, either by a wall, as in the case of Spoonley Wood (Glos.) (fig. 60g), or by a covered portico, as at North Leigh (Oxon.) (fig. 60a), or even by a further range of rooms, as at Woodchester or Bignor. It should, however, be noted that, in a growth which was essentially organic, additional wings were often not joined directly to the parent house, only becoming so as time passed, or, sometimes, even being left isolated, as at Brading in the Isle of Wight.

It is probable that in most cases the enclosed courtyard, which, in embryo, can usually be detected even in winged villas, served as the farmyard. Certainly at Ditchley (fig. 63) it contained a circular threshing floor and a well, presumably intended to supply water not only to the community but also to the stock. The addition of extra wings or buildings round the farmyard may, therefore, be seen as an extension to the farm as a whole and not only to the farmhouse. Granaries, machinery sheds, stock sheds and accommodation for the farm servants may all be expected. In some extreme cases, however, the latter were relegated to an outer court, giving rise to the so-called double-courtyard villa. In these, as at Bignor, complete separation is achieved between the farm and the residence of the owner, enhanced further at Woodchester (fig. 60b) by the presence of a recently identified third courtyard. In all these instances, it is likely that the inner courts were laid out as gardens, although there is little evidence for them so far, most probably because attention has been concentrated on the buildings. Fishbourne, though, reminds us of what excavation can achieve in recovering garden plans, demonstrated even more fully in late medieval and early modern contexts, such as Hampton Court.

Fig. 66. Painted wall plaster from the bath of the villa at Southwell (Notts.). Depicted here is a cupid apparently swimming in a marine environment (*Newark District Council Museum*).

At their peak, villas contained all the comforts and amenities of the better class town houses. Not only were bath-suites provided, but in a number of cases multiple units are known, either catering for different tastes in bathing, as in the baths of dry and moist heat at Chedworth, or possibly providing facilities for some of the farmworkers or retainers. Even when the owner was permanently resident, a large estate like North Leigh or Bignor would have required at least a bailiff. Indeed, the more the owner shut himself away from farmyard activities, the greater the need for a competent manager. Although a retainer, or even a slave, such a man would have had some standing and influence and might well have possessed his own private quarters with a bath-suite. Certainly if we are to assume that simple, second-century villas represent the houses of managers, we ought not to find the same people less well accommodated in the fourth century.

The main reception rooms of the villa were invariably decorated with mosaics, which in the fourth century employed a much wider variety of patterns and designs, often incorporating scenes from classical mythology, such as the Dido and Aeneas portrayal at Low Ham (fig. 65) or that of Jupiter and Europa from Lullingstone. Walls were covered with painted frescoes, a form of decoration which was often extended into the bathing establishments. Some fine paintings of fishes and other aquatic animals come from a bath at Southwell (Notts) (fig. 66), while an underground room at Lullingstone, apparently devoted to a water cult, contained a niche painted with the figures of three water nymphs and dolphins. Often the main rooms were heated with hypocausts, and on occasion, as at Chedworth, the functions of many of them can be identified. There, the main residential wing lay on the west side of the inner court or garden from which it was separated by a covered verandah. At the south end, this verandah could be shut off by a door from its fellow along the south range, so isolating the domestic quarters, containing a kitchen, a latrine and the steward's, or manager's, office, from the main house. The dining-room lay at the south end of the principal wing, close to the kitchen. It was divided visually into two unequal parts by pilasters, probably once supporting an arch across the room, and both parts were floored with mosaics, made by a local firm from Cirencester; the larger mosaic contained panels illustrating Bacchic scenes.

A small antechamber separated the dining-room from three other rooms, two of which formed a self-contained suite and which were presumably bedrooms. The north end of the wing terminated in a bath-suite. Running water was provided by a spring which rose outside the north-west angle; it was collected in a basin surrounded by a shrine, or *nymphaeum*, and then piped to parts of the building.

Chedworth is also an excellent example to consider with regard to the topographical siting of villas, in which act great care was taken (fig. 64). Many occupied idyllic surroundings, but more practical considerations probably carried greater weight. A copious supply of water, either from a spring, well or aqueduct, was obviously of prime importance. Some wells were exceedingly large, such as that at Rudston (Yorks) which was 30 m deep and 3 m in diameter at the top; the large amount of water which it could produce (it contained a depth of 9 m of water when excavated) together with the probability that it did not dry up in the summer, would have greatly helped the maintenance of large herds of stock or sheep, which would daily have consumed massive quantities of water (p. 192). The direction of the prevailing winds was often taken into account, and Chedworth lay at the head of a small combe, surrounded by hills on north, west and south sides, but with a fine open prospect to the east, where it looked across the valley of a minor stream.

From the foregoing descriptions, it can be seen that a typological development can be traced through this form of the Romano-British villa. Nevertheless it is dangerous to attempt a correlation of the types with chronology. While it is true that the majority of large courtyard villas were a fourth-century manifestation, developing over a period of time from humble beginnings, it cannot in reverse be claimed that all simple buildings belonged to earlier periods. It has already been recorded that the growth of villas in Britain was an organic process, representing the fluctuating fortunes of thousands of individuals over many years. Therefore, no reason exists why small houses, so characteristic of first-century construction, should not equally be found in fourth-century contexts, where they would illustrate the later rise to moderate fortune of native farmers, tenants or even immigrants. The term aisled farmhouse is normally used to describe the later examples, since they differ from the modest, early houses. Primarily, each consists of a plain rectangular building, though projecting rooms are sometimes attached. The interior is divided longitudinally by two rows of posts into a central 'nave' and two narrower 'aisles'. At their simplest they could represent granaries, barns or byres. In many, however, parts of both the nave and aisles are partitioned to form separate rooms, in which hypocausts, mosaics and frescoes are not unknown. Small bath-suites also occur, so that it is clear that they provided residential accommodation of a reasonable standard for the farmer. Yet the remaining space in the buildings equally clearly continued to give shelter for farmworkers, animals and fodder, and the overall effect, if allowance is made for the greater sophistication of the living quarters, would have been not dissimilar to the medieval long-house, shared alike by people and animals. The presence of animals is, after all, an excellent form of central heating.

Although villas of this type occur in isolation, such as those at Stroud (Glos.) Exning (Suffolk), Denton (Lincs.), Holbury and Clanville (Hants.), they are also to be found as subsidiary buildings in larger villas: Brading, Ickleton (Cambs.) and Mansfield Woodhouse (Notts.) are good examples. In the latter cases, it is to be assumed either that they were barns or that they provided accommodation for farmworkers of the estate, in which case some form of social distinction can probably be made. It is unlikely that all farmworkers would qualify for heated rooms and baths, and so it may be possible to differentiate between the upper and lower servants.

Another villa, which is a direct development of the rectangular native-style cottage of Roman Britain, to be seen in great numbers in the settlement at Chisenbury Warren (Wilts.) (fig. 46c), is that at Iwerne in Dorset. This villa lacks the tripartite arrangement of the aisled house and contains a living-room, a hall or large kitchen, and a byre, all under the same roof. In essence it probably represents the same class of farmer as the occupant of an isolated aisled villa, but one living in less comfortable circumstances.

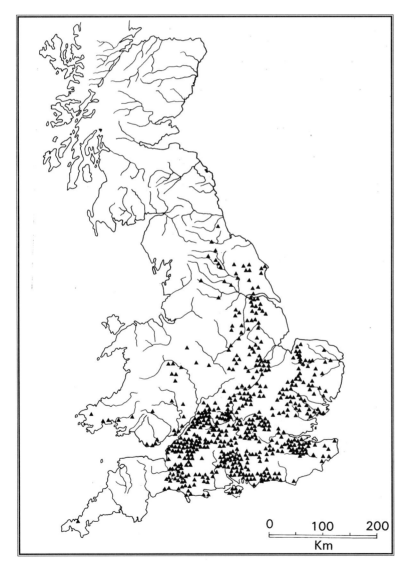

Fig. 67. Distribution of villas in Britain (*after A.L.F. Rivet*).

We have so far considered villa buildings, their types and developments. We must next review the relationship of one villa with another, and with other farming communities, and any evidence for land tenure which may arise therefrom.

If a line is drawn from the Severn estuary to the north Yorkshire moors, most villas will be found south and east of it (fig. 67), a few lie beyond in the Vale of York, in the west Midlands and in south Wales, but these outlying exceptions are matched by an almost total absence in Devon and Cornwall. The area which they occupy represents the greatest concentration of the best agricultural land in Britain, and this is certainly one of the reasons for their selective distribution. But first-class pasture and arable is not unknown elsewhere, if in more restricted quantities. Clearly, therefore, other reasons for their distribution must be sought, and are probably to be found in their relationships with road systems and towns, both of which were a necessary part of the so-called villa system. Where urbanization falters and then fails, so do villas: the latter could not survive without the former.

There are, however, some towns which have a marked villa-free zone about them, even though beyond the zone villas cluster thickly. Such a town is Cirencester with only one villa known in a 6½ km radius circle; Dorchester and Silchester are similar cases. Few villas are known in east Kent, although there are many in the north-west of the county. There are also country areas, remote from towns, almost entirely devoid of villas, such as Cranbourne Chase, Salisbury Plain, the Weald and the Fens, but let us consider the urban cases first.

It is highly probable, as already indicated above (p. 115), that much land around towns was farmed from them. What we do not know, unfortunately, is how it was organized, and several possibilities arise. It may be that few or no villas simply means larger land-holdings. At Cirencester for instance, the one villa at Barton Farm on the outskirts of the town may have controlled the whole of the 6½ km radius; similarly at Dorchester. Alternatively, the land may have been publicly owned, either as common land, following the old Celtic practice, or let out to tenants who resided in the town; or it may have been farmed directly by the civic authorities. Most civitas capitals grew in close proximity to old tribal centres, and the ground on which they stood formed but a small part of the tribal lands, effectively controlled by the chiefs, but probably not theirs to dispose of without approval. In a Romano-British context, can we see in

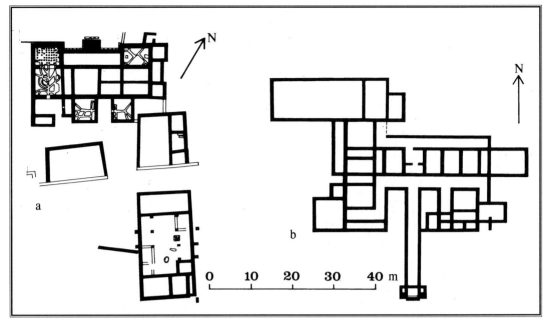

Fig. 68. Urban farms at:
a) Cirencester (*after A.D.
McWhirr*); b) Silchester (*after
G.C. Boon*).

these areas around towns the residue of the 'common' lands, still held
by the tribe (the civitas), administered by the chiefs (the decurions)
and used for the public good (rents from tenants etc.)? If so, then it
would seem that the tribal rulers of the Cantiaci were more
successful in holding off private enterprise, in the area around their
new capital, than were the Dobunni. We might speculate further.
Was the sale of land for private development confined, to begin with,
to tribal margins, and were the profits so obtained sunk in the first
public buildings of the new towns? As time passed more and more
land might have been disposed of until only a residue remained at
the centre, the amount varying from tribe to tribe, according to their
inclinations. This may be a speculative, part solution to the problem,
but it is not the only possibility.

There is increasing evidence to show that a number of towns had
farms, and farmhouses, within their boundaries. Certainly, at
Silchester (fig. 68b), there is a house near the north gate which is
associated with barns or byre-like buildings. Another, of the fourth
century, close to the Verulamium Gate at Cirencester (fig. 68a), is
not only planned like a winged villa, but has, to its rear, ancillary
buildings which can only be interpreted as workshops used by people
engaged in the maintenance of buildings and machinery. Indeed, one
of these structures, had it been found in open countryside, would

Fig. 69. Sandstone slabs for roofs or floors, stacked and ready for use, outside an urban farm at Cirencester (*Cirencester Excavation Committee*).

have been called an aisled farmhouse. The main house does not appear large enough to warrant a permanent labour force of the kind described, but a large estate might well do so, and there is evidence that many large estates employed enough staff to be virtually self-sufficient. Beyond the buildings, in the south-east quarter of the town, there is also known to be a considerable open space, which could have served as a paddock or home pasture. Although it has never been excavated, a similarly planned house shows in aerial photographs of Wroxeter and again seems to be associated with areas that have no buildings.

A late fourth-century house in the centre of Verulamium was designed as a small courtyard house (fig. 44d). In the early fifth century a corn-drying kiln was inserted in a room at one corner of the house, clearly indicating that the owner had grain to dry and, in those uncertain times, was anxious to bring it within the town walls as rapidly as possible. In minor towns, a typical winged corridor house is known at Great Chesterford.

There are, no doubt, many more such buildings to be identified in towns, and urban farms must have been comparatively common. What are they to be called? Stricly speaking, according to Roman law and usage, they were not villas. Yet, is it right to call the house at Barton Farm, some 400 m beyond the walls at Cirencester, a villa while we deny the term to the buildings described above which were just within those same walls? Some authorities consider that the distinction should be preserved. But we may well ask what accident excluded one and included the other within the defences. If the plan of walled Cirencester (fig. 37a) is examined it will be seen as a roughly elongated oval. The Barton Farm house lay at one end of the long axis while the other lay close to the short axis. It would, therefore, have been much easier to have excluded the former if it was an isolated building on the fringes. But to have left out the latter would have required the realignment of the whole of the eastern fortifications. There is little doubt that both were farms before the town boundary was consolidated with a rampart and wall. In the circumstances we would do well to remember the Villa Publica in Rome, which, while hardly a farm, did not lose its name, despite being enclosed within the city walls.

We need not be surprised, therefore, to find farms situated in towns. Indeed it is an extension of the principles which lay behind the deliberate foundation of coloniae. It will be remembered from the preceding chapter that an army veteran would have been given a plot of land in both the town and in the territorium surrounding it. Such land would consequently have been worked from the town, perhaps in time resulting in the establishment of villas. Admittedly, though, villas are not as densely congregated in areas which may represent colonial territoria as in some others. Unfortunately, also, the full extent of these territoria is not known and can only be guessed at. In many provinces the land was divided into regular plots when the colonia was founded, a process known as centuriation, in which it was divided by a grid of accommodation roads into squares with sides of 20 *actus* (710 m). It is to be expected that at least the three military coloniae at Colchester, Lincoln and Gloucester would have been provided with centuriated territoria, although there is some reason to believe that the first foundation at Colchester was not so dealt with. Unfortunately, owing to extensive alterations in land boundaries in the Saxon and Medieval periods, little more than vestigial traces survive of earlier divisions which may not necessarily always be associated with centuriation. It may be, also, that consolidation of the original holdings took place during the Roman period, leading to their obliteration. The plots granted to the veterans were not inalienable and could have been sold by themselves or their descendants.

Fig. 70. Inscription from
Ribchester (Lancs.). It refers to
V. Crescens Fulvianus,
legionary centurion of the
region and commander of the
local garrison, dedicating a
restored temple. Another
inscription refers to a *numerus*
of Sarmatian cavalry and also
to the *regio Bremetennacensis* (the
*Master and Fellows of St John's
College, Cambridge*).

Another form of land settlement for veterans has also been
recognized in Britain. Sometimes retired auxiliaries, especially if they
were recruited from beyond the frontiers, were settled within the
empire. Such a settlement is known at Ribchester (Lancs.), where a
garrison of Sarmatians is known and where evidence attests (fig. 70)
both the existence of the *Bremetennacum Veteranorum* and the *Regio
Bremetennacensis*. These 'regions' became a regular part of the late
empire and were administered by a military officer known as a
regionarius (Chapter 5). At Ribchester a legionary centurion had been
seconded for this duty and he also commanded the auxiliary fort.
There may have been a similar settlement outside the Saxon Shore
fort at Brancaster (fig. 31).

We have seen, therefore, that land around major towns,
particularly where there is an absence of villas, could have been
worked from the towns in which the farms lay. But this is in direct
contrast to the conditions outside many minor towns or lesser
settlements. It has long been recognized that such places as Bath,
Ilchester and Rochester have some of the largest villa concentrations
in Britain around them. Why this should be is not entirely clear, but

is may be that the lesser sites did not provide enough amenities to be attractive to the major landowners. There would consequently have been little or no incentive to reside in the minor towns. The alienation of tribal lands, discussed above, may also have a bearing on the problem. The core of every large fourth-century villa is often a humble first-century cottage. That one could grow to the other means that it was ultimately successful as a farm, and presumably the size of land-holding had to grow with it. Many minor towns tend to lie near the boundaries of civitates, and it is possible that land was at first more easily acquired by private owners on the margins of tribal territories than in the centres. So, ultimately a concentration of large estates might have grown in these peripheral regions, their distribution consequently giving the deceptive appearance of being related to minor settlements, whereas such was not necessarily the case.

Great difficulties occur when attempts are made to relate one villa with another, since so many possibilities arise for which there is virtually no evidence.

It is probably true to say that a very large, residential villa such as Woodchester (fig. 60b) or Bignor lay at the centre of a great estate, but it is almost impossible to say how large it was. Attempts have been made to calculate areas by relating granary capacities, where known, to them. For instance, Ditchley (fig. 63), a comparatively modest villa, has a granary thought to be equivalent to about 300 ha of arable land. Bignor, on the other hand, a major site, is estimated to have had slightly less than 300 ha of arable, but in addition some 200 sheep, which would have needed about 180 ha of pasture, probably on the Downs, together with perhaps 100 head of cattle run on the water-meadows of the River Arun. Woodland for timber, coppicing and fattening swine will also have been part of the estate, which may in all have run to 1,000 ha or more. But if we then try to relate these figures to Woodchester or Chedworth, it is found that other villas would fall within the areas. From this it is possible to conclude that there must be some landowner and tenant relationships, with the main villa acting as a home farm. There are, however, further complications. A large estate might be run by a manager on behalf of a permanently absent landlord, in which case only a modest house would be provided. How then are we to distinguish between the house of the manager and those of the tenants, which might well be larger and more comfortable? It cannot be done in our present state of knowledge, and such conclusions as may be drawn must in the main be restricted to the largest, residential houses. The complexities of the problem are perhaps best illustrated by Lullingstone where there exists not only an extremely comfortable, though modest-sized, villa, but also a barn or granary (fig. 58a) which is almost as big as the residential house. The main house is hardly the dwelling of a farm manager, neither is it really big enough to accommodate the complete family and all the retainers of a large landowner, although it obviously belongs to a man of considerable substance. Can we deduce that it was only used for periodic visits of inspection of a large estate almost entirely let out to tenants, who would have been required to fill the barn as part of their rent? There seems no other worthwhile conclusion to draw, but it is completely speculative.

It is well known, also, that villages and minor nucleated settlements can exist on large private estates, while tenants need not always inhabit subsidiary villas. Native-style farms and villages occur frequently over many parts of Britain, and it is not always easy to relate them to the villas. A number, for instance, are known on the South Downs, not far from Bignor and some other villas on the Sussex coastal plain. At one, on Thundersbarrow Hill, outside Shoreham, a cluster of round houses lie just to the east of an Iron Age hillfort. There is little to distinguish them from similar houses of an earlier period, except the presence of some Roman-style corn-drying kilns, pottery and other objects. The farm, or village, is associated with an extensive series of cultivated fields, while several other similar settlements exist at no great distance. Unfortunately we cannot say whether they belonged to smallholders, owning land of their own or on a communal basis, or whether the occupiers were tenants of one of the nearby villas, or were even agricultural workers billeted on outlying parts of the estate.

Marginal settlements of farmworkers seem to occur on some estates. At Poxwell, south of Dorchester, a rudimentary half-timbered, rectangular building was constructed in the lee of a field terrace in the third or early fourth century. It contained corn-drying kilns and also a furnace for roasting iron ore. A good deal of pottery was found, indicating that people lived there. Although the parent villa is not known, the buildings probably provided accommodation and working space in one of the more distant parts of an estate.

A further puzzle is provided by the detached bath-houses known to exist in some places apparently in isolation from other buildings. The largest number are known in Kent, where three at least occur in areas not noted for the abundance of villas. It used to be claimed that they belonged to timber-framed or cob buildings which had left no trace of their existence: a not altogether satisfactory explanation. They may have been provided for the estate workers who lived in the surrounding areas. But the full explanation is probably still to be sought.

Although they are much larger, the settlements or villages typified by Chisenbury Warren (fig. 46c) in Wiltshire or Meriden Down in Dorset provide similar problems. The former had over eighty rectangular house-platforms as well as a system of lanes, although it is not known if all the houses were occupied simultaneously. Both are surrounded by tracts of Celtic fields. But where do they fit into the hierarchy? Are they again villages of farmworkers on a large estate, or tenants, or are they freeholders farming their own land, either on a personal or a community basis? It has been claimed that a number of nucleated sites such as the walled, minor towns of Margidunum and Godmanchester provided seasonal reservoirs of farmworkers. It is indeed likely that this was at least partly so, in which case the urgent question to be asked is: what was the essential difference between, for example, Chisenbury Warren and Godmanchester? Reduced to this level there appears a strong resemblance between them, yet differences in organization clearly existed but precisely what they were and why, we cannot say.

The case of Chisenbury Warren has been deliberately cited, as it lies on the north-east edge of Salisbury Plain, an area which, together with adjacent Cranbourne Chase, has a marked lack of villas.

Throughout the empire there were areas of land which became the personal property of the emperor, either by conquest, or by sequestration, or by deed of gift. Some of the areas were concerned with mineral extraction, such as the silver and gold mines of Britain but in the main they will have comprised holdings of agricultural land. Two areas command attention in this context. One is that referred to above around Salisbury Plain. It was a region which, with its multitude of hillforts, had bitterly resisted the advance of the Roman army in AD 43. Although there were a few villas, which were generally modest and of late development, there were many native settlements which continued almost unchanged from the Iron Age well into the Roman period, and show little sign of romanization. Yet an assessment of the capacities of their grain storage pits has indicated that, when compared with similar sites elsewhere, between a half and a third of their production was taken away, in place of the normal tax of about a tenth or twelfth. Although such figures should be viewed with caution, they have led to suggestions that the area, in response to its initial hostility, was reduced to an imperial estate, in which the inhabitants were deliberately kept at a low subsistence level in order to provide grain for the Roman army. Later changes support the view that there was an alteration from arable to pasture, as stock enclosures tend to replace, or are added to, the earlier settlements, as at Woodcuts, Rotherley and Tollard Royal. Since these changes went hand-in-hand with the emergence or two of three small villas, such as Iwerne, it is probable that, if it was an imperial estate, a different method of working had been introduced, perhaps involving tenancies.

Imperial estates were managed, on behalf of the emperor, by the provincial procurator. He would have had a number of assistants to run individual holdings, each of which would have been provided with a headquarters. One such building, usually called a villa, is known at Combe Down, outside Bath; it produced an inscription (fig. 54), already referred to in the preceding chapter, which mentions the restoration of a principia by a procurators' assistant in the early third century. We do not know what estate he managed. It has been suggested that it was the one situated in and around Salisbury Plain, although that might be deemed to be too far away. More likely it was connected with the silver mines of the Mendips, or stone quarries in the Bath area. But remembering the number of wealthy villas around Bath, it would not be surprising if it was connected instead with agricultural estates perhaps sequestered after the Albinus fiasco. But the inability to differentiate between this building and an ordinary villa adds yet another dimension to our problems. Who is to say, in the absence of other evidence, which villas acted as centres for imperial estates?

Between them the will of Prasutagus and the Boudiccan rebellion provided Nero with large tracts of land. In the Antonine Itinerary only one villa in Britain is listed, the Villa Faustina at Scole on the Norfolk-Suffolk borders. Why should it have been included as a place to visit on a supposed imperial journey? Presumably because it acted as a centre for a very large imperial estate, derived probably from the aftermath of the rebellion.

Another region often assigned the same status is the Fenlands of Lincolnshire, Cambrideshire and Norfolk. This was an area which, during the Iron Age, was predominantly under water, peat or salt-marsh and consequently only inhabited along its margins and sundry islands. During the early part of the Roman period some of these settlements continued to extract salt from sea water. But during the principate of Hadrian, perhaps as the result of his visit to Britain, large-scale development took place, coupled with a major scheme of land drainage. Hadrian was personally interested in land reclamation, having previously instituted schemes in Africa. Moreover it was he who liberalized the Mancian Law by introducing two important concessions for tenants who took occupancy of waste land on imperial estates. Providing they created a domicile, did not try to sell the holding and kept the land productive, they paid no rent for the first five or ten years, and became virtual owners of the property. Even if, therefore, the Fens were not part of Prasutagus' domains inherited by Nero, we can still make out a strong case on these grounds for them, as reclaimed land, to have been an imperial estate. In support we might cite the scale of the works, which appear too great for private enterprise to have been responsible; only the central government could have provided the necessary organization and capital expenditure. And there is also the nature of the settlements, usually consisting at first of solitary farms, fairly closely placed to one another, each of which then appears to proliferate to about a dozen or so main buildings. These farms look remarkably like the original domiciles of the first settlers, followed by fragmentation of the holdings in the hands of their descendants, so that in time they came to resemble loose nucleations, such as that at Hacconby (fig. 47b). Villas are unknown in the Fens, although a number occur on the higher ground of the Fen edge. Their absence is often considered to be supporting evidence for an imperial estate, which may or may not be so. But it is highly unlikely that a man who aspired to a villa would have placed his house on low-lying insalubrious land, swarming with mosquitoes and other disease-carrying insects.

There is, furthermore, the principia-like building constructed at Godmanchester (fig. 46a) in the early third century. Godmanchester lies on the southern edge of the Fens and on main roads running both north–south and east–west, so it would have been an ideal site for an administrative headquarters. It was built at a time when a general tightening up of imperial administration was taking place, and the more liberal approach of Hadrian towards his tenants had probably long been forgotten. The restoration of the principia at Combe Down would belong in the same context. An alternative administrative centre for the Fens has been suggested at Stonea Grange.

Fig. 71. Aerial photograph of the Fenland village bordering the Car Dyke near Cottenham (Cambs.). Most of the earthworks have now been ploughed out, but enough survives to the right of the photograph to show traces of the blocks of narrow strip fields. See also fig. 59c (*copyright: Committee for Aerial Photography, University of Cambridge*).

The method of drainage introduced in the Fens appears to resemble that used in some places today. Blocks of land were successively crossed by two large roughly parallel dykes, the Car Dyke and Midfendic, into which minor drainage channels discharged. These in turn also cut across the main rivers, which run north-east-by-east into the Wash. Consequently, water flowing from the higher ground to the west could, as necessary, be transferred from one river to another and, by means of appropriately placed sluices, be retained in the system until an ebb tide allowed discharge into the sea. For a long time, the Car Dyke was considered to be a continuous channel, partly natural and partly artificial, stretching from near Cambridge to Lincoln, and intended for both navigation and drainage. More recent work has shown, however, that not only is it made up of discrete sections with causeways crossing it, but also the levels vary considerably along its length; so it could not have been used as a continuous waterway without an extensive lock system, for which there is no evidence.

Navigation and drainage have, in fact, conflicting requirements, the maintenance of deep water being inimical to that of good drainage.

As briefly noted above, there are in the Fens many farms and villages associated with extensive areas of field-systems. They lie almost entirely on the silt Fens and none are yet known on the peats. They vary from single farmsteads through all gradations of nucleation to large settlements covering several hectares and sometimes extending up to fifty. One of the best known of the nucleated sites is that at Cottenham (figs 59c and 71) in Cambridgeshire. There, both banks of the Car Dyke are flanked by farmsteads surrounded by a complicated pattern of fields, droveways, access lanes and paddocks. Some of the fields are arranged in blocks of narrow strips, for long incorrectly identified as 'granaries', thought to have been used for storing grain from the imperial estate before it was shipped to northern garrisons along the canal. It seems more likely that they are to be associated with horticulture or, alternatively, they may have been stock pens for the corralling of sheep and cattle during annual round-ups. Certainly recent investigations tend to show that, while grain production was important, the economic strength lay in stock-raising, and many of the areas between settlements, where few visible field boundaries exist, may have been used as ranches for cattle and sheep.

As in Cranbourne Chase, there is little sign of regular land divisions, probably owing to the tortuous nature of many of the natural watercourses. There are some rectilinear field-systems, such as that near Upwell, Cambridgeshire, but they tend to be rare. Yet some authorities have detected a sense of order in the main arrangements reflecting probably the hand of central government.

Despite a concentration on agricultural activities, it must not be forgotten that the Fenland region also continued to produce large quantities of salt, which may also have been an imperial monopoly. It is likely that shellfish from the estuaries of the Wash provided another source of income; oysters are found in prodigious quantities on most Romano-British sites, while in addition mussels, whelks, cockles and winkles were collected.

Some further sites may also be considered as imperial estates. The villa at Hambledon (Bucks.) was modest in size, but contained in its farmyard a considerable number of corn-drying kilns (fig. 58c–e), suggesting large-scale grain production. In addition, the large number of infant burials would imply a high slave population, while seventy *styli*, instruments for writing on waxed tablets, would point to a measure of bureaucratic control. If not an imperial estate, it probably formed the centre of a large, private holding, run by a manager on behalf of an absentee landowner. A rather similar villa exists at Rockbourne (Hants.), while a dedication to Carinus Caesar at another at Clanville also carries connotations of imperial ownership.

In considering villas, we have also been able to take in much of the related pattern of farming in lowland Britain. There remains one last aspect to be described before we can turn elsewhere.

Villas in Britain were not normally fortified. When they were founded, there was no need; warfare was far away. By the time the real need arrived, the system was already in decline and, although there is ample evidence to show not only the continuance of villas, but also new construction, beyond the barbarian conspiracy of AD 367, it was altogether more modest and lacked the flamboyance of the early fourth century. At best, they were sometimes equipped with a ditch and bank, perhaps topped with a hedge, as at Ely, near Cardiff, or with bank, wall and ditch as at Ditchley (fig. 63); in neither case were they of defensive character. Such structures were intended to afford protection from vagrants, petty thieves and marauding animals, to keep stock in and to provide drainage.

Large, fortified villas are, however, known on the continent, where the idiosyncrasies of wealthy owners were given realism in the form of defensive walls. Such a villa at Anthée, in Belgium, covers some 12 ha. Recently, a site at Gatcombe, a few kilometres north-west of Bath, has been investigated. It was at first thought to be a minor walled town, but there are features which cannot readily be explained by that interpretation. The area enclosed within the wall is about 6.5 ha, and the wall itself is massive, being 4.5 m thick. The angles are not curved as in most urban defences, neither is there evidence for bastions, rampart or ditch. It would appear to have been constructed sometime in the third or fourth centuries. Within the enclosure a number of buildings lie on terraces on the hillside. At least two resemble aisled farmhouses or barns, while there are also traces of iron and lead working. Somewhere, also, is suspected the site of a better class building with mosaics.

If a villa, a conclusion by no means proved, it represents an owner asserting his own individuality in a manner more frequently to be observed on the continent, perhaps in the face of the growing insecurity of the region in the later fourth century. Perhaps too it may denote an emigrant owner from Gaul, for if we are to suppose that Gallic landowners came to Britain for refuge after the third century invasions, there is more supporting evidence for the suggestion in the region around Bath than elsewhere.

The general distribution of villas in Britain has already been considered. Although they are to be associated with alterations in the type of agricultural economy, we cannot be sure that the pattern did not also change elsewhere. The scale of working may well be assumed to have been greater in regions dominated by villas, but general farming practices probably remained much the same everywhere and a large landowner could just as easily inhabit a mud hut as a villa; only his lifestyle would be different.

Some three of four dozen villas occur outside the main area of distribution. One is known at Illogan near Camborne in Cornwall, but its complete isolation in an area displaying vastly different kinds of settlements and farms may mean that it was associated more with tin streaming than with agriculture. A number are also known in south Wales and in the Welsh Marches, but neither the Demetae, the Silures or the Cornovii were greatly attracted by this type of farm. Some are also placed to take advantage of the rich land of the Vale of York, while one at least occurs in Upper Airedale, in the Pennines. The most northerly of all is at Old Durham.

These were, however, the exceptions, representing a fringe to a particular way of life. For the remainder, farms and settlements tended to continue much as they had in the Iron Age. Regional differences, nevertheless, existed but they often owed more to Iron Age antecedents than to any Roman influence. But we must be cautious in some of our assessments as all is not always as it seems.

In the south-west, the predominant form of single farm is one called a round (fig. 72). Their origin seems to lie in the first century BC, and it has been estimated that up to a thousand existed in Cornwall and Devon, often surviving through the Roman period. Despite their name, they appear in a variety of different shapes and sizes, from 0.2 ha–1.2 ha. They are invariably surrounded by a single bank and ditch, frequently of some size. It seems quite likely that hedges were planted on the tops of the banks to give increased protection, and so would appear to be the forerunners of modern Cornish 'hedges', which are a combination of hedge and thick stone-faced and earth-filled boundary wall. These banks were not defensive except insofar as they were intended to keep out thieves and wild animals. Their prime purpose was probably to give protection to the inhabitants and stock from driving rain and wind, while at the same time keeping the latter from straying. The ditch, therefore, may be seen simply as a quarry for bank material. Access was gained by a single entrance, and one or more circular houses lay within the

Fig. 72. Two 'rounds' below the hillfort on Tregonning Hill, Castle Pencaine (Cornwall) (*copyright: Committee for Aerial Photography, University of Cambridge*).

enclosure, usually sheltering in the lee of the bank. It is not possible to say, however, how many family groups might be represented by one round. They are usually situated between the 60 m and 120 m contours and never lie on hilltops or valley bottoms. In some, where evidence has survived, they are related to adjacent field-systems, in which the individual plots are not unlike Celtic fields in size and shape.

Rounds, therefore, seem to represent the class of independent farmer, who, while operating a mixed arable and pastoral system, would, further east, have ultimately erected a villa. But a combination of conservatism and a lack of urban markets and influence acted against it. It is worth emphasising, however, that the existence of the civitas capital at Exeter did not promote any growth of villas even in its immediate neighbourhood, where there was admirable farmland. So we may conclude that the Dumnonii set their faces against the new villa development, and the way of life which it represented, in favour of traditional and well-established forms of dwellings.

That is not to say, however, that no innovations took place. A structure characteristic of the Roman period in West Penwith is the courtyard house. They are usually grouped in small villages on the moorlands, containing perhaps up to a dozen such dwellings

Fig. 73. Aerial photograph of a village of courtyard houses at Chysauster, near Penzance. The *fogou* lies to the right of the main cluster of houses (*copyright: Committee for Aerial Photography, University of Cambridge*).

(fig. 73). The latter are roughly oval in outline and constructed of earth and rubble banks kept in place by drystone walling. The rooms, up to six in number, were built within the thickness of the walls and opened on to a central courtyard, from which a single entrance gave access to the exterior. The rooms were probably roofed with turf, as being less likely to be blown away in south-westerly gales.

In structural respects, therefore, they seem to have developed directly from the rounds, each 'house', or 'room' in the latter having been absorbed, as it were, by a massive, internal thickening of the perimeter wall. We might, therefore, wonder if multiple 'huts' inside a round indeed represent, not individual dwellings, but 'rooms' of one 'house'. If we are right in this assumption, then these villages represent much the same class of people as inhabited the rounds, but gathered together in a community in order to share some of its assets and possibly practising a slightly different type of farming.

At Chysauster (fig. 73), eight of these houses were arranged on both sides of a meandering central lane, with possibly more a short distance away. Each dwelling had its own paddock or garden, while the whole community shared a large underground storage chamber, or *fogou*. The latter are, like the courtyard house, characteristic of the Land's End peninsula in the Iron Age and Roman periods, although they are also found in Brittany and Scotland. They consisted of wide, usually curving, excavations in the ground, the sides of which were revetted by large upright slabs of stone and the whole roofed with similar slabs. Entrances normally existed at both ends, from which ramps led down to the bottom; occasionally there were branching side passages. It is probable that they were used for storing meat, since the through circulation of air would aid its drying and preservation, while an even temperature would be maintained by the surrounding earth.

Each village was also directly connected to large areas of field-systems, suggesting again that they practised a mixed farming economy. In some cases larger rectangular fields replaced the smaller, earlier plots, implying improvements in agricultural methods.

In addition to rounds and courtyard houses, a considerable number of unenclosed round huts, or houses, also existed. Like the two former types they tend to be associated with fields, and probably represent the dwellings of peasant farmers, or smallholders. But as with the relationship between villas and native farms elsewhere, it is impossible to connect them with the more developed forms of settlement. But, if the villa at Illogan represents a romanized manifestation of a round, it is difficult not to imagine that some relationship existed between it and the open hut site at nearby Porth Godrevy.

Despite the general absence of romanized housing in the south-west, there was no lack of other material goods, and even the Porth Godrevy hut produced coins, a samian dish, an amphora and iron nails. Bronze *fibulae*, brooches of Romano-British form, may have been produced in the Isles of Scilly, and it is probable that local blacksmiths, in time, became familiar with the manufacture of better class agricultural implements. Neither must it be forgotten that from the early third century onwards, the inhabitants of even a simple round hut may have been Roman citizens, although we might quite rightly suspect that it made little difference to them.

On considering Wales, we find that regional differences can again be detected in settlement types and patterns. We have already noted above that southern Wales tended to be within the orbit of villas, although it must be admitted that in the south-west the link is extremely tenuous. There, the buildings, which are essentially simple in plan, are often enclosed within a ring-work, possibly belonging to an earlier period. A typical example is known at Cwmbrwyn, not far from the civitas capital of the Demetae at Carmarthen. A rectangular masonry building, approximately 33 m by 7.5 m, was situated inside a roughly trapezoid enclosure, with a bank and ditch, measuring about 42 m across; smaller, wooden sheds were also indicated in the interior. A similar site has been identified not far away at Trelissey. In neither case has it been proved that the defences are contemporary with the buildings, but if the latter were erected within an earlier enclosure, it is difficult to avoid the conclusion that it was done deliberately to take advantage of a fortified site; it is therefore possible that they were replacing earlier wooden buildings. Unlike the Cornish rounds, the bank and ditch are of a scale great enough to warrant the assumption that they were defensive in character.

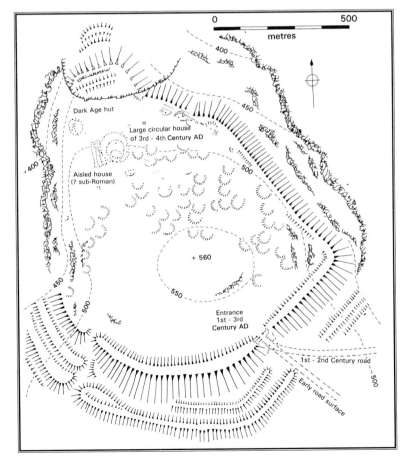

Fig. 74. Native farmstead at Dinorben (Clwyd). It occupies a small Iron Age hill-fort and, with intervening periods of desertion, continued in occupation into the early fifth century (*after W. Gardner and H.N. Savory*).

Elsewhere in south-west Wales, small fortified enclosures of the type just described continued to be used and a number have produced Roman pottery. Exceptional, however, are two sites on the coast, at Gateholm and Sheep Island, where there were clusters of rectangular wooden buildings, probably dating from the Roman period. Their positions would suggest fishing villages, allied to primitive agriculture.

In the west-central part of Wales, bordering Cardigan Bay, no settlements or farms have yet been identified for the Roman period. There are many hillforts in the area, but none have so far been shown to have been occupied after the Iron Age, and indeed casual finds of Roman pottery or metalwork are rare in the region as a whole.

In the north-east, a few enclosed native farms are known containing round wooden-framed houses. Some are related to field-systems. The best-known site is that at Dinorben (fig. 74), where, about the middle of the third century, a landowner built himself a large round house, 20 m in diameter, inside a disused hillfort. Although the house was supplied with a wide range of Roman pottery, metalwork and ornaments, its archaic plan indicates the innate conservatism of even the wealthiest landowners in the highland areas. The large amount of agricultural equipment found on the site indicates the main activity of the inhabitants, and among the latter was an asymmetrical, winged plough-share, of a type which can only have come from a plough with coulter and mouldboard. As noted above, such ploughs were a benefit conferred by Roman technology; a balanced sickle of Romano-British pattern was also found. But surprisingly no visible field boundaries have been recorded in the area, in contrast to this evidence for the existence of arable land. At Dinorben, there are strong indications, therefore, that a land-owning farmer was using the most up-to-date agricultural techniques available, even though he was living in the traditional native manner. This should not be forgotten when comparing other native farms with villas.

Strong contrasts with the foregoing can be seen in the north-western area, which also includes Anglesey. A large number of farms and settlements are known, and it appears that some fairly intensive reoccupation of hillforts took place during the late Roman period. The farms are normally enclosed by a stone wall, and, within each enclosure, there may have been three or four stone buildings, mostly circular, as at Llain-Llan, but occasionally rectangular as at Cefngraeanog. The enclosures themselves vary from roughly oval to polygonal in shape, and are almost always associated with strongly marked terraced fields, the holdings ranging from 1.6–8 ha. They were normally situated on reasonably high ground, so that each farm had access to unlimited hill pasture in addition to its cultivated fields. Occasionally, isolated huts are situated in the fields, while sometimes all the huts of one farm are so distributed.

The density of these farms and settlements has led to the suggestion that they represent official Roman encouragement of new inhabitants during the third century in an area which had been depopulated by punitive action in early Roman campaigns. Certainly the polygonal enclosures and their rectangular buildings might imply Roman architectural influence. But the area is also one where hillforts of the pre-Roman period contained a high proportion of stone-built huts, and a degree of continuity might possibly be expected. Yet, in some cases these enclosed farms overlie earlier settlements of different plan and type, so that rebuilding in the new manner would probably imply a change of ownership, even if there was no change in landholding or redistribution of land.

One of the best examples of a polygonal farmstead is that at Din Lligwy. The enclosure was formed of five straight-sided walls with a single narrow entrance on the east, leading through a rectangular 'porch' or lodge. A circular house stood in the western angle, while three more rectangular buildings were placed against different lengths of the enclosure walls. The masonry was good, and plentiful pottery and coins were recovered. There was also evidence of metal-working. Outside the enclosure are some massive field walls, still in use today, which may or may not represent earlier field boundaries.

Socially and economically these enclosed farms seem to represent the same class of farmer as the rounds and courtyard houses of Cornwall: independent landowners or high-grade tenants. We shall see shortly that comparable systems occur in the north, and if the villa is taken to describe the basic agricultural 'unit' of the lowland zone, so do these farms act in the highland areas.

As in Wales, so in the north, regional distinctions can be seen in the types of settlement, depending on the nature of the earlier Iron Age occupation. For our present purpose it is sufficient to distinguish between the Pennines, the Tyne-Forth area and the Solway-Clyde area. It must also be remembered that, as in other regions where native-style farms remained unaltered, there is a strong element of continuity into the Roman period and that it is not always easy to differentiate between pre-Roman and Roman period sites.

During the Iron Age the Pennines and the Lake District possessed few hillforts: Ingleborough, Mam Tor and Almondbury, to cite those apparently most important, do not appear to have been occupied much after the fourth century BC. It has been suggested, though, that Almondbury became the final headquarters of Queen Cartimandua, while Ingleborough served as the last refuge of her sometime consort, Venutius; but evidence is lacking. For the remainder of the inhabitants of Brigantia, most seem to have been dispersed among a large number of primitive farms and settlements, many of which were not enclosed. The principal activity seems to have been pastoralism, with the breeding of cattle, horses and possibly sheep. The great oppidum of Stanwick, with its banks and ditches enclosing an area of *c.* 300 ha in its final phase, seems to have been designed so as to provide sufficient pasture within the enclosure for large flocks and herds. Recent fieldwork and excavation have confirmed a foundation date at about the time of the conquest and a decline in the closing decades of the first century. While it survived, it was undoubtedly the centre of Brigantian power and wealth, based presumably on the abundant livestock. Elsewhere, some settlements have small areas of fields attached to them, but they cannot always be equated with the pre-Roman period. Nevertheless, a little cultivation of nearby fields probably took place in more favoured places in the Dales.

Beyond the line of the Tyne and Solway the main difference to be detected is the greatly increased number of fortified or enclosed sites. North of the Tyne these frequently began as palisaded enclosures on hilltops, with either one or two rows of posts round the perimeter. More often than not the palisades were later replaced by a combination of ditch and mound or ditch and wall, giving rise to what are, in effect, small hillforts, sometimes with multivallate defences. Circular houses found within the forts or enclosures are normally constructed of timber, such as one, 18 m in diameter at West Brandon (Co. Durham) which was not unlike similar houses further south.

Another type of enclosure has also been recognized, usually known as 'scooped' enclosures. They are situated on hillsides in non-defensive positions and lie within a mound or stone wall. Scoops in the hillside accommodate circular houses and other features.

To the west, in Galloway, settlements are more reminiscent of north and west Scotland, with duns, crannogs and even some brochs, interspersed with fortified settlements. Duns and brochs are normally held to represent single-family occupancy, in contrast to the community settlements, and clearly point to different social origins for the people concerned.

In most of these areas, the one marked development during the Roman period is probably the emergence of circular stone houses to replace timber prototypes; they usually appear in compact groups within stone-walled or embanked enclosures and sometimes overlie earlier hillfort defences. Both single-house and multiple-house types are known. Occasionally such settlements occur in the vicinity of abandoned hillforts, such as that at Jenny's Lantern, Bolton (Northumb.), and clearly point to the non-defensive nature of the enclosure. But by far the largest number have no connexion whatever with earlier hillforts, and seem to date generally from the second to the fourth century AD, or even later. In the single holdings, one, or at most two, round stone houses were built within, or tangentially to, the enclosed courtyard, which is often terraced or scooped from the hillside, as at Ells Knowe (fig. 4a) or Elsdon Burn. In many ways, they are reminiscent of similarly planned dwellings in Wales and the south-west. In the multiple holdings, which are far commoner, upwards of four or five round houses occupy the roughly oval enclosure, which may have a walled paddock within it, such as Knock Hill. The largest known group, containing upwards of thirty buildings, is at Greaves Ash, where piecemeal additions had probably been made to the original nucleus. Sometimes also, loose collections of settlements, perhaps totalling more than a hundred houses, are found in close proximity. In areas nearer and to the south of Hadrian's Wall there is also a tendency for round or oval enclosures to be replaced by rectilinear ones, as at Riding Wood, where four houses inhabited a roughly trapezoidal enclosure with cobbled yards and paved entrance passages. Such settlements are prolific in parts of Cumberland and Westmorland, particularly in the area of the Cumberland plain, south of Carlisle, where, also, probably as the result of Roman influence, rectangular buildings and enclosures are more common; typical sites can be seen at Thursby.

While there is evidence during the Roman period that cultivation of cereals took place in the north, since rotary querns, a Roman introduction, are common finds on such farms, it is often difficult to identify the fields associated with them. Some areas are, of course, exceptional in this respect, such as Ribblesdale, Upper Wharfedale, and parts of Cumberland and Westmorland, where many hectares of continuous, enclosed or terraced fields were opened up in the Roman

Fig. 75. Aerial photograph of Housesteads fort on Hadrian's Wall looking south. Buildings in the vicus can be seen clustering round the south gate, while beyond lie numerous terraced fields; not all are necessarily Roman, but some almost certainly are (*copyright: Committee for Aerial Photography, University of Cambridge*).

period, to increase quite markedly the amount of cereals produced. Yet the impression remains of a predominantly pastoral economy, linked with the unlimited upland grazing, good pastures for wintering in the valleys and in the small stockyards of the farms and settlements.

Ultimately the northern farmer was probably better placed than his north Welsh or Cornish opposite numbers to take advantage of the growth of towns and vici. Carlisle and Corbridge must have commanded considerable markets, while both, together with the numerous vici, would presumably have contained resident farmers and farm-workers who went out each day to their work, acting as the counterparts to the many workers from towns and minor settlements much further south. Some of these sites may have even contained farms. Certainly the reason for the growth of so many agricultural establishments in the Cumberland plain might be explained by the presence of nearby Carlisle.

Nor must we forget that, in the third and fourth centuries, soldiers could become farmers and cultivate land around forts. We might, therefore, expect some sign of fields in their vicinities; one such fairly extensive system is known at Housesteads, parts of which may be of Roman date (figs 26 and 75). Their activities must have had some effect on the overall farming pattern.

Having considered farming and its various ancillary aspects in different parts of Britain, it requires no great extention to take in horticulture.

It is probable that Iron Age man, when desirous of fruit, vegetables or herbs, collected them from the wild, and there is little evidence for any cultivation. Indeed, there was little need, since most vegetables were probably valued for their medicinal qualities and not as foodstuff. The Roman period saw not only the practice of horticulture being introduced, but also many new varieties of fruit and vegetable. Unfortunately the evidence for botanical material is not easy to find, surviving in Britain mainly in waterlogged deposits, or as pollen in acid soils, while evidence for the actual borders or flower beds are even more difficult to trace in the course of excavation.

In other respects we are more fortunate in having excellent contemporary pictorial representations on wall-paintings in Italy, and also good accounts of horticultural practices written down by authors such as Columella in the late first century, not that it is necessarily valid to relate such evidence directly to Britain.

It is difficult to estimate, even within the widest limits, the place of vegetables in the Romano-British diet, but it is probable that most horticultural work will have aimed at producing vegetables or fruit (fig. 76). Ornamental gardens were well known in the Roman world, but it is likely that only the very rich could afford, or even be bothered with, such layouts, and the great central garden at the Fishbourne palace is an excellent example to consider (fig. 61). Its general plan has already been described earlier in this chapter; as with the building, it was probably laid out in the most fashionable manner available, and it is interesting to compare what we know of it with the almost contemporary descriptions of Columella and Pliny. It seems to have combined excessive formality with areas of wild garden, a favourite association in the classical world, which can be seen illustrated on wall-paintings. The middle walk was flanked by arbours or parterres, alternately semicircular and rectangular, backed by hedges, which may have been of box. The bedding-trenches provided for the latter can be closely matched in Columella's

Fig. 76. 'Roman' garden at Corinium Museum, Cirencester, with plants of the period (*Corinium Museum*).

descriptions, where he advocates that, to sow a hedge, the seeds should be fastened at the correct intervals to a piece of rope, which is then laid in a trench and covered with soil. Further walks surrounded the whole garden, but in the two central areas so formed, no formal layouts seem to have been made, except for some pergolas flanking the paths, and we might suppose that they supported a variety of ornamental shrubs or fruit trees; Pliny mentions roses growing on pergolas. Unfortunately, the evidence for the plants grown, apart from weeds, was restricted to one species; some seeds of *Lathyrus*, an everlasting pea, were found in one room. But it should not be forgotten that in addition to various native species which might have been naturalized in a garden, such as the crab-apple, bullace, sloe, elder, or possibly the vine, several new forms were possibly introduced during the Roman period: a black plum, not unlike the Carlsbad variety, the cherry, medlar, walnut, mulberry, rose and the flowers, lily, violet and pansy. Greater emphasis than today was probably placed on pot-herbs for seasoning and medicinal purposes, and native species again could have been introduced into gardens to

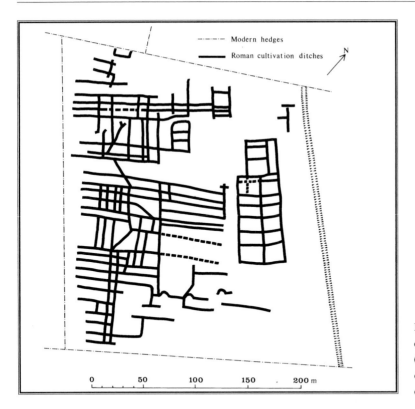

--·--·-- Modern hedges

——— Roman cultivation ditches

N

0   50   100   150   .   200 m

Fig. 77. Horticultural enclosures at North Thoresby (Lincs.). Alternatively, they could have contained fruit trees or even vines (*after D.F. Petch*).

save the trouble of collection from the wild: parsley, fennel and coriander. Introductions apparently included dill, alexanders, chervil and the opium poppy. Many other varieties of native plants would also have been worthy of a place, such as mallow, foxglove (also useful for a drug), St John's wort, marjoram or thyme.

Apart from Fishbourne, and although a garden court may be suggested for the possible governor's residence in London (p. 165), the only other evidence for formal flower beds comes from the villa at Frocester, near Stroud. But it seems inconceivable that the open spaces, often walled, which were associated with town houses and villas were not put to similar use, although the accent will probably have been strongly utilitarian, rather than on visual effect. Nevertheless, box clippings as well as the seeds of many ornamental plants were found at Silchester, and it is as well to remember that many plants normally grown as food can make quite attractive displays when interspersed with other types. Neither should we forget that bee-keeping was a supplementary activity, probably practised by many households, as honey provided the main sweetening agent in the diet. The growing of suitable flowers for the bees would have been a logical extension, while almost all dyes for cloth were obtained from vegetable matter, of which we might mention dyers' bugloss and madder, both suitable for cultivation. Apart from Silchester, both York and London have recently provided abundant botanical material; much of the evidence is confined to wild plants and to what would now be called weeds, but cultivated species also occur.

There are upwards of 300 wild food products, including fungi, growing in Britain today. Not all were available to the inhabitants of Roman Britain and some, such as cabbage, broad bean, pea, parsnip, celery, mustard and possibly turnip were introduced during that period. The Celtic bean had of course been grown before, while such fruits as hazelnut, strawberry, raspberry and blackberry were abundant in many areas, and suitable for transplanting to gardens. It is not always possible, when presented with the evidence of seeds or pollen from an excavation, to say, if they represent the wild or cultivated varieties; indeed both probably continued to be used. But it is worth mentioning that, during the nineteenth century, good-sized parsnip roots were obtained from wild stock inside ten years, simply by selecting seeds from the best-developed plants each year and sowing in well-prepared ground. So some form of plant improvement was well within the compass of experienced gardeners in the Roman period, and was probably recognized as one of the benefits of cultivation, the other being easy availability. Yet most vegetables would have been both tougher and stringier than modern day varieties, and a preliminary pulping or crushing to break down the coarser fibres would have made them more tender. Perhaps this is the reason why so many *mortaria* – shallow, fairly heavy, bowls with gritted inside surfaces – are such common site finds; they would have been ideal for the preparation.

What then of the small rectangular plots attached to Fenland settlements as mentioned above (p. 142)? They could well be plots for roots or greens, either or both for human or stock consumption, and the Fens today are, after all, noted for their excellent vegetables.

Not far from the Fens at North Thoresby in Lincolnshire, another site of interest in the present context has been discovered (fig. 77). There, an area of some 5 ha, overlying a clay subsoil, was covered with a network of ditches, about 1.5 m wide by about 1 m deep, and placed about 7.5 m apart. The fill of the ditches had been highly organic and incorporated large quantities of pottery, bones, chalk and stones. The area was suggested by the excavator to have been an experimental vineyard, with the ditches representing prepared trenches for the vines. The spacing between the rows might be thought rather large for vines, but recent excavations near the small town of Irchester in the valley of the River Nene, have produced just as widely spaced trenches; here there is little doubt over the existence of an extensive vineyard, since a good deal of vine pollen was recovered from the trenches. The areas between the rows could have been interplanted with vegetables, a practice still common in the Mediterranean region.

We have looked then at the development and improvement of agriculture and horticulture during the Roman period, and must now consider its decline.

In any period of agricultural recession, it is likely to be the most advanced and sophisticated systems which slip first. The more basic the requirements of a community, the better are its chances of survival. We have already seen how villas, despite setbacks, outlasted the ordeals of the third century, which seriously affected the standard of living of many households. As then, so in the later fourth century, it was the villas which probably first felt the onset of depression. But it was by no means a uniform process; some proved more resilient than others in resisting the changes, which were many and various.

The beginning of the end for the villas as an agricultural system is probably to be seen in the barbarian conspiracy of the late 360s. Villas were easy prey for wandering bands of raiders, while desertion of slaves or tenants, hitherto bound to the land, in the general confusion would have had much the same effect. A number of villas in Somerset, Hampshire, Hertfordshire and Yorkshire seem to have been sacked and burnt, but this form of violent destruction was not as widespread as is sometimes made out. Nevertheless, the experience must have been demoralizing for many villa owners, even if not actually destructive. Some of the burnt houses, such as Langton (Yorks) were rebuilt immediately afterwards, but a number of others not apparently affected by the hostilities seem to have been abandoned, their owners presumably seeking safety in the nearest towns. However, by far the larger number continued as before, and the fairly strong measures taken by Theodosius for the safety of the provinces seem to have reassured many owners, who, for the time being, remained on their estates. Moreover, we must not conclude that those where the houses had been abandoned necessarily ceased to act as farms, although we might suggest that a reduction in the overall number of profitable farms will at first have strengthened the position of the survivors.

From then on, however, the growing insecurity of the countryside will have had its sequel in the gradual running-down of establishments, as markets became more difficult of access and profits declined. If we could detect the changes, we might find shrinkages, in that less land was being cultivated, or that fewer stock were being kept. Outlying bands of farmworkers on large estates may have been brought further in, so saving on building maintenance; certainly the workshed at Poxwell (p. 137) seems to have been abandoned at this time, with a new corn-dryer left unused, and it might indicate that the ploughing of marginal lands was discontinued.

Many villas, however, survived until well into the fifth century, although we may suspect continuous contraction in most, showing perceptibly as a decline in the standard of living: corn-drying kilns being inserted into bath-wings or through mosaic floors. Some certainly ended abruptly in flames in the early fifth century, such as North Wraxall and Lullingstone, but for most it was decay following abandonment. We should also remember that the burning of standing crops – a recommended method of Saxon warfare – could be highly destructive to a large estate, even if the farm itself could be defended against attack.

Finally, it was probably the complete breakdown of the economic system, of which villas had been a part and on which they had depended, that caused their end. Lack of maintenance of roads and the general insecurity of the countryside will have made it increasingly difficult to get even the surviving produce to markets in towns or to country fairs. We should suspect, therefore, that villas more distant from towns would be the first to be affected, but this was not always so. Other factors are consequently involved. It is probable that the markets themselves were dwindling and the number of people relying entirely on farm-produced food may have been reduced also. Moreover, as we have already noted, towns were becoming more self-reliant with regard to food production in circumstances which must have been partly forced upon them by the villas' increasing inability to deliver the goods. One factor acted on another and produced a chain effect.

Some of the richer landowners seem to have tried to protect their estates by the introduction of small bodies of troops, or, after 408, by federate Germanic soldiers, for no less than nine villas have produced the bronze buckles supposedly characteristic of these people. But the aim may have been self-defeating and have merely attracted a more vicious attack, for two out of the nine houses so defended were burnt to the ground. If, however, reliance was being placed on mercenaries to protect villas, it may be that they were given land in exchange for their services, as happened in Gaul. Attempts have sometimes been made to show continuity between villas and Anglo-Saxon villages. There is certainly, sometimes, a remarkable coincidence between the site of a villa and that of a parish church, such as at Lullingstone and Woodchester. Early settlements of Germanic mercenaries on villa estates might well provide an element for continuity, the death of the villa carrying with it the birth of the village. But, in general, the evidence is far too ephemeral to draw any but the most speculative conclusions, and, as with the relationship between Romano-British and Anglo-Saxon towns, accident of geography may have had more to do with it. Indeed it might be taken to show how well sited villas were in the first place to take advantage of the best facilities and land.

St Patrick, in the account of his life in Britain, before being captured by the Irish, gives details of villas still inhabited by their owners as late as 430, sometimes in insecure positions. Gildas, writing a century later, knew nothing of them; not even a tradition had survived. What happened in those intervening years we cannot say, but the dilapidation of the buildings themselves cannot have been long deferred after the collapse of the economy on which they had depended for their livelihood.

A contrast, however, exists in the south-west, Wales and the north. Admittedly the farmers were less troubled by Saxon immigrants, but there were still raiders from beyond the Wall and Ireland to be dealt with. Yet one suspects that being nearer to the soil and to a subsistence level of agriculture, and with less to lose, they would have been more troubled by refugees from the east, causing an increase in population and resulting land-hunger, which ultimately generated a migration to Brittany. But there is ample evidence to show that many farms in all three areas continued without any perceptible change into the fifth century and beyond. There was, however, one major change, mainly in Wales and the west, pointing to the growing lawlessness of the times. A considerable movement back to the hillforts occurred, some of which were refortified for protection. To what extent this reflects the transfer of Cunedda and a large body of Votadini from southern Scotland to north Wales in order to drive out Irish settlers, is not known. But in the preceding decades, pressure from Ireland possibly forced the abandonment of unfortified farms and homesteads, which may have been taken over by the new arrivals, in favour of the better placed hillforts.

CHAPTER 5

Organization and Management

The Roman empire was broadly divided between senatorial and imperial provinces. Since the emperor paid the army, those provinces containing garrisons, and which were often the latest acquisitions, tended to fall into the latter category. Britain was so treated and consequently, in effect, the emperor was the governor of the province. But, for obvious practical reasons, he appointed a personal representative, an imperial legate, to act for him as a kind of viceroy.

Most provincial governors were drawn from the senatorial order, the highest social class in Rome. By means of a carefully graded career structure, a young man might aspire in time to the highest office of consul, having first held other ranks such as the command of a legion and the praetorship. The governorship of a province was an accepted part of his promotion, and he may, at first, having served as praetor, have been sent to a province with a small army containing no more than one legion at his disposal. Thereafter, having in the meantime returned to Rome for his consulship, he might have been appointed to one of a whole range of imperial provinces, containing larger garrisons, and ultimately, if he continued to prosper, to the governorship of the senatorial provinces of either Africa or Asia, which were considered the peaks of achievement, and certainly the best paid.

The governor of Britain, therefore, down to the late second century, in view of the presence in the island of never less than three legions, was an ex-consul. But if he had retained this status in an imperial province, difficulties of protocol would then have arisen if the emperor visited the province in person, for the emperor himself might have held the consulship more recently and so be 'junior' to the governor in the supreme senatorial position. This factor serves well to illustrate the peculiar dichotomy which existed between the emperor and the Roman senate. To overcome this difficulty a consular governor serving in an imperial province invariably took the next lower title and was officially referred to as *legatus Augusti pro praetore.*

The governor of a province, until the early fourth century, was both general officer commanding the army and also chief justice. A high degree of versatility was therefore expected and the stages in his career were constructed with this in mind. We know the careers of several British governors, and they almost invariably included the governorship of some lesser provinces which would provide related experience. Britain was perhaps considered a difficult province since a succession of some of the ablest men in the empire became governor, and a large proportion went on to take plum jobs in the imperial service. Quite frequently, also, some had served earlier in Britain as military tribunes or legionary commanders, so were not unfamiliar with the problems presented. This system, whereby more was expected from a man than might be thought humanly possible, tended to weed out the ordinary, leaving only those with an extraordinary and varied capacity. It has been said that a provincial governor was either a wonderful success or a gigantic failure, and both types served in Britain.

An imperial governor was usually appointed for a term of not less than three years, and some were known to have remained at their posts for much longer; Agricola in Britain served twice the normal term. On appointment, he would subscribe to the *lex provinciae*, a form of written constitution for the province containing details of boundaries, and probably taxes, put together when the province was inaugurated. He was allowed to nominate from among his friends or relations an unofficial staff to assist him in his duties. In addition to them, he would also be able to call for advice from a number of other officers, of whom the legionary legates – or commanders – were the most important. Also attached to his headquarters was a permanent administrative staff, mainly clerical and sub-clerical, who were frequently centurions or soldiers seconded from legions, whose duties might take them anywhere in the province. On appointment, also, he would have been given his instructions for the management of the province by the emperor and also a large cash float to pay for the administrative expenses. Strictly speaking he was not bound by any of the decisions of his predecessor, but a man would have been unwise to ignore them altogether or reverse them except for very sound reasons.

In a province such as Britain, with its exposed frontiers and long history of frontier wars, the military duties of a governor will obviously have been important. In major campaigns he would have led the army in person, conducting the battles and, with his staff officers, laying down general strategy and tactics for the regulation of the frontiers and the control of military areas. During much of the first century, the British governors were so actively engaged in this way that no permanent headquarters seem to have been provided and it is difficult to say either where his administrative staff was housed, or where the more static processes of government, such as record keeping and report writing, were carried out. For the governor was expected to keep the emperor informed in all matters by regular dispatches carried by the imperial postal service.

But, as already noted above, in addition to his military duties the governor was also required to carry out a variety of judicial functions. To him fell the task of making the circuit of assize centres in the province. Apart from acting as a court of appeal, all cases, both civil and criminal, involving either large sums of money or the death penalty were referred directly to him by local courts in the towns. Additionally, Roman citizens could appeal to the emperor for relief from the governor's verdict, but the expenses of doing so were probably so great as to deter most litigants except in the gravest cases. Non-citizens, however, had to abide by his decisions, from which there was no appeal. When it is remembered that the cases he tried might well involve disputes of Celtic Law as well as Roman, or conflicts between the two, the difficulties of the governor are seen to be manifest. In the circumstances, assessors might be appointed to help try the cases and, in extreme instances, points of law were even referred to Rome for decisions or guidance.

As the complexities of empire grew, intolerable burdens were, therefore, being placed on single men. Some relief, however, was to come under Vespasian, for he instituted a new post, *legatus iuridicus*, to aid a governor in his legal duties. As with the position of governor, that of law officer was a personal appointment of the emperor, although the man nominated was subordinate to the governor, and did not relieve the latter of his final responsibility. But the iuridicus would have carried much of the routine, day-to-day administration. At least two of the officers first appointed in Britain were eminent

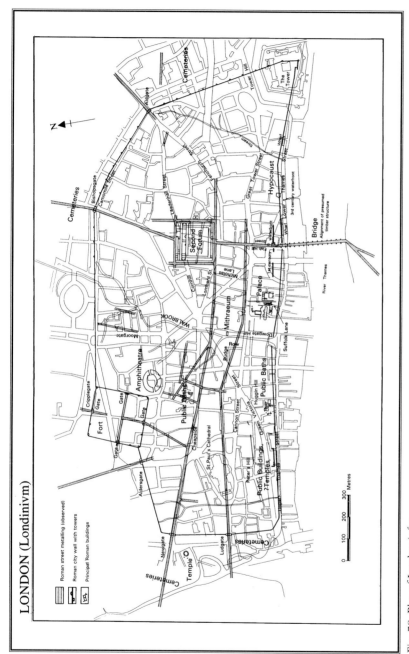

Fig. 78. Plan of London (*after
Museum of London Archaeological
Service*).

lawyers, at a time when, under the governor Agricola, attempts were being made to work out a final solution to the British problem and when many thorny legal questions had probably to be resolved.

The main reservoir of Roman citizens in Britain at first lay at Colchester, so that the principal and, probably, only assize centre at first lay there too. But it seems likely that the number of citizens living in London rapidly passed the population of Colchester, leading perhaps to a change in venue for the assize or to the creation of another centre. Certainly it was in London (fig. 78) that the provincial administration had ultimately settled by the end of the first century, although the financial offices were earlier located there.

A large building (figs 78–9) has been identified in the area of Cannon Street station, London, and has been interpreted as the possible *praetorium* of the governor. As with the almost contemporary palace at Fishbourne (p. 118) it was constructed round a large open court, or garden, containing pools and probably fountains. North of the court was a range of monumental structures, at the centre of which was a massive hall, approximately 13 m by 24 m, possibly flanked at either end of the range by an apse or rotunda to provide an imposing architectural façade. The east range of the building was made up of a wing containing groups of small rooms, perhaps providing offices or living accommodation for higher members of the administrative staff. Unfortunately, more recent excavations, particularly under Cannon Street station, have shown that the building was by no means symmetrical on the west side and that not all parts so far excavated are contemporary. Nor has any more evidence been found for the south wing, which, if a palace, would probably have extended down to the river and would have provided the main residential quarters. The river frontage would also have displayed an elaborate and impressive architectural façade. Consequently, opinion is divided over the initial interpretation and it may be that the praetorium is to be sought elsewhere; indeed an alternative has been suggested in Southwark, in the area of the medieval Winchester Palace, where a massive and elaborate building has been partly excavated. Most interesting here were fragments of a marble inscription containing a list of names of some soldiers belonging to several different legionary cohorts, who could have been seconded for duties connected with the governor.

London has produced other evidence from which can be inferred the presence of the governor. A tombstone erected in memory of a man named Celsus, records that he was a *speculator*, an officer

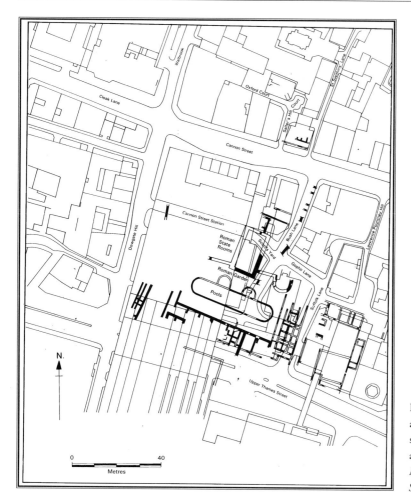

Fig. 79. Buildings beneath the area around Cannon Street station, sometimes interpreted as the governor's palace (*after Museum of London Archaeological Service*).

attached to the governor's staff. There were usually thirty seconded for service from the legions and their duties consisted of the apprehension, the custody and, where necessary, the punishment of state prisoners. Another tombstone depicts a centurion, Vivius Marcianus, carrying a scroll; he has been identified as a centurion in the clerical staff in government house, the *princeps praetorii*.

During the late first or early second century, a fort of exceptional size was erected on the north-western outskirts of London (fig. 78). It occupied nearly 5 ha of ground and was ultimately incorporated in the town when the civil fortifications were built. Its presence helps further to illustrate the special arrangements made at London; no other town in Britain, with the exclusion of York, was so closely associated with a garrison, and the fort was probably intended to house the military detachments required for special duties in the capital, although where these people were accommodated before its construction is not known.

The only sphere over which the governor had no legal control was that connected with provincial finance, which was managed by the *procurator Augusti*. He was appointed by the emperor from the ranks of the equestrian order of Roman society, which was below the senatorial order. The equestrian order also had its own career structure, by which a man might rise from prefect to tribune of an auxiliary infantry regiment, then to be prefect of a cavalry regiment, after which he might be promoted to the procuratorial service, so, as with the governors, gaining wide experience of both civil and military matters.

The procurator, as a nominee of the emperor and probably dependent to a greater extent than the governor on the whims of his imperial master, was given increasingly wide powers as time went on. Sometimes procurator and governor quarrelled, and he was a wise governor not to meddle in matters of the imperial treasury. In Britain, the rapacity of the procurator, Catus Decianus, played a large part in promoting the Boudiccan rebellion, while, after its suppression, Suetonius Paullinus, the legate, disagreed so radically with the new procurator, Julius Classicianus, over the punitive measures to be adopted that Nero arranged for an inquiry, as the result of which Paullinus, not Classicianus, was recalled. On the other hand Agricola was praised by Tacitus for not interfering with procuratorial matters when he was legate of Aquitania; yet Agricola, so we are told, also corrected many matters relating to unfair tax extortions in Britain, and cannot have remained as aloof on his arrival here.

The procurator could hold his own courts and hear cases related to tax collection or other sources of imperial revenues and he also commanded soldiers to assist him in his duties. Again at the time of the Boudiccan rebellion Decianus sent 200 men to the aid of the colonia at Colchester. Procurators could also be governors of minor provinces and it has been suggested that, when Britain was divided into two provinces early in the third century (see Chapter 2) one of them was, to begin with, governed by a procurator. Certainly by the third century the chances of a procurator being so promoted were much greater than earlier.

Imperial estates also came within the competence of the procurator and he would have a number of junior assistants to act as managers. Through these assistants, he was responsible for leasing mining concessions and for all the myriad activities which went on in the settlements attached to the mines: renting shops, running bath-houses, or places of amusement. The recruitment and training of gladiators was yet another duty.

The principal task of the procurator, however, was to assess the level of and to collect taxes, of which there were several kinds. In a newly occupied province they were calculated by carrying out a detailed census, not only of all landholdings and their status, but also of the productivity, in which the procurator would have been assisted by the tribal leaders. Every so often a complete new census was ordered, for which special commissioners were sometimes appointed, while in between the records were kept up to date by the tribal leaders, or local magistrates, as they later became. There were two main types of revenue, a land tax based on a percentage of yield of crops or animals and a poll tax, which was more generally applied to movable property and trades, and which was in effect a tax on income or wealth. Roman citizens were sometimes exempt from these taxes but they were subject to death duties, which yielded increasing amounts as more natives were given the franchise. But all alike had to pay customs duties as a percentage of the value on goods passing the frontiers and sometimes also crossing provincial boundaries. For the latter purpose some provinces were grouped together in what were in effect customs unions. Finally there was the *annona*, the compulsory requisition, probably at a controlled price, of corn or other appropriate goods for army use (fig. 80); this tax was not, however, evenly applied throughout the imperial period. Each branch of revenue raising was probably supervised by an assistant procurator, and there would have also been a permanent staff of clerks and orderlies.

London early became the financial centre of the province, acting so possibly before the Boudiccan rebellion. Julius Classicianus, procurator after the rebellion, died in office and his fine tombstone was found to have been later incorporated in the city fortifications. In addition, an unused writing tablet, branded with the procurator's stamp, and also an iron stamp for marking soft metals with the legend M.P.BR – *Metalla Provinciae Britanniae* – are hardly likely to have been lost far from the main office. Moreover, there seems in addition to have been a government brickworks, managed by the procurator's department, situated near London, with its output devoted to official buildings. An interesting structure (fig. 81) beneath the second-century forum has been interpreted as an earlier, much smaller forum dating to just after the Boudiccan rebellion. It contained an open court, numerous offices and a hall and superficially it resembles a forum and basilica in plan. But its presence would

Fig. 80. Bronze corn measure found just outside the fort at Carvoran, south of Hadrian's Wall. It carries an inscription in which the name of the emperor Domitian has been erased after the *damnatio memoriae* decreed after his death. It was originally suggested that it was a measure for the *annona*, but it is more likely to have been for measuring soldiers' rations (*Crown Copyright: English Heritage*).

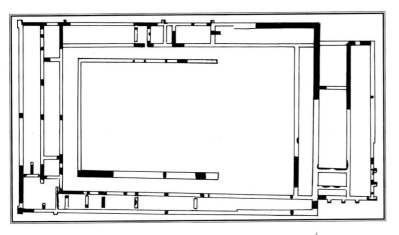

Fig. 81. The building which preceded the second-century forum in London. It has been variously interpreted as an early forum, a market, or the offices of the procurator (*after Museum of London Archaeological Service*).

imply a municipal status for London which it probably did not then possess; there are also other objections. Alternative interpretations should, therefore, be considered; it might have been a macellum (p. 88), not dissimilar in plan to a forum, the offices of the procutator, or less likely an early palace for the governor.

It can be seen, therefore, that the total personnel employed to administer the British province was not large and at first probably did not exceed a few hundred people; lack of numbers was largely made up by their versatility. Today we are so used to everyone having their own rigid, small specialities, that it is difficult to grasp the wide range of experience which was available to the governor and procurator among so few people.

At regional or local levels, the affairs of the central government were superintended by various officials stationed in the places concerned. Among their duties will have been running the imperial postal service, the *cursus publicus*, collection of the *annona* and the security and transport of other supplies for military areas. The officials were normally called *beneficiarii consularis*, but were seldom above the rank of legionary soldiers. We know of such men stationed at Winchester, Dorchester (Oxon.), Wroxeter and Catterick, as well as at many northern military sites. At Catterick, the only site where two such men have been attested, there was a large *mansio*, or official inn, for members of the imperial post.

This service, largely organized by Augustus, covered the whole empire with a network of land and sea routes, primarily for the transport of military dispatches, but it was soon adapted for the carriage of any official messages, persons or goods. Nevertheless, licences to use it were not freely given and even governors of provinces had to justify its employment, perhaps because the cost of the service, which was heavy, had to be borne by local civitates and municipalities; but abuses were apparently common and difficult to prevent. Couriers were known to travel, on average, some 80 km a day, although in emergency this might have been increased threefold.

Mansiones and the lesser *mutationes* were placed in major towns and minor centres. The latter consisted simply of stations where changes of horse could be obtained by the messengers or wagoners, while the former contained overnight accommodation, secure parking, storage areas and stabling. Several mansiones are known in Britain, although they are not easy buildings to identify, often appearing in plan like any other large domestic residence. Yet the well-known example near the south gate at Silchester contains features which help to distinguish it from a private house: it has a large bath-house, far larger than would be required for even a substantial household, and numerous suites of three rooms, arranged in groups in the north and south wings, which flank a central court. The west wing contained the large public rooms. The overall size of the building also tends to distinguish it from the other houses in the town. Since Silchester lay on several routes of the postal service, the mansio would have needed to be large to accommodate the relays of messengers, and it would have been permanently busy.

The mansio at Catterick was somewhat smaller in size, but still had a large bath wing and two main suites of rooms, as well as piped water (fig. 82). It had been built in the second century by a ninth cohort, probably of Legio VI from York, in contrast perhaps to the Silchester building, which is more likely to have been erected by the civitas Atrebatum. It is possible that the two beneficiarii mentioned above (p. 169) as being stationed at Catterick successively managed the mansio, or were otherwise connected with its running.

It is fortunate that a large part of the postal routes of the early third century seem to have been recorded in a document known as the Antonine Itinerary, while an earlier version is known in a much more fragmentary state in the Ravenna Cosmography. These two sources give the names of towns, forts and villages which lie on routes, the distances between them and usually the total distance between the terminals. For instance the so-called Iter II for Britain gives the distance from Hadrian's Wall at Carlisle to the port at Richborough in Kent as 481 Roman miles, but the route goes via York, Chester, Wroxeter and London, by no means the most direct way. The latter fact has led some authorities to doubt its value as a

Fig. 82. Ornamental fountain situated in the central courtyard of the mansio at Catterick. It was fed from the main water supply to the town. The front stone of the tank was unfortunately missing, but the stone-cut channel for carrying the overflow can be seen in front of its position (*Crown Copyright*).

true representation of the postal service. Nevertheless, it indicates where mansiones and mutationes are likely to be found and also provides useful corroborative detail for the equation of Roman and modern sites.

The identification of mutationes is more difficult than that of mansiones, but a comparatively small, rectangular masonry building with massive walls, lying just within the north gate at Thorpe-by-Newark, might be so interpreted.

One last aspect of imperial management must be considered: the supply of coin. Roman coins reached Britain in three ways: in the hands of traders and itinerant immigrants, sale of British goods in other provinces; and, by far the largest quantity, in the pay-chests of the army and civil service.

The coinage consisted of issues in three main metals or their alloys, gold, silver and copper (fig. 83). The coinage therefore had the inbuilt weakness of all trimetallic systems. A variation in the actual value of one of the metals immediately imposed an artificial value on the others, and although the values of the earliest Roman coins were related to the amount of metal they contained, being issued at so many pieces to the pound weight of metal, this soon came to be meaningless and individual coins simply became valuable tokens with their 'price' governed by the proportionate amounts of goods they bought. Nero was responsible for starting the steady devaluation of the coinage which continued slowly until the early third century, when the monetary reforms of Caracalla increased the rate of depreciation. The third century was also a time of extreme inflation which in itself was exacerbated by the rapid decline in the standards of coinage. During the reigns of Gallienus and the other rulers of the independent Gallic empire, the base 'silver' coins became virtually valueless.

Diocletian again reformed the coinage, reissuing good gold and silver, but thereafter the lack of standards, particularly in the copper coinage, constantly affected values and it may be that coins came to be treated largely as bullion. One of the remarkable manifestations of the late fourth century is the number of silver coins of good quality in circulation in Britain, no doubt due to a revival of interest in silver deposits there.

During the early empire the principal coins were the gold *aureus*, the silver *denarius*, the brass *sestertius* and the copper *as*, with equivalent half-value coins in each metal and an additional quarter-value copper. Caracalla introduced a new silver coin, usually called an

Fig. 83. A selection of Roman coins

1. *Gold aureus of Claudius I (AD 41–54)*
Gold coins such as this piece, which
celebrates the triumph over Britain, soon
swept away the inferior British staters.

2. *Silver denarius of Mark Antony, 32 BC*
Until after the end of the first century, more
than half the Roman silver coinage consisted
of old, worn, Republican *denarii*, many of
them of this legionary issue made just before
the battle of Actium.

3. *Copper as of Claudius I (AD 41–54)*

4. *Contemporary forgery of no. 3.* The sudden
imposition of the Roman coinage and
currency system led to a shortage of ready
money. Combined with widespread
unfamiliarity with imperial coins, this
created a situation which forgers of all levels
of competence were quick to exploit.

5. *Brass sestertius of Vespasian (AD 69–79)*
(obv. only) These fine coins, generally with a
laureate obverse portrait, formed the largest
base metal denomination in circulation
down to the 260s.

6. *Brass dupondius of Hadrian (AD 117–38)*
(obv. only) Half the value and weight of the
sestertius, this denomination was often distinguished from the very similar as by the
Emperor's radiate head.

7. *Brass sestertius of Gallienus (AD 253–68)*
(obv. only) From the later years of the second
century, the Roman mint often struck
sestertii on blanks with two parallel sides.
Galloping inflation led to the brass and
copper denominations being discontinued
after 260.

8. *Base silver denarius of Severus (AD 193–211)*
Inflation was also reflected in the increasing
debasement of the silver coinage. This piece
celebrates Severus' victories in Britain.

9. *Base silver 'antoninianus' of Caracalla (AD
211–17)* (Obv. only) We know neither the
real name nor the value of this multiple
denarius denomination. In a period of
rapidly rising prices, it quickly superseded
the ordinary denarius in general use. Note
the Emperor's radiate portrait.

10. *Base silver 'antoninianus' of Tetricus I (AD
271–4).*

11. *Contemporary forgery of no. 10* The silver
currency reached a nadir of style, technique

and fineness with the coins of the Gallic emperors and their Roman contemporaries. Several mints now worked at full pressure to supply
currency needs, and the rapidly degenerating size and style of the imperial coin made a golden opportunity for forgers.

12. *Base silver 'antoninianus' of Carausius (AD 276–93)* Even in Britain, the usurpers of this period required more than one mint. This coin,
vainly invoking peaceful co-existence with the continental emperors, was struck at London.

13. *Base silver 'follis' of Diocletian (AD 284–305)* (obv. only) This fine coinage was part of a vain attempt to stabilize, or even to reverse the
inflationary spiral. It was struck at Trier.

14. *Base silver centenionalis of Constantine II (AD 317–40)* In 318 yet another coinage reform was instituted. This piece was struck in London
c. 320; the London mint closed in 325

15. *Base silver centenionalis of Constantine I (AD 306–37)* These coins honouring the cities of Rome and Constantinople are among the
commonest Roman coins of the mid-fourth century.

16. *Bronze coins of Constantius II (337–61)* (rev. only).

17. *Contemporary forgery of no. 16* (rev. only) The ineptitude of the Roman government in dealing with currency problems is well illustrated by
the events of AD 354. The coinage of that year (no. 16) was intended to supersede all earlier pieces; the effect was not merely to give rise to
forgery on an enormous scale, but also to provoke the hitherto unprecedented overstriking of authentic coins by false dies.

18. *Bronze coin of Honorius (AD 395–423)* The latest Roman bronze coins to enter Britain in quantity were these little, ill-struck pieces of
c. 400. Their currency was largely restricted to southern and eastern Britain.

19. *Clipped silver 'siliqua' of Arcadius (AD 395–408)* After the cessation of Roman government in Britain, the surviving silver coins were
severely clipped. No coinage was produced at this time, for its use depended on the Roman fiscal system, rather than the needs of internal
commerce.

antoninianus (fig. 83, 9) by numismatists. Its original weight was 5.75g as against 3.0 g for the denarius, but its weight and fineness fell rapidly, so that by AD 270 it only weighed 3 g with a silver content as low as 3 per cent, yet its value then was supposedly worth 5 denarii (fig. 83, 10–12). Such was the measure of inflation. In the fourth century the aureus was replaced by the *solidus*, of lesser weight, and the denarius was revived. Copper coins also appear with a silver wash on their surfaces, but the rapidly changing standards caused a good deal of variation in type and size.

In the early period, the emperor was chiefly responsible for minting gold and silver, while the senate continued to mint brass and copper; the latter coins therefore carry the letters SC (*senatus consulto*) on the reverse side. Various mints were used for the manufacture of coins, but it was not until the late empire that they were each distinguished by a code of letters included on the coin. From Britain, an interesting find at Verulamium was the hard bronze die for stamping Hadrianic denarii. How this came to be in Britain is not known as no official mint is then thought to have existed; it cannot have been incidental to Hadrian's visit to the province since the type of reverse is much later in date than the visit. In the third century, however, mints were established at London (fig. 83, 12) and possibly Colchester under Carausius, but were closed by Constantine about AD 325.

Coins of the Roman period were extensively used for conveying propaganda to the people, either by depicting imperial works in artistic form with an appropriate legend, or by straightforward invocations of an abstract concept, such as *Gloria Exercitus* (our glorious army) or *Fel Temp Reparatio* (a return to happier times) on fourth-century issues. Needless to say, imperial victories were often commemorated, and an extensive series is known referring to British campaigns. Indeed one of the commonest coins of Antoninus Pius is the Britannia issue. It is of interest that Britannia as an emblem on coins first appeared on an issue of Hadrian's dated to AD 119–22.

Few coins reached Britain after the closure of the Gallic mints at the beginning of the fifth century, so that the number of coins in circulation rapidly declined, ceasing finally, so it is thought, about AD 440.

The Roman side of the provincial administration was matched by the native provincial council. This council was formed by delegates from the constituent municipalities or civitates of the province. One of its principal duties was the care and promotion of the imperial cult (see Chapter 7), and the president of the council was also chief priest. The council in Britain was centred at Colchester, where was also the main temple of the cult, the Temple of Claudius, founder of the province. The temple may not at first have been inside the colonia, although it later became enclosed within the walls. South of the temple and its precinct lay a number of buildings which were probably connected with the council. It has been argued, partly on the evidence of a dedication to the emperors on behalf of the British province, and partly because of a tombstone of the wife of a provincial slave, that London superseded Colchester as headquarters of the cult. While it is possible that the administrative buildings were moved to the provincial capital, we need not doubt the continuance of the Colchester temple as the most important in the country. Moreover, it was not unknown for the provincial council to be based elsewhere than in the cult centre.

The other functions of the council varied from province to province, and unfortunately we have no specific information regarding Britain. It would certainly have had to raise money and promote annual games and festivals in connexion with the cult; more often than not the money came out of the members' own pockets, as they never obtained the power to raise taxes or legislate. They were, however, allowed to communicate directly with the emperor, so that, in law at least, excesses or injustice in the provincial administration could be reported, but we know of no such cases from Britain and it is more likely that the council remained a largely ceremonial body. They could, however, select a patron, usually an influential man holding high office in Rome, who, in return for various honours, could plead British affairs in the right quarter.

For the exercise of local administration, Britain must be considered in two parts: that which remained under military government and that which achieved a measure of civilian self-government. When taken over the whole Roman period, it can be seen that considerable changes in these respective areas took place.

At first, when the frontier cut across the Midlands, most of the province would have been under military rule. Exceptions of course were the two client kingdoms of the Atrebates and Iceni. What is not known is whether they lay inside or outside the province. From the evidence of geography and some vague literary references, it could be argued that the former lay within the province, but the latter outside it; if so the Iceni may have had slightly more freedom from interference, not that it did them much good when Ostorius

Scapula decided to put down a minor rebellion in their ranks in AD 48. It is not improbable that both client states maintained their own armies and indeed Cogidubnus may even have sent troops to help Ostorius against the Iceni. These armies would also have helped to keep order, collect taxes and raise recruits for the Roman army in their respective kingdoms. From about AD 50, there was also a chartered, self-governing city at Colchester as well as three civitates. By AD 90, the two client kingdoms had been absorbed and further civitates and chartered cities had been established; the numbers were added to yet again under Hadrian. But a return to military control of some of the latter areas took place before the end of the second century, and the arrangements then recorded represent about the maximum area given over to civil administration, until its complete separation from military government in the early fourth century.

Within areas of military government it seems likely that regions were allotted to each legionary commander who as a member of the governor's staff will have been intimately concerned with the formulation of plans. So we can see, in the final and permanent phase of legionary distribution, much of south and central Wales being allocated to the legate at Caerleon, while the remainder of Wales and also some areas to the west of the Pennines came under the Chester command; east of the Pennines and the whole northern frontier region were probably controlled from York.

Each legionary command contained numbers of auxiliary forts, whose commanders will have been of varying rank and seniority. To what extent the latter interacted is not known, but each local commander probably had responsibility for his own area, and it will have been he, or his men, who were in closest touch with native Britons, passing on regulations originating from the governor. Where a compact tribal organization existed before the conquest, it is probable that such instructions would have been relayed through the tribal leaders, in which case it is not surprising, for instance, that we find a fairly senior officer, the prefect of a cavalry ala, ultimately stationed at Cirencester, close to the main Dobunnic centre. He would have ranked above any neighbouring infantry commanders. Some degree of tribal autonomy must, therefore, have been respected.

In regions, however, where no such united tribal structure existed, greater responsibility must have rested with each auxiliary commander to run his own area. We know, from several sources, the wide range of duties which might be expected of such a man with relation to the civilian population. He would be expected to settle disputes, keep the peace, take censuses and collect taxes and subject to overriding orders from a superior officer, he would have had the last word in many matters.

But the natives were encouraged to play an increasing part in the management of affairs. Where vici had grown outside forts, the people were allowed to run their own petty affairs through the two elected magistrates and possibly a council of villagers in a properly constituted manner, although we do not know in Britain the precise boundaries which must have existed between the civilian and military jurisdictions. Certainly the latter retained responsibility for all roads, and possibly the placing of buildings within a vicus, but the former could most probably have settled internal disputes between villagers and made corporate dedications to deities. But as with most matters of this kind in the empire, a good deal of flexibility will have existed and much would have depended on the character of a particular military commander and the amenability, or otherwise, of the local population. So the native inhabitants would have been introduced to the Roman way of doing things and given valuable experience for the time when full self-government might be conferred.

We have already seen, in the Midlands and south, how many vici associated with forts of the Claudio-Neronian period formed the kernels of later towns and villages, and the implications which this development had in the sphere of local government. The communities so formed joined the ranks of self-governing organizations of which there were, as already noted in Chapter 3, several different kinds.

At the head were the chartered cities of varying grades: the coloniae and municipia, each of which would have had either full Roman, or only Latin, rights. Full Roman rights were normally only conferred on communities containing a predominance of citizens, and the charter of constitution enforced the practice of the Roman legal code. Latin rights could be earned by a city composed almost entirely of non-citizen inhabitants, who may have been permitted to retain many of their native laws. Promotion could, however, take place from one grade to another.

The charters by which these cities were founded or constituted were once considered to be conferred by the imperial government and modelled on the constitution of Rome, but it now appears that most were concocted locally, although leaning heavily on established precedent. These charters were written constitutions for the regulation of the communities and seem to have incorporated many common features. Consequently, though we know nothing of those which applied to the British coloniae or municipia, we can, by analogy, make some general deductions of the ways in which they were managed.

The ruling body was the *ordo*, a council of up to about a hundred members, *decuriones*, which, certainly by the second century, was virtually a self-perpetuating oligarchy, when there was a shortage of candidates for election and nominations were made by the magistrates. Membership of the ordo was restricted by both age and wealth and, moreover, a man had to be free-born. No ex-slave was therefore eligible, no matter how wealthy, but his sons could be.

From four to six executive officers carried out the day-to-day affairs. At first they were elected by the popular assembly of the town's people, but increasingly appointed by the ordo. They were grouped in pairs: *duoviri iuricundo*, *aediles* and sometimes, but not always, *quaestores*. The former pair were the most senior and had charge of the law courts, trying petty criminal cases and civil cases below a certain value. When remitting more serious cases to the governor's court, they would have provided transcripts of the evidence and a summary. One or other acted as chairman to the ordo, or if both were unavoidably absent, a prefect could be appointed. They also had charge of the imperial cult, the local militia and the junior officers. Although they were nominally subservient to the ordo, there seem to have been occasions when they could rule contrary to the ordo's instructions and the system appears to have been constructed to include some degree of cross-checking between the parties. Every fifth year, two especially distinguished men were appointed as duoviri. This year saw vacancies in the ordo filled, public contracts renewed and new levels of tax assessed.

Duoviri would almost certainly have been members of the ordo before appointment, but the aediles not necessarily so, since their age of appointment was below that required for the council. Aediles were responsible for the upkeep of public buildings and roads, the aqueducts and water distribution systems and sewers. They could also, it seems, act in place of the duoviri in the courts.

Not all cities had quaestores but, where they existed, they were responsible to the magistrates for the financial arrangements. None are attested in Britain, but then neither is there firm evidence for duoviri; yet they must have existed. Inscriptions do, however, record decurions.

Other important people in the municipal hierarchy were the six priests – *seviri Augustales* – charged with the ceremonies connected with the imperial cult. These positions were open to manumitted slaves, freedmen of considerable wealth, for they personally had to underwrite the cost of the rituals.

The municipal exchequer was financed from a variety of sources. Chief among them were probably the fees exacted on election to public office; moreover, the people appointed were also expected to make some valuable gift to the town, such as a public building, or to stage an entertainment in the theatre or amphitheatre. Rents from public land, money from its sale, rates on water supplied to private users from the aqueduct, fines in the courts, and dues exacted on goods entering or leaving the town, all contributed; but it remained a fact that many cities and towns were always chronically short of money, and depended mainly on private donations for major public works. As already recorded (p. 100) this often led to considerable delays in building programmes. On some occasions, the emperor remitted taxes due to the imperial treasury. Hadrian was noted for doing so, and it may be that remission of taxes to some poorer towns in Britain during his visit enabled work to be resumed or commenced on a variety of public buildings.

Many of the larger and more important cities were subdivided into constituent quarters, or vici. Indeed the normal definition of vicus is the smallest unit of built-up area having its own administration; consequently use of the word was not always restricted to villages or settlements outside forts, and constituent vici are known at Lincoln. They were probably allowed a pair of elected officers, but their duties would have been largely religious or ceremonial, and the full administration devolved upon the parent organization of which they were a part.

The methods of local government so far described would, in Britain, have been appropriate to the four coloniae at Colchester, Lincoln, Gloucester and York with their associated territoria; the probable municipium at Verulamium; and almost certainly London.

In the tribal territories a similar system was adapted to the differing circumstances, and it is here that we see, most adequately demonstrated, the Roman flexibility to problems of local government in the provinces.

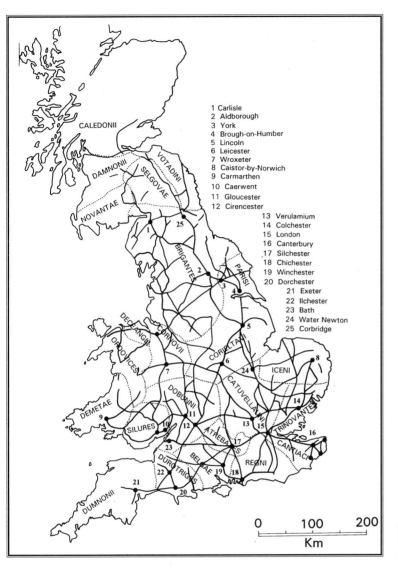

1 Carlisle
2 Aldborough
3 York
4 Brough-on-Humber
5 Lincoln
6 Leicester
7 Wroxeter
8 Caistor-by-Norwich
9 Carmarthen
10 Caerwent
11 Gloucester
12 Cirencester
13 Verulamium
14 Colchester
15 London
16 Canterbury
17 Silchester
18 Chichester
19 Winchester
20 Dorchester
21 Exeter
22 Ilchester
23 Bath
24 Water Newton
25 Corbridge

0   100   200
Km

Fig. 84. The civitates of Britain and the principal towns.

Britain, like much of Gaul before its conquest, possessed a clearly defined tribal structure and these areas became the basic units in local government, each one being given, as in Gaul, the title of *civitas*. In some cases where the units were too small to be viable on their own, as in Kent and Wessex, amalgamations took place; or where a reduced client kingdom was too large, as was that of Cogidubnus, it was split.

Civitas in Latin strictly means citizenship, but an extension of the meaning embraced communities of citizens also, so the *civitates peregrinae* came to mean communities of citizens of foreign, i.e. non-

Roman, origin. In many places where the term was used to describe such communities, it became synonymous with town or city. But in the three north-western provinces of Gaul and in Britain its meaning was once more adapted to apply to whole tribal communities or their equivalents. There has, however, been much argument over this definition and there are authorities who still maintain that, in Britain, civitas equals town and that the tribal land around it was attributed to it as a territorium, as in the case of coloniae and municipia. Certainly down to the early third century, the weight of evidence is against such suggestions; thereafter changes occur which will be considered below.

In Britain, therefore, as in Gaul, a civitas was basically the whole tribal territory constituted after the Roman manner (fig. 85), with closely prescribed rights and duties, within the framework of the provincial government. In the middle was the capital town, used as an administrative centre, and the selection of sites for these towns has already been considered in Chapter 3. As far as can be judged in Britain, the organization of a civitas closely resembled that of the chartered town, with magistrates and a council, but it must be admitted that variations may have occurred both in the structure and in the names used to describe the officers. Yet a quaestor is known from Carlisle and an aedile from Brough-on-Humber.

What then of the status of the civitas capitals? Most, as we have already seen, started as vici attached to forts, and vici they probably remained, despite their often considerable increase in size and importance. There is a little evidence to suggest that some may have been subsequently promoted, but it is not entirely reliable.

Within each civitas there were probably country districts called *pagi*, and additionally there were probably other vici, some of which may have acted as pagus centres. The pagi may correspond to earlier, pre-Roman tribal subdivisions, and some of them are known to have lived on in areas of Britain. Indeed one, the Carvetii, was destined for later promotion to an independent civitas. Otherwise there is little evidence for their existence in Britain, but they were possibly the last link in the administrative chain by which instructions were relayed to the great mass of country people. They may well have proved more important in those civitates which remained strongly orientated towards the country, such as the Dumnonii and Cornovii.

We have already seen that two different legal codes, native and Roman, were in force in Britain, certainly down to the early third

century; thereafter the grant of the franchise to all freeborn members of the empire should have virtually eliminated the use of native laws. In fact governors were specifically empowered to continue trying cases under local law at their own discretion. In the main these would have been concerned with inheritance, with land-ownership, with the general relationships of servant and master, and landlord and tenant, and with parental and family matters.

Claims have been made that the native laws of Britain were largely later enshrined in a codified version of Welsh law, dating to the tenth century AD. Two principal forms of landholding have been detected in them. In one, the land was held in common by a whole community, and the apportionment between its members of arable and pasture was governed by changes in the total population and not simply in family groups, so that reallocation took place when someone died or reached the age of majority. In the other, the reverse of primogeniture, the original freeholding was divided equally among all the sons on the death of the father and so on down to the fourth generation, when the cycle was restarted. But it was open to any member to contract out of the system whenever he liked to go off on his own. Indeed it has been claimed that it was the latter system which gave rise to the multiplication of residential blocks in some of the larger villas. Such a system could have brought about a massive fragmentation of the original landholding, unless a degree of cooperation was secured between members. It is as well to tread delicately on such unsure ground, and remember that, though interesting, these suggestions lack proof. Nevertheless, Celtic law was undoubtedly the mainstay of ordered life for a considerable time in the Roman period of Britain.

Fig. 85. Inscription recording the dedication of the forum at Wroxeter, under Handrian (129–30). It was erected under the authority of the whole *civitas Cornoviorum*, not just of the town *Viroconium* (*Crown Copyright: reproduced by permission of Her Majesty's Stationery Office*).

181

Roman law, like so many things in the empire, developed on a piecemeal basis, with its roots firmly established in the republic. It was compounded of a mixture of case law and statute law, with the former predominating to begin with, but with the latter taking over entirely at the end of the empire. In case law, earlier decisions of the courts were binding in subsequent similar cases, unless upset by a superior court; statute law took the form of edicts, issued by the emperors. From time to time, when the weight of case law became overwhelming, codified forms were issued, the first we know of being the Institutes of Gaius, put together in the second century AD and followed much later by the Theodosian Code and the Digest of Justinian, among others. The rulings contained in the latter received legislative force after their publication.

A sharp distinction was made between public and private law. The first regulated the powers and structure of public bodies and their relations to the private citizen, while the second, as might be expected, was concerned with the actions of citizens one with another, but this is not to say that a considerable body of law was not enacted by the state to regulate the latter, and so became part of public law. Within this structure, it is possible to detect three kinds of relationship. There was that of a citizen to the state, an absolute condition which came within the realm of public law; there was that of the members of a family to its head, which was again absolute in its condition, but where excesses were guarded against by further applications of public law; and there was that of one family against another which was the sphere of all private law.

Apart from offences against the state, such as certain types of murder or treason, where the state apprehended and tried the criminal, it was left to the wronged person to bring an action against the malefactor. Many offences, now deemed to be criminal in their content, such as theft and assault against the person, were then considered no more than civil offences, so that, in a wide range of circumstances, someone seeking justice had not only to arraign the accused person before a court, but also to collect the evidence and witnesses. In cases of malicious accusation, a penalty could be enforced against the accuser, often equal in value to the amount supposedly in dispute. These provisions were necessary, since professional informers, especially in cases involving crimes against the state, often hoped to be rewarded on obtaining a conviction from the confiscated estate of the accused.

The different types of court have already been considered above. Civic courts of petty jurisdiction could only inflict minor penalties, mainly fines. Imprisonment was not a recognized form of punishment and was used primarily by magistrates for persons waiting trial and as a method of coercion to arrive at the truth or to extort a penalty. But it would seem that by the late empire, few powers of correction were left to local magistrates in criminal cases. The governor's court technically had power of sentencing to death or to hard labour in state mines or quarries, but ultimately, in fact, almost all death sentences had to be referred to the emperor. There were also different classes of society, the *honestiores* and the *humiliores*. No legal definition of the classes has even been traced, and discretion seems to have been left with the courts to decide. Broadly, however, honestiores were treated more leniently, often being spared the death penalty, certainly in its more extreme forms. Neither could they be condemned to the mines; in place, banishment to a remote province or island, with or without confiscation of their wealth, seems to have been the rule. It should perhaps be remembered that Britain may have been considered a suitable place to which people could have been banished from the central provinces. Humiliores, in contrast, as well as slaves, could be examined as witnesses under torture.

One of the most important applications of the law in Britain must have been in connexion with slavery. Before the occupation, Britain was a slave-owning society and the manacles and slave-chains from the Llyn Cerrig Bach hoard and other sites are eloquent evidence for it. It is likely that the number of slaves increased during the Roman period, and the laws regulating their sale and treatment were many. They had no rights, but were supposedly protected from the worst abuses by edicts issued by several emperors, especially by Augustus and Hadrian, and in time their lot improved. It was open to a free man to discharge a debt by selling himself into slavery, but the supply was chiefly kept up partly by frontier warfare and partly by interbreeding among existing slaves, since the children of slaves were the property of the master and the number could be controlled by the practice of child exposure. The large number of infant burials at the villa at Hambledon, as already noted (p. 142), implies the existence of a slave-run establishment.

Slaves often reached management posts, particularly in the imperial civil service, and many laws had to be enacted to take the new circumstances into account. They could often amass considerable wealth, by means of the *peculium*, or perquisites, and as a result purchase their freedom. Many slaves were also freed by their masters as a gift, while others obtained freedom on their master's death. But a freedman still had obligations to his ex-master, which, if ignored, might in extreme cases lead to his reduction to slavery. Although many freedmen achieved great wealth, usually as merchants, they still had disabilities in that certain offices, such as that of decurion, were not available to them; moreover, even though one freed by a Roman citizen became a citizen himself, he could not enter the equestrian or higher orders, although his sons could do so. In all, freedmen formed a numerous and important class in society in the empire, frequently occupying prominent positions in the emperor's service; a freedman of Claudius was sent to settle the mutiny of the army at Boulogne in AD 43, while one of Nero was charged with an inquiry into events after the Boudiccan rebellion.

The management of the empire was a continuously developing process, affected alike by imperial edict and provincial attitudes. Many of the changes which reached full flower in the fourth century can be traced back to Hadrian's reform of the imperial civil service. He instituted for the first time a separate career structure for civil servants which did not embrace military service, so bringing about a fundamental change in the types of people holding public office. It undoubtedly brought about greater efficiency and also specialization, but in times of civil war or anarchy, such as in the 190s or later in the third century, put the civil service at a distinct disadvantage. Senatorial provinces had been impotent to interfere in earlier, similar catastrophes, because they contained no large number of troops. Hadrian's actions, therefore, theoretically enhanced the power of the army still further.

In Britain, as in some other provinces, the first major changes came about as the result of the civil war of the 190s, and after Severus had retaken the province from Albinus.

The division of Britain into two provinces somewhat naturally caused a duplication in the administrative offices. London remained as the capital of Upper Britain (*Britannia Superior*) under a consular, while York became the seat of the governor of the Lower province (*Britannia Inferior*), but it is probable that the governor of the latter, of praetorian status, combined his duties with command of Legio VI. But the two military commands did not remain entirely separate and legionary vexillations from Superior are known to have served at Corbridge, as well as orderlies from the consular governor's staff at Chesterholm and Greta Bridge.

However, the most drastic changes in the provincial administration came about in the early fourth century, as already indicated. The four provinces which now made up the British diocese were: Maxima Caesariensis, Flavia Caesariensis, Britannia Prima and Britannia Secunda. Each was at first governed by a *praeses*, a man of equestrian rank, whose title had now entirely replaced that of procurator; the title of legate also disappeared. Later, however, Maxima appears to have been promoted to have a proconsular governor. London was almost certainly the seat of the diocesan *vicarius* and also the provincial governor of Maxima. There too would have been the offices which, in the fourth century, partly replaced the old-style imperial procurator's department: the *rationalis rei privatae per Britannias* and the *rationalis summarum Britanniarum*. Between them they continued to collect revenue payable in bullion and to supervise imperial property. Most remaining taxes were by now paid in goods and the organization of the system was combined with the other governmental duties of the praeses.

The separation of military command from civil government was a further measure enforced, together with the reform of the army, as already noted in a previous chapter (Chapter 2). Changes in judicial processes also occurred, summary trials without a jury becoming the norm rather than the exception. Most of Diocletian's new laws intimately affected every person in the empire, particularly those that made certain employments hereditary. The overall result was to remove all the last traces of fictitious republicanism, fostered since the time of Augustus, and to replace it with an undisguised absolute monarchy. Versatility and a slightly amateur approach to administration now gave way completely before more narrowly based, professional specialists; excessive centralization and control became firmly established. The resulting bureaucracy may have been necessary to save the empire from disintegration but in the long run it was hardly beneficial. Indeed it was recorded that the increase in the official class was so enormous that the receivers of public money seemed to outnumber the payers. In the end, tax-collectors were demanding the means for an administration which ruled but could no longer protect, and people who might before have aspired to the rank of decurion, now sought the greater security of comparatively humble posts in the emperor's service.

Not all the measures were, however, successful. Diocletian's edict of prices, which was issued partly to preserve the purchasing power of soldiers' pay in the face of severe price rises, and by which a maximum price was fixed for all the necessitites of life throughout the empire, was a complete failure. It had to be withdrawn, despite the savage penalites for breach of the codes.

At local government level there were also many changes, brought about chiefly by the interference by the central administration in local affairs. One development was a considerable extension of the system whereby officials of the governor were placed in charge of regions; at first the *regionarii* or *stationarii* were often seconded centurions (p. 135 and fig. 70), later probably civil servants. Their principal duty was probably to see that taxes in kind were correctly returned, but they may also have had some police functions in order to control brigandage; one such centurion is known from an inscription at Bath. The third century had already seen a great rise in the number of *beneficiarii consularis* placed round the provinces, probably for much the same purpose. But, as with many of the reforms of the fourth century, the beginnings lay much further back in time. Occasionally in the second century, when financial difficulties caused by mismanagement or extravagance beset a town, the emperor appointed a *curator* to clear up the muddle. They were frequently citizens held in high esteem in the town, who perhaps were, or had been, *duoviri quinquennales*. It is possible, also, that the emperor, having remitted taxes to help a municipality, saw the need for some central government control to see that the money was not improperly spent. Curatores, therefore, were additional magistrates with special financial responsibilities, appointed first when the need arose. By the third century, however, they had become a permanent feature of the municipal scene, and since they were appointed by the emperor, assumed seniority over the other magistrates, replacing the duoviri as chairmen of the ordo.

The diminution of the power of the ordinary magistrates went hand in hand with an increase in their burdens. By the fourth century, the ordo was being compulsorily filled from the ranks of those with requisite wealth, and under Diocletian, not only was the office made hereditary, but also more and more laws were passed to prevent decurions escaping their liabilities. Despite the wealth qualification for entry to the ranks, subsequent bankruptcy was no escape. The requirement that held decurions personally responsible for making good the deficits in taxes of certain dependants must have weighed particularly heavily, and it is no surprise that every means to escape was attempted.

In contrast to administrative matters the management of business affairs fell broadly into two classes, public and private.

As we have already seen, the provincial procurator was responsible for most public business, chiefly through the imperial estates. Unfortunately we have no detailed knowledge from Britain of their management, but we can probably assume that they were run no worse than those in other provinces. That being so, it is fair to consider the evidence from the silver and copper mines at Vipasca in Spain, as representing the likely state of affairs in Britain. It is probable that most mining rights were held by the emperor – although the commonly occurring iron ores in Britain may have been exempt – so that careful control could be kept on production. Since the economy was to a large extent managed and not entirely free, we find that production of metals in Britain was sometimes limited in favour of the Spanish mines.

The evidence from Vipasca comes in the form of two inscriptions, one of which, dating to Hadrian's principate and probably originating in the local procurator's office, gives instructions to the manager on the conditions of mine tenure and operation. They are extremely detailed and all-embracing in their scope, and cover not only tenancy agreements, but also the removal of ore from the mines (only between sunrise and sunset), safety (all diggings to be carefully propped; no props to be removed; rotten ones to be replaced) and drainage (no work to be carried out within a certain distance of the ditch which carried away water from the mines).

The other inscription, probably of the same date, concerns the ancillary services provided by the mining settlement. Even auctions of the metals were carried out under a concession, the concessionnaire taking a percentage of the sale price. Further concessions were made to people who ran the bath-house, acted as barbers or launderers or made shoes. A modern trade unionist might well appreciate the definition of a shoemaker as one who 'drives or sells shoemaker's nails'; other restrictive practices abounded. Schoolteachers were exempt from taxes, a point of interest to present members of the profession. Also, rights were granted, at a cost, for reworking slag-heaps.

Before leasing a concession to a private individual or company, the procurator had to be satisfied that sufficient working capital was available. This probably accounts for the fact that most silver mines in Britain were at first worked direct by legionary detachments using convict and slave labour. Lead ingots, or pigs as they usually known, a valuable by-product of the silver industry, have been found with cast inscriptions of Legio II, from the Mendips, and Legio XX, from the Welsh borders. But entrepreneurs were soon in the field and one, C. Nipius Ascanius, probably a wealthy freedman from Italy, was working in Somerset by AD 60 and later in Flintshire. Another, Tiberius Claudius Triferna, had mines in Somerset as well as in the Peak District. By the end of the first century, however, companies were active. One, the *societas Novaec*, was working in the Mendips, while in the second century the *societas Lutudarensis* was heavily engaged in Derbyshire. Another was working copper in Anglesey, the *societas Romae*.

These companies, or partnerships as they might be better called, were governed by various laws of contract. In multiple partnerships, two of the members would be appointed executives, as joint *magistri*, and the names of some of the magistri of the societas Lutudarensis appear on lead pigs. In some cases, leases on mines were obtained by the local ordo, or perhaps they were even given the duty of working them, for lead pigs bearing the names of the Brigantes of north England and the Deceangli of Flintshire have been found.

There is one further interesting point concerning lessees of all imperial estates, whether single operators or partners. Normally they had full rights to dispose of their tenancies, or shares in them, for the highest price they could get, simply by registering the transfer with the procurator. But they were not allowed to divest themselves if they were in debt to the imperial treasury. Consequently as taxes became more onerous, more and more people found themselves bound to the land or to the mines, often in time becoming little better than serfs.

It is difficult to trace the activities of other business partnerships in Britain, although they assuredly must have existed; the nearest we can come to suggesting others is probably in the pottery industry. Five different people with the common name of Sextus Valerius made *mortaria* (see Chapter 6) at Colchester and would seem to represent a family business. It is noticeable that in this particular field of manufacture, many of the early producers were Roman citizens, and may either have been sponsored by rich patrons, or were wealthy proprietors in their own right. Towards the end of the second century, one or more German firms from the Rhineland tried, not altogether successfully, to make samian pottery at Colchester. The capital required for such a venture is more likely to have come from partnerships.

Management of shops and other trades must often have been put in slaves' or freedmen's hands. An inscription (fig. 51) from Norton, east Yorkshire, mentions a slave running a goldsmith's shop. It has also been suggested that a certain block of shops built to a standard pattern at Verulamium in the early years of the town, was leased out to tenants or managed by slaves on behalf of a wealthy, Catuvellaunian landowner, who had constructed the block as an investment. When it was rebuilt after the Boudiccan fire, fragmentation of the original holding took place, suggesting perhaps that individual owners had bought themselves in.

In the early days of the empire, the state looked with great suspicion on all kinds of free associations, suspecting them of political agitation. Consequently such associations, whether connected with a trade or with a benevolent purpose, had to be registered and the laws controlling them were strict. Yet, flexible in all things, the state then proceeded to make use of those societies which served imperial purposes.

Trade associations, or *collegia*, existed all over the empire, including Britain. Although they were frequently composed of people following the same occupation, at no time were they comparable either to guilds or trade unions. Trade standards, higher wages or improved conditions were no part of their business, and they were primarily intended more as clubs to form centres for social activities on behalf of people with similar interests. It is probable that they also acted as burial clubs for their members, which were the commonest types of associations and the only ones permitted to be run inside forts and fortresses. They, therefore, played an important part in society, since they permitted both slaves and freemen to meet on common ground during life and assured them decent burials afterwards. Burial clubs frequently held plots of land in cemeteries (see Chapter 7), and often used communal graves, or *loculi*, in which compartments for cinerary urns or coffins opened off a central space; one has been suspected at Lincoln, where also two guilds formed from districts of the city are known. One of the best attested examples in Britain is the smiths' club mentioned on an inscription from Chichester (fig. 15). It was sufficiently wealthy to be able to erect a temple to their patron deities, Neptune and Minerva, very soon after the conquest. Here, the authority for recognizing the legality of the club was not the emperor, but the client king, Cogidubnus. The inscription, therefore, provides a useful sidelight on the areas of law in which the ruler of a client state was competent to act on his own authority in matters normally reserved for the emperor. In an ordinary province, the legality of a club could not be decided by the governor alone; the matter had to be referred to the emperor, as did Pliny to Trajan when he was governor of Bythinia. Maintaining an illegal society was an act of treason.

The organization of a society or club revolved round a set of rules which were approved at the time of its inception. The names of the officials are reminiscent of municipal magistrates and the titles *quinquennalis, decurio* and *curator* all appear. The latter term, usually taken to mean treasurer, occurs on an inscription from Lincoln. Another inscription from Caerwent refers to a man being excused all further subscriptions, presumably for some signal service, while some inscribed fragments from Silchester attest the presence of what might best be called a Travellers' Club, no doubt to take care of the body, if a member was sufficiently unfortunate to die away from home.

Supreme in the area of management and organization was the Roman army, for which there is a tremendous amount of information from widely different sources. The fundamental organization of the army and its fighting capacity have been considered in Chapter 2, but it remains to look briefly at some closely related matters which went to make it the most efficient army in the ancient world.

Recruits were obtained from many sources, both within and without the empire. Every major acquisition of territory brought its quota of men, and to begin with care was taken to station them away from their homelands, so that Britons are found serving in Germany during the late first and second centuries. In time, however, this regulation was greatly relaxed, with the idea of giving a man a stake in the defence of his own home. Recruits from the outer provinces were normally placed at first in auxiliary regiments, but as time passed greater numbers aspired to the legions, for which, until the early third century, Roman citizenship was the passport. On enrolling, a man had to swear an oath of loyalty and give a statement as to his status. It seems that notes were made in the records of any physical pecularities, such as scars.

Assigned to his regiment and equipped, the new recruit underwent a lengthy primary training programme to accustom him to discipline and methods of warfare. Needless to say such training remained a considerable part of peace-time duties. Foot-drill, route marches and swimming in full kit, weighing up to 27 kg, weapon training, surmounting obstacles, and constructing fortifications were all recommended for infantry, while cavalry likewise trained in squadrons in the principles of attack and retreat. More specialized training probably included exercises such as constructing bridges of boats, or artillery practice with *ballistae* or *onagri*; the former fired an iron bolt, the latter hurled a lump of stone. It was also recommended that recruits and young soldiers should be drilled morning and afternoon, but that experienced men should only have weapon practice once a day. For wet weather, most legionary fortresses had large drill sheds. No doubt also there were many fatigue duties to be learnt and carried out, and there was always equipment to clean and polish, or clothing to wash and mend.

The logistical problems of the army were immense. The basic foodstuffs were wheat for bread (fig. 86), bacon and cheese, supplemented by some vegetables, meat, fish, shellfish, salt and olive oil, together with beer or a thin wine, normally mixed with water. Fodder had to be supplied for animals, timber and other materials for building construction, and leather for tents and clothing. It is not always possible to calculate the quantities which must have been required, although it is known that each soldier was allowed approximately 330 kg of corn a year (fig. 80), so that the total annual consumption of the army in Britain was of the order of 20,000 tonnes, all of which had to be collected and distributed. The diet also implies wine and oil from Gaul or the Mediterranean. One of the most recent, interesting British finds has been a series of wooden writing tablets from the fort at Chesterholm, just to the rear of Hadrian's Wall. Dating probably to the end of the first or early second century, they appear to include records of food issues or purchases, but whether as part of the regular diet or for a special occasion is not entirely clear. It must be remembered that soldiers had sums deducted from their pay to cover the cost of their basic diet and also clothing, and they probably had to purchase other foods out of their pay.

On active service and when away from permanent bases, accommodation was in tents made of calf leather. Fragments are found from time to time in waterlogged deposits, and when added to other information, enables us to make some deductions about quantities. It has been estimated that a tent for eight men (the normal arrangement for private soldiers) required some fifty leather panels, and that the skin of one calf would only provide two panels. The second-century garrison in Britain, therefore, possessed tents equivalent to some 200,000 calves. Admittedly they would not all be made at once, and many would have come from overseas, but nevertheless the repair and replacement of worn-out tents must have called for considerable resources of livestock.

Fig. 86. Bread ovens in the
fortress of Legio XX at Chester
(*Grosvenor Museum*).

The logistical problems of supplying the cavalry regiments of the
Roman army are not often appreciated. A quingeniary ala, with
about 500 men, would probably have required some 600 horses on
its strength in order to allow for sick and injured beasts. A single
horse given extra feed in winter still requires 0.6 ha of grazing to
keep it reasonably fit and healthy, so a single cavalry regiment of this
strength would have needed some 360 ha, a figure that could be
reduced perhaps by a quarter if supplementary feed was given all
year; nor should we forget the 5,000 hl of water needed daily. On
modern figures a single working horse consumes some 64 standard

bales of hay a year, which would be over 38,000 bales (= 1,378 tonnes) for one regiment, all to be harvested and properly stored (wet hay is mouldy hay and mouldy hay is the quickest way to lung disease for both man and beast) and then distributed. Reduction in these figures is difficult to envisage if a regiment was to be kept in peak condition for active service. Britain contained on average one milliary and some ten quingeniary regiments of cavalry in its garrison, although the number varied from time to time. A total of about 4,300 ha of permanent pasture and 16,500 tonnes of hay per year would have been needed, and this does not take into account any of the part-mounted cohorts or baggage animals, or the quantity of hard feed which might amount to another 600 tonnes a year for a single regiment. But these figures can only be taken as a rough guide to the supply of the cavalry, since many variables would have operated.

It has been calculated that about 16,000 cu m of structural timber were required for the Agricolan legionary fortress at Inchtuthill (fig. 13a), weighing nearly 17,000 tonnes. To this must be added another sum for cladding and nearly a quarter of a million each of roof tiles and shingles, with appropriate supplies of nails and nearly a thousand tonnes of mortar. The question is: where did all this material come from? Tiles could have been made locally, although there is no evidence for their manufacture. The iron for 1½ million nails (6–10 tonnes) can only have come from further south, the nearest sources being around the area of Hadrian's Wall, if indeed they were then being worked. Neither was lime for mortar available locally. As for the timber, it could have been cut and worked on or near the site as needed, in which case it would not be seasoned, although some claim that for oak this would be an advantage. But it would have added immensely to the overall task of almost completing the fortress in three years. But there is ample evidence to show that, when forts were evacuated, much of the recoverable timber was salvaged, presumably for re-use, and many forts in the Midlands were being dismantled at or before the same time as Inchtuthill was being constructed. Moreover, there is evidence from Caerleon that wood for the first fortress was cut and worked off site and as much as five or six years before it was actually required. This in turn suggests the existence of stockpiles and also allows for a period of seasoning. Indeed, the creation of such stockpiles during the non-campaigning periods of winter, when the wood was in the best condition for felling, would have been ideal employment for the legions. Taking all these factors into consideration, a strong case can be made out to suggest that timber for Inchtuthill had been prepared in advance and was carted to Scotland from dumps further south, possibly from as far away as the Midlands and presumably by sea and river. Nor must it be forgotten that Inchtuthill was not the only fortress to be built in the decade or so surrounding Agricola's governorship. Three other fortresses were under construction as well as some eighty auxiliary forts in Wales, northern England and Scotland, all requiring their quota of timber and perhaps adding as much as a further 176,000 cu m or more to the total. It has been calculated that approximately one hectare of natural woodland can only provide 9 cu m of suitable structural timber, so the full quantity would have required the felling of over 200 sq km of forest. It seems inconceivable that so much could have been provided in the short space of time, and with the tools then available, and indeed the evidence from Caerleon strongly suggests that it was not. We can only conclude that much of the preparation had been started before Agricola's campaigns began and that stockpiles were kept in readiness which, added to the recyling of wood from dismantled forts, would have been adequate for any eventuality which faced the Roman army. Such figures, of course, can only be extremely general and tentative, and may indeed be conservative, but they are worth quoting as they can help to quantify the efficiency of the organization which lay behind the operations. We might also remember the 11 tonnes of iron nails of all sizes which could be written off from the stocks at Inchtuthill without a qualm, to save transport when the fortress was abandoned. The order to do so probably caused near heart failure for some quartermaster, who, no doubt, had to account for their absence in his stock returns.

We know, also, that full records of requisitions and supplies, daily duties, outpostings of men, registers of correspondence as well as accounts were kept, with returns sometimes having to be duplicated or even triplicated. Moreover, manpower returns had to be made to show the state of recruitment, and copies of these documents presumably ended up in Rome. One of the most interesting surviving documents from the late empire is the Notitia Dignitatum. It is a list which shows the composition of all the military commands and offices of state and the placing of military units, government factories, and civil service officers. Many arguments have taken place as to the date and origins of the Notitia and, indeed, as to its internal consistency. It seems most likely that not all sections are strictly contemporary and represent dispositions in different parts of the empire at different times. Neither can we be certain that it is an official document, or simply a copy made by someone with access to the records. Nevertheless, it is invaluable in showing the extent of late Roman organization, both civil and military, and reflects the many changes which had occurred. Army administration continued, on paper, as efficiently as before, but we may suspect that the increasing bureaucracy was in the end self-defeating.

CHAPTER 6

Work

The everyday work of the province, as with the administration, can be broadly divided between military duties and civilian employment, but there is a comparatively large area of overlap, since the Roman army, as already noted in Chapter 2, aimed at self-sufficiency in many matters.

The first duty of every Roman soldier was to achieve proficiency in the art of war. It has long been recognized in all warfare that a few well-disciplined and highly trained men can be more than a match for superior numbers of inferior quality. Consequently the training given to the men of the Roman army always had this objective firmly in mind, and was, moreover, supported by the provision of first-class weapons and armour.

The main offensive weapon of a legionary soldier was a short but broad, double-edged sword, about 0.6 m long, which was most effective when used for stabbing rather than slashing. Such use is more economical of movement, inflicts the more serious injuries and does not expose the swordsman so much to attack. He was also provided with special throwing spears, or javelins, some 2 m long, which had a square-sectioned iron point connected to the wooden shaft by a shank of untempered metal. It could be thrown considerable distances and could kill at up to about 10 m, but its chief purpose was to lodge in an enemy's shield. The trailing weight of the shaft then bent the soft iron shank, so hooking a large encumbrance firmly to the shield and causing it to be discarded. For his protection, the legionary was given a composite bronze and iron helmet with neck, brow and cheek guards, body armour of overlapping plates attached to leather backing (fig. 87) and a rectangular plywood shield curved to fit round the body. It is highly probable that much of this equipment would have been manufactured by the army and certainly maintained by armourers and blacksmiths attached to each regiment.

The weapons and armour of auxiliary infantry and cavalry (partly displayed in fig. 120) varied much more. In the first place a cavalryman needed a greater reach and therefore had a longer sword; the rectangular shield would have been cumbersome on horseback and so was substituted by a circular or oval variety. Lances and spears were issued, the different lengths, shapes and styles equating with their use. Specialist regiments of archers, slingers and spearmen were also maintained with their own individual weaponry.

In addition to the personal fighting equipment of each man, the army also deployed artillery in the form of *ballistae* or *onagri*. The former, usually mounted on carts and each with a team of ten men, were not unlike large crossbows and fired iron bolts with a killing distance of up to a hundred metres or more, while the latter hurled rocks up to 250 kg in weight for considerable distances. Various other 'engines-of-war' could also be assembled as need arose and were used mainly in sieges or for storming fortified positions.

Fig. 87. Reconstructed suit of body armour – *lorica segmentata* – based on fragments found in a wooden chest buried beneath the principia of the Flavian fort at Corbridge (*C.M. Daniels, Museum of Antiquities, University of Newcastle*).

In Britain, despite its long history of warfare during the Roman period, there is unfortunately little evidence for the sites of battles, or for the ways in which they were fought. The military historian, Vegetius, writing in the late fourth century, tells of tactics and strategy then in use and applies them to battle formations, but in a somewhat idealized form; it is likely also that he was relying heavily on the earlier, now lost, account of Julius Frontinus. The latter, governor of Britain in AD 74–8, wrote yet another work, a surviving account on tactics and strategy, which takes the form almost of a training manual for officers. It is more than likely that Frontinus would have practised his tactics in his campaigns in Wales, but unfortunately none can be related to specific sites.

The Roman soldier was most effective when working in close formation on carefully chosen ground. Almost all the serious defeats of the Roman army happened when such tactics could not be followed; the Varus disaster in Germany in AD 9 took place in the Teutoberger Forest, and the defeat of a legionary force in Silurian territory in the early fifties probably occurred in equally difficult terrain.

But the effectiveness of Roman tactics in attacking fortified positions is perhaps demonstrated best in Britain by the battles which excavations show to have been fought at the two Dorset hillforts of Maiden Castle and Hod Hill in the year of the invasion. At Maiden Castle a direct frontal assault was mounted on the complicated structure of the east gate, perhaps after the timbers had been fired by incendiary missiles. There we can imagine the use of a *testudo*, linked shileds held overhead to protect the assault force from missiles thrown from rampart tops. A cemetery of the defenders killed in action produced ample evidence for the power of Roman arms, one skeleton still containing the fatal ballista-bolt embedded in the spine, after it had penetrated the upper chest.

At Hod Hill (figs 10 and 14), on the other hand, no assault seems to have been necessary. Instead, an extremely accurate artillery bombardment took place on the chieftain's house which, fortunately for the Roman army, lay within range, at a distance of some 180 m from the south-east corner. But to carry out the bombardment, a siege-tower at least 15 m high would have been required to give the gunners, or their observers, visibility over the ramparts. The accuracy of the fire can be judged by the fact that only two bolts appear to have missed the target completely, while eight actually struck the house, causing, so it would seem, an immediate surrender.

Other hill forts and oppida such as Spettisbury, Old Cadbury and Sutton Walls have shown the Roman army at war, if in less graphic ways. But of the great battles of Romano-British history little is known. Attempts have been made to show that the battle of the Medway in AD 43 was fought near Rochester, that Caratacus was finally defeated near Caersws, in central Wales, that Boudicca's forces were annihilated somewhere along Watling Street near Mancetter, and that Agricola defeated the Caledonians in the battle of Mons Graupius near Ythan Wells in north-east Scotland, but at no site can positive evidence be produced. An altar at Corbridge records revenge taken after the Brigantian rebellion in AD 155, and it used to be thought that the siege works at Burnswark (figs 89–90), north of Carlisle, belonged to the same campaigns; but more recent research now relegates them to practice works.

Not all members of the army were actively employed in fighting and the support services were equally important, although all could fight if need be. Foremost among them were the medical orderlies, usually under the command of a non-commissioned Greek officer. The Greeks were noted for their medical knowledge and skill in the ancient world and many entered the ranks of the army. Greek doctors are known from inscriptions left at Chester, Binchester and Housesteads, while a field-dressing station is depicted among the scenes on Trajan's Column. Most medical work was of a highly empirical nature. In battle it would have primarily involved the dressing of physical injuries, amputations, removal of foreign bodies and the recovery of

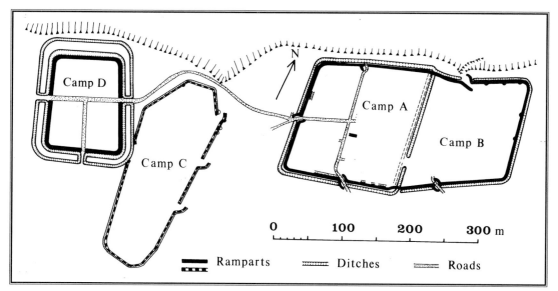

Camp D

Camp C

N

Camp A

Camp B

| 0 | 100 | 200 | 300 m |

━━━ Ramparts ┈┈┈ Ditches ░░░ Roads

Fig. 88. A series of camps at Cawthorn on the N. Yorkshire moors, which have been interpreted as practice works. One at least resembles a fort (*after I.A. Richmond*).

the wounded from the battlefield. Surgical instruments, in many cases of a surprisingly sophisticated design, enabled quite major surgery to be carried out, but of course without anaesthetic. Good base hospitals, moreover, existed in most forts and fortresses and were equipped with wards – at Inchtuthill one for each century (fig. 13a) – and operating theatres. The maintenance of good health among the ranks was a well recognized need and sick parades must have been a normal feature of peacetime soldiering. The importance of diet in curing ill-health was also known and special diets for invalids were sometimes ordered, while army convalescent stations may have been maintained in a number of provinces, including perhaps one at Bath.

Although every legionary was something of an artisan, trained carpenters would have been on hand during battles for the construction of siege works or defensive shelters. If the engagement took place anywhere near the sea, or on a river, special boat parties would have been present, not only to provide transport but also for constructing bridges, and the important parts played by the naval arm in the campaigns of Agricola, or later, of Severus in Scotland must not be forgotten.

It was, however, in peace time that the full versatility of the Roman soldier became apparent. Some of their duties as administrators have already been considered in the preceding chapter, but beyond that there was scarcely a job of any nature, that the army could not undertake, in addition to remaining always ready for battle.

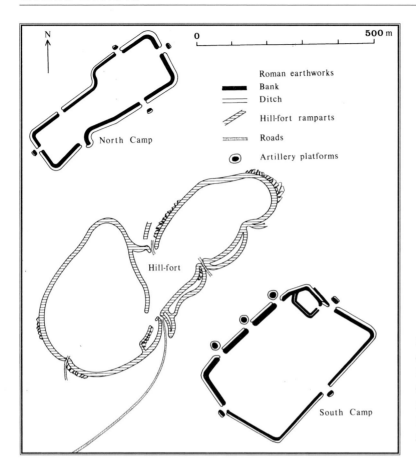

Fig. 89. Practice siege camps on either side of the disused hillfort at Burnswark, north of Carlisle. The southern camp has three emplacements for ballistae facing the fort (*after the Ordnance Survey*).

Battle-readiness was maintained by an unceasing round of drills, training and manoeuvres. Army drill instructors were attached to all legions and had charge of foot-drill and weapon training, and so instilled that habit of implicit and unhesitating obedience to orders, which is called discipline. In the field, practice camps were constructed as part of training programmes, and good groups of these could once be seen just outside the legionary fortress at York, while they still exist on Llandrindod Common and at Tomen-y-Mur in Wales, among others. Most of the Welsh examples occur near auxiliary forts and were therefore probably constructed by the local regiments. All these camps are small, but nevertheless demonstrate the principal defensive features of Roman fortifications, such as the turf ramparts with rounded corners, the ditches, and either titulate or claviculate entrances. Each camp may have represented a day's work on the part of a detachment of new recruits.

Turf cut to a standard-sized block was commonly employed by the army for defensive fortifications, especially in the first and second centuries in Britain. Certainly practice would be required in its handling, as, clumsily laid, it would slump and peel away from the core. But properly laid and compacted it would give a solidity which is absent from dumped earth or rubble. Great care was therefore taken in selecting good quality turf. At both Glenlochar in south-west Scotland and at Brough-on-Humber it was brought some distance, since the local turf was too friable. It had the added advantage also that the grass exposed at the outer edges continued to grow, so ultimately rooting the whole surface together and giving increased stability. One of the summer fatigue duties would almost certainly have been cutting the grass on the rampart slopes. Practice camps of an entirely different nature, probably derived from large-scale manoeuvres, can be seen at Cawthorn (fig. 88) on the north Yorkshire moors. There a succession of three camps, or forts as they might more correctly be called, was constructed, but never permanently occupied.

At some time, also, a full-scale mock assault was made on the empty native hill fort at Burnswark, north of Carlisle (figs 89–90). The fort occupies a prominent hill in the coastal plain of the River Solway and can only be approached by a steep climb. Military camps were constructed on the lower edges of the slopes on both north and south sides of the hill, and that to the south was also equipped with three projecting ballista platforms, suitable for mounting a preliminary bombardment of the type noted above at Hod Hill. In siege-craft it was often Roman practice to construct a continuous circumvallation around a besieged site. Such a work was carried out at the unoccupied hill fort at Woden Law in the Cheviots, presumably again as part of a battle-training exercise.

To what extent ordinary soldiers were trained in other fields than martial arts is not entirely known, but the rudiments of carpentry and masonry were probably imparted to all. An inscription from Chesterholm refers to the testing of recruits who, having passed, went on to construct a masonry building. But for the major construction work specialist soldier-craftsmen, under the command of the *architectus*, were at hand to carry out the technical work. It should not be forgotten, however, that they were still soldiers and could be called upon to fight if the need arose. But the rank and file legionaries will have provided most of the unskilled or semi-skilled labour, perhaps supplemented by civilian corvées.

Apart from the construction of fortifications of various types and the normal run of military buildings, the army was also responsible, on many occasions, for surveying and building roads, aqueducts, sewers, and even pottery and tile kilns, which they also operated.

For the ordinary legionary, the most fatiguing aspect of all this work was probably the provision of the raw materials: timber, stone, lime, sand, gravel, clay, metals. Every man had in his personal equipment an axe, an entrenching tool, a saw and a basket for carrying earth, and so was basically fitted out for such tasks, and only needed supplementary tools suited to the type of work. For instance quarrying would require heavy hammers, metal and wooden wedges, 'jumpers', crowbars and lewis or scissor equipment for lifting large blocks by derricks, cranes or shear legs. Quarries used by the Roman army are well attested to the rear of Hadrian's Wall, where the units working them frequently carved their names and those of their officers on the rock face; the Written Rock of Gelt near Brampton (Cumbria) is one of the best known examples, and records the activities of a vexillation of the second legion (fig. 91). If Hadrian's Wall had been completed to the full gauge of 3 m, over 1½ million cubic metres of masonry would have been required for the Wall alone. If allowance is made for the reduction in width and for the fact that the masonry is composed of puddled clay or lime mortar as well as stone, it is probably not too rough a guess to suggest that over half a million cubic metres of stone had to be quarried for the work, a proportion of it dressed, and then often carried some little distance before it could be used. Add to that the sand and clay which had to be dug, the stone to be quarried for lime-burning, the mortar to be mixed, and it is not difficult to see why, at first, the employment of three legions was necessary and that they had only progressed a little over half way before the change to turf-work took place to speed up the rate. The employment of perhaps 15,000 men on such a multiplicity of jobs, all with one object in view, is again eloquent testimony to the discipline and organizing ability of the Roman army; a job with such a large number of men working without it would soon have become a shambles.

Apart from the quarries mentioned above, which, unfortunately, have now been largely destroyed, the best examples of the Roman quarryman's art in the area are to be seen in the sectors where the hardness of the whinstone prevented the full excavation of the fronting ditch. At Limestone Corner, between Chesters and Carrawburgh, can still be seen great blocks of rock as the Romans left them. One such block, which must weight upwards of 13 tonnes, lies on the northern

Fig. 90. Aerial photograph of the southern, practice siege camp at Burnswark (*copyright: Committee for Aerial Photography, University of Cambridge*).

Fig. 91. An etching of the Written Rock of Gelt from a quarry face on the north side of the River Gelt, near Brampton (Cumbria). The left-hand portion refers to a detachment of Legio II Augusta working under an *optio* (a junior NCO), Agricola (*by courtesy of D.J. Smith*).

lip; another, unsplit, still remains at the bottom of the ditch, and the holes cut in the upper surface for inserting the wedges to split the block are visible (fig. 92). Steel-tipped wedges, of a type suitable for such work, have been discovered embedded in the Wall at Milecastle 26, further to the east, while a lewising chisel was found at Chesterholm; heavy hammers are comparatively common finds in Britain. But even given mechanical lifting aids, of which a number of different types were known in the empire, the work must have been laborious and slow and would have called mostly for brute force.

The skilled masons' work would have been no less arduous, and the preparation of several million roughly dressed facing stones for the Wall and its forts would have been a task of considerable magnitude. It also called for more exacting work in the construction of specific buildings, with the preparation of voussoirs for arches, monolithic slabs for sills and lintels, and frequently ornamental work for more important and elaborate buildings. Much of the better masonry was dressed by chopping or by pecking the surface of the stone with a special hammer on which one end was pointed and the other chisel shaped, but the finer work called for a hammer and a variety of chisels. Plumb-bobs, squares, rules, dividers and straining pegs for lines would all have been necessary equipment, and examples are sometimes found.

Many pieces of the military masons' craft have survived in Britain. As might be expected, they show a degree of workmanlike competence rather than artistic merit, although some of the better examples, such as the Corbridge lions, if they were indeed executed by a military mason, can stand comparison with most provincial art. The fountain-head from the Catterick mansio depicts a dolphin and a sea horse, somewhat woodenly drawn, but with a pleasant imaginative touch, for one of the front legs of the horse was portrayed so as to be dipping below the surface of the water in the tank (fig. 82); it may have been the work of a mason from Legio VI. It is likely that a large number of the surviving army tombstones were the work of military masons. Some are undoubtedly of better quality than others, but, although they form an interesting and informative collection on their own, they do not fully measure up to the best civilian work. Military altars form yet another corpus of their work, but generally provide less scope for artistic portrayals, although in their own right interesting for the varying calligraphy they display.

We have already seen in the preceding chapter (p. 193) that the demands of the Roman army for the supply of timber would have

Fig. 92. Block of hard quartz dolorite still lying in the ditch of Hadrian's Wall at Limestone Corner. The upper surface shows the slots cut by wedges in the attempt to split the stone for removal.

been considerable. Timber is at its best when cut down between late autumn and midwinter, a period which would have coincided with the non-campaigning season of the army. Since stocks were probably maintained, it is likely that much of that time was occupied in felling and preparing the wood. Felling and trimming were presumably carried out with axes, and the work involved in dealing with a mature oak must have been very considerable, with the amount of waste probably exceeding that of today. Saws were certainly in use, but most of those found are too small for felling, and were probably restricted to preparing standards and planks from the trunks. Precisely how this was done is not known, but the longitudinal sectioning of a large, hardwood tree would be no easy job without either circular saws or even large two-handed saws. The manufacture of the latter, however, was within a contemporary blacksmith's competence, even though none are known, but their effective use would have required saw-pits. Mechanically-driven saws for stone-cutting were known and similar devices may have been employed for timber, using either water or animal power. The design and construction of such equipment would again have been well within the ability of Roman engineers, who were familiar with gear systems and crown-and-pinion equipment. There is, however, only slight and tantalizing evidence for the use of the cam and crank, in order to turn rotary into vertical or horizontal motion. Certainly, water-driven saws for cutting stone were used in the fourth century in the Ruwar valley in Germany, although it is not known how they worked, but there seems no good reason why similar machines should not have been employed for wood. Large lengths and sections of sawn timber have sometimes been recovered from waterlogged deposits in Roman forts in Britain, so that there is no doubt that the army could manufacture the products, and, in view of the quantities involved, it seems inconceivable that it was done entirely with small, single-handed saws. Admittedly, a single standard could have been cut from one tree by chopping and adzing, but the waste would have been appalling, and the total requirement of trees for the Agricolan building programme would have to be trebled or even quadrupled. But, once again, we might wonder at the amount of physical effort which went into such construction, mainly with somewhat primitive equipment, and anyone who has attempted to cut a single cross-section of a large, hardwood tree with even a modern steel handsaw will be in a better position to appreciate it. We need not doubt, therefore, that a very large number of man-hours went towards the

Fig. 93. Restored eastern gate of the Neronian fort at The Lunt, Baginton, near Coventry. It gives an excellent impression of the scale and complexity of the work which would have been required of Roman army carpenters (*Brian Hobley*).

maintenance of the timber stocks and that doing so would have been one of the principal midwinter duties of the men.

Many timber buildings of the army were made within broadly standard limits of size, owing no doubt to the measuring rods supposedly carried by the centurions during the building operations. Consequently a degree of prefabrication might be envisaged, which was nevertheless sufficiently flexible to allow some variations within the module and which would also help to make recycling of used timbers much easier. For instance barrack wall uprights might be sawn to the same length with mortice holes for the horizontal members – also sawn to lengths – cut in the correct positions, in advance of use. Wall sole-plates, where used, could likewise be sawn to certain lengths, with the number of specially prepared corner pieces manufactured to a given ratio of side lengths. In the buildings of the Claudian fort at Valkenburg (Holland), where timber survived in the wet conditions, the corner unions of the sole-plates were made with half-lapped joints and with the corner post morticed through the junction to act as a retaining peg. The standard of joinery was, therefore, very high, and numerous carpentry tools, ranging from hammers, gouges, different bits to be used in bow-drills, chisels, rasps, saws and planes have been found in Britain from time to time, many on military sites. Derricks were employed to erect large timbers in a vertical position, and smaller post-holes set beside the main gate-timbers at the fort at Oakwood in south-west Scotland are evidence for their use to haul the larger pieces upright.

There is no doubt, also, that timber was recovered by systematic dismantling when a fort was evacuated. At both Inchtuthil and Fendoch, foundation timbers had been dug out of the ground, and nails removed with a claw, judging from the number of curved and bent examples found scattered around the bases of posts. Such timber was then presumably inspected for rot, and, if sound, returned to stock. Somewhere there must lie extensive compounds used for stores depots, and it is most likely that the large fortified annexes connected with many forts, such as that at Thorpe-by-Newark, which is several times larger than its parent fort, were so used, providing space for storage and parking areas for the numerous carts and wagons employed in the distribution.

Among other building materials produced directly by the army were the metal fittings for woodwork, mostly of iron, and brick and tile. Blacksmiths would have been posted to every unit, while legionary fortresses contained large manufacturing workshops, such as that uncovered at Inchtuthil, with its buried stock of iron nails and spikes. No doubt such men also acted as farriers, and although their duties may have included the manufacture and repair of military weapons, perhaps kept separate from general smithing, it is probable that an equivalent, or even greater, weight of metal had to be turned into structural ironwork. Apart from the wide range of nails and spikes, varying from big, 28 cm lengths to small, hollow-headed hobnails, all made on a special anvil, large quantities of door locks and hinges, binding straps, ties, hooks and holdfasts would have been needed. Wagons and carts would have required tyres, hub-rims, lynch-pins and chains. Carpenters, joiners and masons needed tools; even agricultural implements may have been manufactured. Bronzesmiths, probably fewer in number, must have worked closely with the blacksmiths, since many pieces were of a composite bronze/iron structure. The two enclosed compounds which were constructed at Corbridge in the early third century seem to have been set up as arsenals for making military ironwork, and the excavators found, in one furnace, a half-completed iron beam which had been in the process of manufacture. The *classis Britannica*, the British fleet, seems to have maintained an iron-smelting works in the Weald of Kent, although the supply of timber for shipbuilding would have been a useful secondary activity.

The manufacture of brick and tile, which was mainly undertaken by the army during the first and second centuries, called sometimes for specialist depots. The best known of them is that at Holt (Denbighshire) where Legio XX maintained a centre to supply the fortress of Chester. The site consisted of a small fortified enclosure containing at least three barracks and some other buildings, while outside lay a bath-house and a house, perhaps providing accommodation or offices for the officer in charge. There was a range of workshops and drying rooms, besides the firing kilns, which were arranged in a solid bank and served by a single stoking area. The kilns themselves were more elaborate and better constructed than the normal run of civilian types, and possessed sectional floors which could be removed for cleaning the fire chambers beneath. Nearby were the clay-pits from which the raw material was extracted. The situation of the depot close to the River Dee will have enabled the finished products to be shipped by water directly to the fortress.

The kilns, eight in number, not only produced brick and tile, but also pottery, mainly of early second-century types, and including some fine, glazed wares. The site seems primarily to have been established at the time when the Chester fortress was being reconstructed in masonry and the production of pottery was probably introduced as a sideline, although the depot was not finally given up until the fourth century.

It is almost certain that the other two legionary fortresses at York and Caerleon likewise had their own manufacturing centres, and sometimes also auxiliary regiments were similarly equipped, such as the tilery near the fort at Tomen-y-Mur in Wales. Another, worked by Legio IX, has been identified at Scalesceugh, near Carlisle.

We can conclude, therefore, that the Roman army contained competent potters and brickmakers as well as the trades already mentioned. Butchery and tanning will have been an additional qualification for others, as the supply of large amounts of leather, already noted (p. 191), would have called for works devoted to these skills. It is likely that such a depot existed at Catterick, run by an auxiliary regiment. The Brigantes, with their extensive pastures, and in whose area the fort was placed, would have provided cattle instead of grain as their tax levies. Presumably the live animals were delivered to the depots, slaughtered and skinned. The meat would not be wasted, but was probably salted or dried for later use, while glue and size would have been important by-products. But the skins, when tanned, were the most valuable. The process was a lengthy one, lasting perhaps a year, so some degree of forward planning would have been necessary. The skins were first cleaned of surplus flesh and hair by scraping with convex-bladed knives after treatment with some alkaline material, such as stale urine, lime or ashes. They were then packed in layers in deep pits, each layer being separated by the tanning material, usually wood bark or chips from suitable trees. The pit was kept topped up with water throughout the process. Finally, the tanned skins were washed, and then stretched backwards and forwards over a beam to make them supple. A wooden 'slicker' for this purpose has been found at Chesterholm and suggests perhaps, the site of another tannery. At Catterick, a long timber structure might be interpreted as a shed for the initial cleaning process, while a great rubbish dump, waterlogged since Roman times, produced many waste fragments and offcuts, showing the manufacture of finished goods was also carried on. Among the rubbish was a large quantity of animal bones and many discarded boots, shoes and tent panels. More important, however, for the interpretation of the site, were some small punches which would have been suitable for embossing patterns on the finished goods.

The construction of roads was, at first, yet another army duty, although local labour may well have been impressed to assist. As with streets in towns, roads were invariably surfaced with the best locally available materials, such as gravel, flints, crushed stone, or even iron slag, but during the fourth century, paved surfaces became more common, and needed less frequent repairs. During the construction, a wide strip of land was first cleared of trees and undergrowth and drained by two ditches dug on both edges of the strip. The size and position of the ditches could, however, be varied to suit local conditions, the object being not only to create boundaries but also to carry away surface water, and where necessary to drain the subsoil to give a firmer base. If very wet or marshy ground could not be avoided, a substructure of brushwood or baulks of wood was first placed in position, as on Watling Street leading to the Medway crossing at Rochester. The material excavated from the ditches was then heaped into a raised mound in the centre to form the agger, which facilitated drainage of the final surface. Large, heavy stones were usually placed over the agger as a foundation course and were topped with a rammed layer of finer aggregate some centimetres thick, which provided the running surface.

Quite frequently, also, numerous quarry pits for providing the aggregate are to be seen flanking stretches of main road, such as those by the Fosse Way at Thorpe-by-Newark and Brough. Sometimes, exceptional methods were employed in the construction, such as the excavation of a considerable thickness of peat to expose a firm, rock surface at Blackstone Edge on the borders of Lancashire and Yorkshire or at Graik Cross (Dumfriesshire).

Wherever possible bridges were constructed over rivers and streams. In most cases, they were probably entirely built of timber, like that which carried the Gartree Road from Leicester to Colchester over the River Nene at Aldwinkle near Thrapston, where huge, iron-shod, wooden piles, some 50 cm square, had been driven into the river banks and bed to support the bridge (fig. 94). But in the frontier region masonry abutments and piers were more commonly used in conjunction with wooden superstructures, such as those at Piercebridge, Newcastle or Corbridge, or at Chesters, after the bridge had been rebuilt; the latter, in its first stage, was probably arched, since voussoirs were found to have been incorporated in the later work. The construction of the piers and abutments will have called for the use of coffer dams, built of timber and carefully plugged with clay, of a type well demonstrated at the bridge which crossed the Moselle at Trier in Germany.

Fig. 94. Edge of a wooden bridge at Aldwinkle (Northants) where the Gartree Road crosses the River Nene, it was revealed in the side of a gravel quarry (*D. Jackson; Britannia*).

Small streams or shallow rivers with gently sloping banks, were sometimes crossed by fords, which might or might not have been paved; the crossing of the Trent at Littleborough appears to have been so treated.

Milestones were also an integral part of the arterial road system. Early examples usually took the form of large cylindrical pillars, often standing a metre or more high. Later, however, much rougher blocks of stone were used, perhaps as the result of the repeated cutting down of the original pillar when new imperial dedications were required. Some milestones were uninscribed but most carried an inscription invoking the name of the emperor in whose principate the road works were carried out, so providing valuable evidence of date. Sometimes also the name of the place from which the distance was measured is included, sometimes only the distance was given. Both milestones and bridges are yet further evidence of the work of military masons and carpenters.

Behind all this construction work of different sorts, however, lay the hand of the army surveyors. Surveying was a skilled and well-practised art in the Roman world and its practitioners received some degree of formal training. Apart from laying out the lines of camps, forts and buildings, for which unfortunately little evidence is likely to survive, they were also responsible for road alignments. Despite their normal high standards, errors did, however, occur and it is only necessary to look at the plan of the fort at Fendoch (fig. 17b) to see how the irregularity in the laying out of its defences had to be repeated in the internal buildings to avoid the barracks impinging on the rampart. But the extraordinarily contorted barrack at Longthorpe (fig. 13d) is so badly planned that it is hard to conceive it as the work of a qualified surveyor. Indeed, it might be said that the irregular outline was caused by less skilled legionaries trying to put together a building from partly prefabricated members and getting the pieces inextricably muddled. There seems little other excuse for such irregularity, even given, perhaps, the haste with which the building may have been erected.

It is, however, in the road system where the work of the surveyors can best be demonstrated. One of the most striking roads in Britain is the Fosse Way which links Seaton in Devon with Lincoln in the north-east, a distance of some 320 km. Despite the fact that, like all Roman roads, it was made up of a series of discrete, straight sections, the road never deviated more than 10 km either side of a straight line joining the two terminal points. This degree of accuracy must have required a considerable knowledge of the local geography as well as the ability to project an established bearing over the whole required distance, which, in the absence of magnetic compasses, could only be done by relating direction to positions of the sun or stars at certain times of the day or night. Hence some astronomical knowledge was also required. It has also been suggested that the release of homing pigeons might have been used to indicate directions over long distances.

Study of the Fosse Way alignments is also instructive to show how individual sections were surveyed. Where possible the road clung to high ground, but where this requirement caused deviation from the overall alignment, corrections had to be made from section to section as convenient. North of Leicester, it caused a gradual swing towards the north until reaching the high point of Cotgrave Gorse, where it was returned to the north-east. Further turns in the same direction are made where the road almost touches the Trent at Thorpe and again at Potter Hill, before it finally runs into the southern suburbs of Lincoln.

The same road also provides information on the approach to sharp gradients. In its course across the Cotswolds (fig. 95), several deep combs had to be crossed and the line was usually adapted to take the

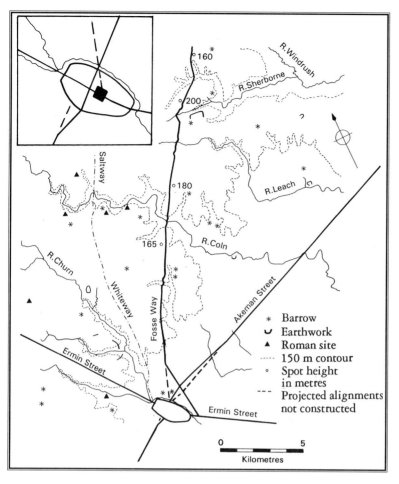

Fig. 95. Road alignments north of Cirencester. The deviations made by the Fosse Way to cross steep-sided river valleys can be appreciated. On its approach to the early fort, the final line chosen aims between two barrows directly at the north-east gate. But for some unexplained reason, the actual road was constructed to pass to the east of the fort, crossing Akeman Street and ultimately joining Ermin Street. South-west of the fort the alignment is again corrected in the direction of Bath. Ermin Street also changes direction at the fort so as to aim for Gloucester.

road on a more gentle, angled slope down the hill and up again the other side. Yet steep inclines were not unknown and in the approach to Lincoln from the south side, the road climbed directly up the limestone scarp at a gradient of less than 1 in 6; but ascent was aided by a series of shallow steps.

The instruments used by the surveyors were chiefly the *groma*, a form of cross-staff, and the *dioptra*, a more elaborate sighting device which could be used for measuring both angles and heights. The *chorobates*, a levelling instrument not unlike a huge spirit-level, was principally used for surveying aqueducts, but another form of level could be fixed to the head of the dioptra. A type of hodometer for measuring distances was also known.

Since the fleet was considered an extension of the army, it is not surprising that we also find soldiers undertaking seafaring duties. An altar from York mentions a soldier from Legio VI being seconded for duty as a river pilot, probably on the treacherous waters of the Humber, and the manning of military transports, as opposed to warships, was mainly undertaken by soldiers.

In describing the work and duties of the Roman army in Britain, we have to a degree anticipated some forms of civilian employment. This is not entirely surprising since many British tradesmen would first have learnt their craft, soon after the conquest, from army technicians. Broadly, however, civilian work fell into a number of recognizable categories, much as it does today: the professions, such as the law, teaching, possibly medicine, when practised at its higher levels, and some forms of local government service; trade, which included all manufacturers, shopkeepers and travelling salesmen; the construction industries, with masons, joiners, carpenters, plasterers, tilers, thatchers, painters, plumbers and floor-layers; seafarers and their ancillary trades, such as sailmakers, shipbuilders and dockers. Consequently, when the total sum of civilian experience is added to what we have already obtained from a study of the army, a fairly full picture emerges, restricted only in certain areas where evidence is scarce owing to the perishable nature of material.

We do not know to what extent the law was practised by British advocates, but it is not unlikely that the province produced its quota of jurists, and Juvenal refers to Britons being trained to plead by Gauls. Men versed in both Celtic and Roman law would have been needed, not only to act as assessors in court but also to argue cases. At least one British case reached the emperor's courts, and since it involved both legal codes, British jurists would probably have advised on it at one or more stages. We should remember also the many scribes and clerks employed in this, and in other ways, to keep records, write letters and prepare documents. *Styli* for inscribing on wax-covered writing-tablets are exceedingly common site finds in Britain and point to a high level of literacy in most business affairs, while the tablets themselves are not infrequent finds in waterlogged sites; notable examples have come from the fort of Chesterholm, to the rear of Hadrian's Wall, and from London. No doubt the bazaar letter-writer was as common in Roman Britain as he was in British India. Ink-wells are known, although more rarely, and there is also the evidence of impressions on Iron Age (tin) coins showing that papyrus reached Britain before the conquest, and surely afterwards as well. The script employed by these people made use of the Roman capital alphabet adapted for a freehand style, since no lower-case letters existed; it is referred to as cursive script.

In a province such as Britain, where presumably Celtic and Latin were spoken side by side, and where, in addition, there is evidence for the use of both Greek and Palmyrene, interpreters would often have been required in the courts as well as in daily life.

There must have been teachers since Tacitus mentions that the British learnt readily and that the sons of the gentry came to speak and write passable, if somewhat archaic, Latin. As noted in a previous chapter, Plutarch records a conversation with the schoolmaster Demetrius, who had recently returned from Britain, and who may possibly be identified with the Demetrius who dedicated at York to the gods of the governor's residence. The word *equus* inscribed on a painted wall at Verulamium and *pavo* scratched on another at Leicester, together with other stilted phrases, might suggest somewhat unorthodox writing practice. A stone disc from Dorchester with its repetitive words is also best interpreted as part of a similar lesson.

The practice of medicine at its worst probably gave rise to much quackery and was probably indistinguishable from trade; nevertheless there were respected physicians and surgeons in the empire, often of Greek extraction and frequently freedmen. Many, as we have seen above (p. 198), enlisted in the army. A case of surgical instruments is reputed to have been found with a burial at Wroxeter, and another has recently come to light in one near Colchester, while similar instruments are not uncommon elsewhere in Britain and other provinces; tongue-depressors, artery forceps, surgical needles, retractors, probes and scalpels have all been found, but some of the most interesting are bronze catheters from Baden in Germany and Pompeii. Other common finds are the stamps used for imprinting descriptions, and the instructions for use, on cakes of ophthalmic ointments. Medical information can also be obtained by a study of skeletal remains from burials. A case of gout has been identified at Cirencester; many broken bones were obviously carefully splinted to promote good reunions, while cases of osteoarthritis, spondylitis and tuberculosis were not uncommon. Medicines were largely made from decoctions of herbs, often taken up in a pleasant-tasting base such as honey or wine. The properties of belladonna, opium, colchicum, henbane, wormwood and many other drugs, often still recognized in modern pharmacopoeias, were well known.

Priests should also, perhaps, be included among the professions. Certainly, as with teachers, they were exempt from taxes. Many of the larger temples must have had residents, and houses closely associated with temples can be observed at Wroxeter and Caerwent. A priestly burial which included ornamental sceptres has been excavated near Brough-on-Humber in Yorkshire, while several ceremonial crowns have been found, including some fine examples from Cavenham, Suffolk. A *haruspex* or augurer is recorded on a statue base at Bath. With the rise of Christianity we know of the Bishops of London, York, Lincoln, probably Cirencester and possibly of Silchester also.

A far larger number of people will have been engaged in commercial or manufacturing activities, and there is much evidence for them. Some were engaged in the import and export trade, such as Verecundius Diogenes and M. Aurelius Lunaris from York, and Antonianus, who dedicated an altar at Bowness-on-Solway before setting out on a trading enterprise, probably to western Scotland. Merchants from the Rhineland came to Britain and one of them, Fufidius, died at Mainz, while another, a pottery merchant M. Secundius Silvanus, dedicated an altar at Westcapell at the mouth of the river. There must have been many firms engaged in the import of samian from Gaul, and one lost a cargo in a shipwreck on the Pudding Pan Rock in the mouth of the Thames. Losses to another merchant were caused by a crate of samian being dropped between the quay and the ship's side in the London dock. If the distribution of some good quality glass vessels is to be taken as a guide, there were merchants dealing directly between the Rhineland and the north of Britain. Trade in wine, oil and condiments, such as fish sauce, was considerable judging from the large number of amphoras and flagons to be found on British sites. These vessels sometimes bear stamps denoting the origin of the contents, or notes scratched or painted on the walls giving the quantity or quality. For instance a painted example on an amphora from Chesterholm may have contained 'prime mackerel sauce', while another gives the tare and total weights of the vessel when filled. One amphora from Chester records in black paint, 'spiced, and flavoured, vintage; for the stores', while a stamped example from Cirencester refers to oil or wine from an imperial estate in Spain, imported during the early third century. Yet another, from Carpow, refers to horehound cough mixture for the army, and is a commentary on the British climate.

Metalwork was also imported into Britain in quantity, coming at first from Italian, later from Gallic, workshops. Bronze jugs, candlesticks and brooches, and silver tableware all speak of merchants in what would today be called the upper end of the market. For a brief period during the early second century, enamelled brooches from Britain became fashionable in the Rhineland, an operation which must have been tantamount to carrying coals to Newcastle. British lead is also known from Gaul, but is more likely to have come from official consignments transported from the imperial mines. But in the same upper bracket there were probably merchants dealing in silk from China, as well as more humble cloths, and a fragment of damask silk has been found in a burial at Holborough in Kent. Cloth-merchants can also be discerned in the mention of British woollen goods in Diocletian's price-regulating edict. Other merchants probably specialized in furs and skins, while oysters from Britain certainly reached Rome; which, although they normally travel well in barrels of salt water, must have represented a slightly hazardous commercial activity. By way of trinkets, jet ornaments from Yorkshire reached the Rhineland, perhaps carried on outward journeys by merchants seeking pottery or glass.

Within the province we can point to many commercial enterprises, and the premises for them have already been considered in Chapter 3. As today, they can broadly be divided into service and manufacturing industries, but with a different emphasis on each category. It must be remembered that most manufacturing was carried out in small workshops which formed part of the premises where the goods were for sale, so resembling many modern eastern bazaars. Only in certain industries, which either required specialist facilities or large open areas of ground, would the two activities have been separated, with middlemen sometimes brought in to market the goods. Moreover, many manufacturers would have carried on repair work, particularly in the various smithing trades.

The six metals of economic value in Britain all had their own manufacturing areas close to the sources of ore. All except iron are easily smelted in small bowl-shaped furnaces with charcoal as fuel, sometimes after a preliminary roasting to convert the ores to the more readily refined oxides of the metals.

Gold, of course, since it occurs naturally as the metal, requires no such process and, after extraction from the ore matrix, has only to be melted and cast into ingots. The only known mine at Dolaucothi, as already indicated above (p. 91), was probably under imperial control. The mines themselves were worked both by open-cast and by adit processes, the latter often leading to extensive galleries which were kept drained by means of waterwheels, arranged one above another in series, so that the water was raised from the mine sump to the surface. The work was carried out by convicts or slaves and conditions must have been appalling despite the strict terms of operation; indeed being condemned to the mines was looked upon as being little better than the death sentence. Economy of working was enforced so that, sometimes, little more than the veins of gold-bearing quartz was chiselled carefully from their beds, making the passages narrow and tortuous. Ventilation was occasionally provided by extra shafts in the larger continental mines, but there is no evidence for such provisions in Britain, so that the air must have been foul, the conditions both cramped and wet and the only light provided by primitive oil-lamps: both Pliny and Lucretius refer to the bad air in mines.

At Dolaucothi, with its ample water supply from at least two aqueducts, a process known as 'hushing' also seems to have been used. In this, a reservoir of water was accumulated above a slope where ore veins were expected to outcrop. By releasing the water down the slope, soil and vegetation would be carried away, so revealing the ore. The same process could also be used for clearing the mining debris, so exposing new working surfaces.

After the ore had been extracted it was crushed on the dressing-floor and then panned in wooden cradles, one of which was found at Dolaucothi, under running water. The water carried away the rocky detritus leaving particles of gold in the cradle, which could be collected and melted into blocks or ingots.

Despite the fact that most of the gold production went to the emperor, some was sold onto the open market, for evidence for goldsmiths' shops, or working, has been found near the mines, at Norton (Yorks.) (fig. 51), and at Cirencester, Verulamium and London. The most interesting remains are those from the latter town where a workshop existed in the Neronian period beneath the site of the possible palace (fig. 79). A number of crucibles and their lids were recovered, together with the remains of clay luting used to seal the two together. The luting had been stamped with impressions of a lion and a boar within a rectangular panel, and had been intended to give a gas-tight seal for the enclosed vessel; it is likely that the stamp was applied to prevent pilfering of the vessel's contents. These closed containers were used for refining gold, by heating it for a considerable time between layers of brick dust in the presence of organic acids such as urine. The impurities in the gold were dissolved and absorbed in the brick dust.

At Verulamium, a goldsmith's shop was identified in Insula XIV, and a number of very small crucibles, some containing residual traces of metal, were recovered from the shop floor. The slave-managed shop at Norton has already been referred to (p. 89), and the evidence from Cirencester is in the form of a crucible fragment from the market-hall.

Most lead-silver mines appear to have been open-cast and the extraction process will have been closely akin to quarrying. It is, however, claimed that some shaft mines in the Pennines above Swaledale are of Roman date, but no proof is as yet forthcoming. After the ore had been crushed it was roasted and then smelted to given an alloy of lead with a small percentage of silver. In order to extract the silver a cupellation furnace was employed, in which the alloy was remelted in a bowl-shaped container lined with a thick layer of crushed bone ash. A blast of air was directed at the surface of the molten alloy so as to oxidize the lead, the product of which, since it was in a molten state, was absorbed by the bone ash, leaving behind a small pellet of silver. In order to recover the lead, the bone ash mixture was resmelted with further quantities of charcoal. The process is reasonably efficient and desilverized lead from Britain often contains no more than 0.01 per cent silver. Some lead 'pigs' carry the cast inscription *ex argentariis* – from the silver works – from which we may deduce that silver was the most important of the two products.

As with gold, most silver will have gone to augment supplies of imperial coinage, but some again reached the open market. A silversmith's workshop of some size is known at Silchester, where the owner was not only manufacturing, but also cupelling, low silver alloys. Another is known at Wroxeter, while the goldsmith at Verulamium was also working sometimes in the less precious metal. A glass manufacturer at Leicester (fig. 52) was, as a sideline, carrying on the business of separating silver from base silver coins, a process prohibited by law and carrying the death penalty as its punishment.

Lead would have been much more readily obtainable by private individuals and was put to a very wide number of uses. Somewhere, as yet unknown, factories for the manufacture of lead sheet of a very regular thickness must have existed, for it was the starting point for many finished objects, such as water-pipes, coffins, bath-linings and probably roofing. Water-pipes were made by wrapping strips of lead sheet around a circular former and then soldering together the overlapping edges of the joint; sometimes, as in the case of pipes from Chester, an inscription, cast onto the surface of the pipe, recorded the circumstances of manufacture. The largest pipe yet known in Britain comes from York and carried water across the bridge over the River Ouse; it was 180 mm in diameter and would thus have fallen within the 30-digit category of Vitruvius, requiring about 40 kg of lead per metre length. The great bath at Bath was once lined entirely with lead sheet, and excavations revealed the small plumbers' furnaces used in its fabrication. Similar furnaces around the Cirencester basilica point perhaps to lead-covered roofs, or to the jointing of large blocks of masonry by means of iron masons' 'dogs' set in a lead seal. Lead coffins are comparatively common in Britain and are sometimes extensively ornamented. These, together with decorated lead water tanks, are excellent examples of the plumbers' craft. Lead was also a primary constituent of pewter, much used for tableware in the fourth century. A factory for its manufacture existed at Combe Down, outside Bath, where stone patterns, into which the pieces were beaten, or cast, have been found. Another existed at Camerton, and no doubt both were using Mendips lead. Since tin is the other constituent of pewter, and Cornwall the only place where it is found in workable quantities, it is not surprising that stone moulds have also come from St Just, although others have been found as far afield as Yorkshire and Wiltshire.

Copper ores were to be found in Shropshire, and also Wales and Anglesey. Adit mines occur at Llanymynech, but elsewhere collection of ore nodules on the surface appears to have taken place on a local basis. Copper is also an easily smelted metal and industrially can be used either by itself, or as an alloy with other metals, the most commonly occurring being bronze, an alloy with tin. Bronze and coppersmiths must have been almost as ubiquitous as blacksmiths in Roman Britain since the metal was used for many different products, ranging from small personal articles like pins and brooches to large castings for furniture and harness. Manufacturing smiths are known from a number of places: both Verulamium and Catterick have produced evidence for workshops in the form of wooden-lined waste-tubs used for separating bronze filings and waste from lighter dross by flotation in water. The smith at Catterick seems to have been engaged in enamelling and the shop produced several examples of the craft. Bronzesmiths' crucibles of the late first or early second century have been found at Wroxeter, while at least two smiths are known by name, Celatus who was working near, or at, Lincoln and Cintusmus from Colchester. One of the most interesting recent discoveries has been an ingot of brass weighing 9.3 kg and stamped

V.H.ET.B from an industrial area to the west of Colchester, where there was other evidence of practising smiths. Another firm, manufacturing bronze brooches, may have been working on N'or-Nour in the Isles of Scilly, perhaps using Cornish tin and copper, although recently some doubt has been cast on this interpretation.

Roman interest in British tin was not great. Spasmodic attempts were made during the first century to develop the industry but it was not until the fourth century that more deliberate efforts were introduced to capitalize the resources. Most tin ore was probably obtained by streaming, although limited mining of surface veins may have taken place. Smelting, as with copper, is comparatively easy, and at least one tin ingot, possibly stamped with a late imperial imprint, has been found near Camborne. Despite the lack of government interest, considerable quantities of tin must have been required by Romano-British industry for the manufacture of bronze and for coating finished objects, since tinned bronze was a much-favoured material for personal ornament.

Of all the metals in Britain, iron was not only the most commonly occurring, but also the most difficult to extract from its ores, since it melts at a somewhat higher temperature than the other metals so far considered. If melted, cast-iron is produced, and, although Romano-British technologies seldom achieved such high temperatures, they had to reject the product, since they were unable to use it. Consequently the ores, after a preliminary roasting, were smelted with charcoal in either a bowl or shaft furnace. The former was the more primitive device and the rate of extraction was lower, but, providing a high enough temperature was produced, probably with bellows, to liquefy the slag, the end product was a spongy mass of sintered iron with many slag inclusions called a bloom. Before the bloom was removed from the furnace, the slag would be run off into a separate pit. The bloom was then reheated in a smithing furnace and hammered while still hot to squeeze out the slaggy impurities. The result was a lump, probably weighing about 1–2 kg, of reasonably pure wrought iron.

Shaft furnaces seem to have been up to 1.5 m high and 30 cm in diameter, judging from examples found at Ashwicken in Norfolk, although others of smaller diameter are known elsewhere. They were lined with clay and, at the bottom of the furnace, there was an arched opening for drawing off molten slag and for allowing access of air. The furnace was charged from the top, layers of ore probably being interspersed with layers of fuel. The height of the furnace induced the draught and so increased the temperature, but bellows could

Fig. 96. Remains of a shaft furnace for smelting iron at Wakerley (Northants.). Draught would have been induced, and slag drawn off, through the vent in the far side.

additionally have been employed. The slag will have been more fluid and greater extraction would have taken place, while in addition larger blooms were probably produced. Moreover, the higher temperature of operation increased the carbon content of the metal, so making a harder iron. At Wakerley in Rutland, a number of shaft furnaces were found, together with some interesting shallow linear furnaces (figs 96–7). The latter would have been appropriate for preparing iron strips, a form in which the metal might most suitably have been marketed.

The art of the blacksmith was practised widely in Roman Britain and some splendid examples have survived, yet strangely enough few blacksmiths' shops have been definitely identified. The inscription from Chichester, mentioned above (p. 189) indicates that there were enough smiths in the town to form a guild. A tombstone from York depicts a blacksmith with the tools of his trade. Hoards of ironwork have been found from time to time at Silchester, Great Chesterford and Chedworth which illustrate their activities. One fine piece of forging is represented by the great pot-hanger from Cirencester with its three hooked chains fastened to a central rotating pivot. At Cirencester, also, estate blacksmiths may have manufactured and repaired agricultural tools in a smithy associated with a farmhouse inside the town.

Fig. 97. Horizontal iron-working hearth at Wakerley (Northants). It could have been used for preparing strips and bars.

Some of the most interesting and largest fabricated pieces are the iron beams made to support hot-water boilers over the stokeholes of bath-houses, often 1.5 m long and weighing as much as 250 kg. They were made by welding together individual blooms by an alternating process of heating and hammering. But, in fact, examination of their internal structures has shown that the welding only occurred at the outer surfaces and that the interiors of the beams remained very much as separate blooms. Inadvertently, therefore, the smiths had discovered one of the strongest forms of structural support: the box girder. Smiths were acquainted with the process of carburization, whereby the surface of a knife or implement could be case-hardened to form a mild steel. It was also known that tempering, by heating and quenching the metal in water or oil, produced superior quality products. Specialist toolmakers are also known, with a cutler, Basilius, selling his goods in London, while the knives of another, Victor, of Vienne, reached Catterick; Martinus made chisels which were also on sale in London.

Two other manufacturing processes were normally carried on close to the sources of raw materials: pottery and brick, and glass.

Glass was made in a number of places in Britain during the Roman period, but the quality always remained poor and production seems to have been confined mainly to window glass and the more utilitarian vessels. At no time does fine glass, either coloured or decorated, such as was imported into the province from the Rhineland or the Middle East, appear to have been made.

The principal constituent in its manufacture was silica, either in the form of sand, or crushed flint or quartz. This was fused with bone ash or wood ash according to the type of glass required, the former providing a glass with a higher softening temperature. Owing to traces of iron in most of the raw materials, natural glass so produced was usually coloured green or brown, the intensity depending on the amount of iron present. This glass was considered suitable for most ordinary vessels or for windows, although decolourizing could be done by adding traces of manganese salts. Similarly, other colours could be imparted by the addition of different minerals: copper or chromium for green, antimony for yellow, cobalt for blue and finely divided gold for ruby red. None of the colours was apparently used in Britain, although many imported pieces display a wide spectrum.

Glassworks have been identified at Caistor-by-Norwich, Leicester, Mancetter and Wilderspool, mainly through the discovery of suitable furnaces and waste material. The factory at Caistor-by-Norwich was a comparatively large establishment, occupying most of a big house. At Leicester, in contrast, a single small furnace was used in one of the shops of the market (fig. 52). It is not entirely clear what was the total repertoire of these manufacturers, as few vessels can be associated with them, but glass bottles and jars of varying shapes and sizes seem to have been the normal run, in addition to window glass. Strangely enough, none of the characteristic implements of the glassworker, usually made of iron, has ever been identified in Britain.

Window glass occurs widely in Britain and was obviously used in considerable quantities for both public and private buildings. Two distinct forms have been detected. The earliest tends to be naturally coloured, rather thick and opaque, with one surface having a sanded appearance. Later, a thinner, colourless and clear material was manufactured, a distinct improvement apparently having taken place in the processing. It used to be thought that the panes were made by casting the glass on sanded surfaces in moulds, so giving the characteristic appearance to the early types. More recently, however, it has been suggested that it was manufactured by first blowing a cylindrical bottle in a mould, after which the top and bottom would be removed and the resulting cylinder cut longitudinally with shears. This cylinder was then placed in an annealing furnace at a temperature just sufficient to soften the glass, when it unrolled and assumed a flat shape.

The importance of the process is that it removed the stresses inherent in cast glass which might otherwise have caused it to crack on cooling. It is also thought that, at first, the annealing furnaces were slightly overheated, so causing pitting of the under surface, but as ability to control the process was improved, so the quality improved with it.

Glassware, both imported and locally made, was undoubtedly offered for sale in many towns and settlements, judging from the quantity of broken fragments found on most sites. But only one shop has so far been posivitely identified in Britain at Colchester. There, at the time of the Boudiccan rebellion, a hardware shop was burnt down. Glass vessels on upper shelves melted and ran down over nests of samian bowls standing on the floor, so sealing all together.

The Romano-British pottery industry, together with the trade which it generated, is probably the best attested of all manufacturing processes, since the material it produced was largely indestructible, although easily broken, so that large quantities, illustrating many different styles, were needed to satisfy the markets. The production of good quality wheel-turned vessels had started in south-east Britain some decades before the Roman invasion, so that the increasing demands made upon the industry, especially at first by the army, seem to have been met without undue difficulty. Fortunately, the distinctive fabrics and forms of many of the vessels enable centres of production to be pinpointed and the marketing patterns worked out, although much still remains to be done in this direction.

The manufacture of pottery is most conveniently carried out close to the sources of raw materials. Clay, water and fuel are the principal requirements, although access to good transport facilities, particularly by water, is an important secondary consideration. Much pottery is known to have been carried by water in the Roman world, not only because it was cheaper, but also, since pottery is both bulky and breakable, there was less risk of damage and larger amounts could be carried by boat. Readily available supplies of fuel must also have been a decisive factor in the siting of a kiln, as modern experiments have shown that consumption was prodigious. The supply was probably maintained by regular coppicing of woodland. In view of these considerations, it is not surprising that many of the main production centres were situated close to, or within easy reach of, navigable rivers, and it is possible to demonstrate by means of distribution maps that these were often the chief routes to the markets.

The manufacture requires several different processes. The clay has to be dug and then worked up to make it suitable for throwing on the wheel. In the raw stage, certain additives were sometimes included, such as crushed grit, shells or old potsherds, or sand, to make the vessels less liable to crack during firing. No potter's wheel has been found in Britain from the Roman period, since they were probably made of wood, but some objects have been interpreted as spindles. Many vessels were made wholly on the wheel, but a large number of types seem to have been hand-moulded before being finished on it. After throwing, the vessels were allowed to dry to a leather-hard state, at which point decoration or an external coating could be applied. Drying sheds have been tentatively identified at some potteries, but there is little to indicate the actual use of the buildings and many were probably of an ephemeral nature, as indeed

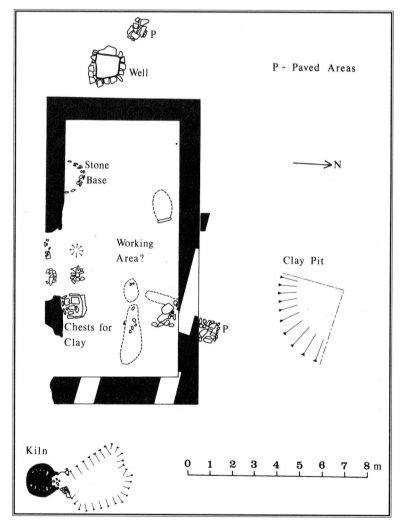

Fig. 98. Potter's workshop at Stibbington, near Peterborough. Close by were a well, the clay pit and the kiln (*after J.P. Wild and G.B. Dannell*).

were other workshops. One has, however, recently been discovered at Stibbington in the Nene Valley; it consisted of a simple rectangular building, some 6.4 m by 12.2 m, with a well outside, and with the bases for four stone-lined tanks, in one of which a quantity of prepared clay, mixed with crushed shell, had been left (fig. 98).

While these stages of manufacture were being carried out, other processes, providing the firm had sufficient employees, could have been going on simultaneously, such as cutting wood and preparing the kiln. Remembering that a single small kiln could hold upwards of two hundred medium-sized vessels, a reasonable time would have been necessary to prepare for a single firing. But it is likely that many one-man firms were operating in which all the processes would have been carried out consecutively.

The commonest type of Romano-British pottery kiln consisted of three parts. The furnace chamber was dug below ground level and, for obvious reasons of drainage, was usually constructed on a sand or gravel subsoil. The wall of the pit, so dug, was then lined with a thick layer of clay. The furnace chamber communicated with the stokehole area, situated on the same level below ground, through a flue arch, which likewise had to be constructed of stone or clay. The oven, in which the pots were placed for firing, was separated from the furnace chamber by means of a floor supported in one of several ways. In some kilns, a central or off-centre pedestal supported prefabricated fire-bars, which, in turn, carried a perforated clay floor. In others it is clear that the clay floor was carried temporarily by timber framing, and burnt away during a preliminary firing, during which the clay hardened in its place.

Once the floor was made the prepared pots could be stacked upon it and then covered with a bee-hive shaped arrangement of withies over which a clay and straw, or grass, mixture was plastered, leaving a vent at the top. Firing could then commence and might have lasted twenty-four hours or more, according to the size of the kiln, after which it was allowed to cool before the pots were extracted. If red or brown pottery was the desired end product, excess oxygen was allowed at all times, but, if black or grey wares were required, the kiln had to be effectively sealed in the later stages to prevent the admission of oxygen, or, if it accidentally entered, to be consumed by a surplus of fuel.

It is becoming increasingly clear, however, in the light of recent discoveries, that many kilns were built wholly above ground, using perhaps blocks of turf for the walls and prefabricated fire-bars to support the floors, with the top of the oven sealed by a clay lid. Less effort would certainly have been involved in their construction, but, being even less permanent structures, they unfortunately leave little evidence for their presence.

One other type of kiln, common in the Surrey area, is worth mentioning. In this, the stokehole, firing chamber, oven and flue are all situated at the same level below ground. It is not likely, however, to have been more technically advanced, and, indeed, may have suffered disadvantages.

At best all the kilns so far described would have been only semi-permanent, being used for perhaps some half a dozen firings before they were replaced by new structures. That their life was short is demonstrated by a Nene Valley kiln, where the floor had partly collapsed during the last firing, so spoiling a number of vessels.

The principal centres of production were many and altered with the times. At first, the industry seems to have been largely in the hands of small producers, manufacturing primarily for local markets, but from the late first century onwards, mergers seem to have led to an increasing concentration of production in the hands of larger firms, whose products ranged much more widely. The local man never entirely disappeared, however, and, in east Yorkshire for instance, it is possible to find pottery in third- and fourth-century contexts which owes more to continuing, handmade, Iron Age traditions than to the Romano-British industry.

In considering production centres, it is also possible to look at marketing patterns, although the subject is too large to be considered here comprehensively, and examples will be taken at random. One of the most informative groups of vessels for such an examination is the stamped mortaria of the first and second centuries. Many were made at potteries between London and Verulamium, at Hartshill, near Nuneaton and nearby Mancetter; others at Lincoln, Doncaster and Corbridge to name but a selection of sites. One particular manufacturer, Sarrus, was first producing at Hartshill during the middle of the second century. His markets lay mainly in northern military sites up to and including the Antonine Wall, and it is likely that he had obtained an army supply contract. Later, however, he moved to Doncaster, probably to be nearer his markets and to cut down on transport costs, since the new site had better access to navigable rivers and the east coast sea-routes.

During the first and early second centuries, as already noted above (p. 207), some military detachments manufactured their own pottery. An abrupt change can, however, be discerned about AD 120, when a new, centralized source of supply replaced the earlier, localized system. The lucky firms to win these valuable contracts seem to have been situated in the Isle of Purbeck, Dorset, or possibly Somerset, and they produced a number of standardized bowls, jars and dishes in a not unattractive, black-burnished fabric. It is not, perhaps, taking the evidence too far to suggest that from AD 120, the legions in Britain, who until then had been the main producers of military pottery, were expected to be more than fully extended in building the new frontier. It is probable, therefore, that they were divested of a purely peripheral activity and the burgeoning British industry given the task of providing the army with pottery. It must have been a decision made at the highest level, since both the Welsh and northern garrisons were henceforth supplied with this ware until the middle of the century, while little of the production reached civilian markets in the south-east.

Some of the most interesting marketing patterns appear in the fourth century, a time which, moreover, saw the concentration of the industry at even fewer centres, such as the Nene Valley, the New Forest, the Upper Thames Valley and east Yorkshire, notably at Crambeck, Castle Howard. Nene Valley pottery, for instance, is seldom found in the south-west or west of Britain, areas normally dominated by the New Forest and Thames Valley industries. There is some degree of overlap between the two latter industries, but it varies according to the type of the vessel. In this respect there was obvious competition between the centres. Also, whereas New Forest pottery is hardly ever found north of the Thames, Oxford wares occasionally travelled into areas dominated by the Nene Valley industry and even reached Brough-on-Humber. The most remarkabe concentration of production came in the north in the last decades of the fourth century. There is hardly a site occupied then, north of a line from the Humber to the Mersey, which did not receive Crambeck ware in its supplies. Yet the cut-off line is remarkably sharp, and although a piece has been found at Lincoln, it rarely travels further south. Whether or not this was a return to official manufacture is not known, but the Crambeck potters, supplying both military and civilian sites, must have been successful beyond all their expectations. Yet, despite their extensive range of vessels and the quantities produced, there was still room for Nene Valley pots to be marketed in considerable numbers in the northern areas.

The retail trade in pottery is indicated by the two burnt Colchester shops which occupied sites on one of the main streets, and possibly by a nearby warehouse, stocked with flagons and mortaria.

An itinerant merchant is known to have lost his stock of Gaulish samian bowls and Mancetter mortaria in the forum fire at Wroxeter.

The manufacture of pottery was largely in the hands of private firms and individuals, whereas the production of brick and tile seems to have been more highly organized and included public utilities. Brickworks run by the imperial procurator near London and Silchester have already been mentioned (p. 168), while the municipal works of Gloucester are well known from the number of products stamped RPG (*Rei Publicae Glevensium*). Other companies such as the *Arveri*, or those which stamped IVC DIGNI or TPF on their products also existed in much the same area.

Tile kilns are not as commonly found as pottery kilns, probably because the products were more often fired in large clamps above ground. But a tile kiln near Canterbury, incidentally associated with pottery kilns, was constructed with a long, narrow firing chamber in which the tiles were stacked. All too little is unfortunately known about the processes of manufacture, although we might imagine that considerable cleared and levelled spaces must have been required for moulding the pieces and for laying them out to dry under cover from both sun and rain. The repertoire included the large roof tiles with upturned flanges, possibly moulded, but with the rebated end, intended for interlocking with the next tile on the roof, cut out by means of a knife; curved and tapered tiles for capping the abutted flanges, probably made on some type of wooden or stone former; curved and slotted ridge tiles, made similarly; roughly triangular tiles, often decorated, for fixing to the ends of the roof ribs at the level of the eaves; hollow rectangular flue-tiles; tubular water-pipes and a variety of large and small floor tiles and wall bricks, the size depending on their intended use. The latter were probably moulded by hand and trimmed by knife to the required shape.

When production was sufficient for a firing, the items were apparently stacked loosely on the ground until a sufficient pile had accumulated, which was then covered with a thick dome of clay and grass, or straw, apertures being left at ground level for the fires, and vents in the roof. An interesting item relating to the life of one brickmaker was found in London. It was a floor tile on which, while the clay was still plastic, its maker had recorded a message for his master, to the effect that a fellow worker, Austalis, had been absenting himself without leave for the last thirteen days.

The other extractive industries carried on at source were quarrying of different kinds, including coal, and salt production.

Salt was produced, as already indicated (see Chapter 3), by the evaporation of sea water or brine from mineral springs, a process practised on many coastal sites round the Wash, and the Thames and Severn estuaries. The process requires careful control in order to remove salts other than sodium chloride, since their presence renders the final product deliquescent and also unsuitable for tanning. Evaporation seems to have been carried out in large clay pans set over fires, the impurities fortunately crystallizing out before the sodium chloride. Salt was an important item in the Roman economy, being required for preserving meat, fish and skins and as a condiment. In the Diocletian edict of prices, the value was fixed at the same as wheat, so that it was comparatively expensive.

Outcropping seams of coal were quarried in a number of places in Somerset, south Wales, Nottinghamshire, Yorkshire, Lancashire and Northumberland. It was used on many military sites, both for heating and for industrial purposes, and sizeable quantities have sometimes been found, such as the deposit in the guard-chamber of the east gate at Housesteads, which seems to have been converted to a coal-bunker at a late date. It was also used in the Corbridge armaments depot.

Coal also appears on civilian sites, at considerable distances from the fields, where it was used for heating hypocausts and baths, and for sundry industrial purposes. There is an extensive distribution around the Fens, and it may possibly have been used for the extraction of salt. It was also used on the altar of the temple of Sulis and Minerva at Bath, a fact recorded by a contemporary writer, Solinus.

Other forms of quarrying covered the extraction of stone, chalk, clay, gravel and sand, mostly for building work, of which something has already been said in considering military duties (p. 202). But stone quarries are known just outside the town at Cirencester, while a chalk-pit was discovered during modern working near Canterbury. Stone from the better class quarries travelled long distances, despite its heavy and bulky nature. Indeed there must be many more quarries to be found, since the total amount of stone used in civilian building construction was considerable. Reference (p. 202) was made earlier to the walls of towns, but it is worth recording that Cirencester alone required some 84,000 cu m of masonry for its fortifications, while every time the streets were resurfaced, which was not infrequent, about 11,000 cu m of gravel or stone rubble were needed. Indeed the total aggregate which ultimately went into the

streets of the town was of the order of 155,000 cu m, representing a not inconsiderable quarry hole, 100 m by 50 m and 30 m deep (fig. 99). Considered in terms of labour, also, a very big task.

Two quarried stones are of especial interest: Kimmeridge shale and Whitby jet. The former was used extensively for furniture, and some fine, carved table-legs have been found at a number of places, such as Dorchester, Verulamium and Silchester. It was also used, as with Whitby jet, for trinkets. Bangles, for instance, were turned and cut on lathes and the central discs, removed during the manufacturing process, are not uncommonly found in areas round Kimmeridge.

The quarrying of building materials leads us logically to the construction industry, which, as today, covered a wide field of craftsmen and technicians, ranging from surveyors to joiners, masons, plasterers, painters and floor-layers. There is some evidence for all of them in the civilian industry of Roman Britain. Surveyors'

Fig. 99. Street running westwards from Cirencester towards the amphitheatre, showing the latest, very rutted and pot-holed surface, which was never repaired. Before this, repairs would have been made by spreading and compacting a new layer of aggregate. Such repairs would have been comparatively frequent, so leading to an inexorable rise in street levels in the town (*Cirencester Excavation Committee*).

work is difficult to identify, since it is essentially ephemeral, the quality of the buildings alone being the surviving guide to their competence. But the surveyors laying out the apse for the Cirencester basilica had employed special marked stones as base points, from which the curve could have been computed by bisecting chords. At Verulamium, also, a wall left unfinished had been marked out by a line secured to a square peg, a feature presumably more normally obliterated by the masonry of the completed work.

Wherever possible local materials were used in most domestic construction. Consequently the appearance of Romano-British towns would, as today, have altered according to the part of the countryside in which they were situated. In the south-east, where good building stone was hard to come by, a predominance of brick, flint and tile occurred, with occasional public buildings clad in greenish-grey Kentish rag-stone. In the Cotswolds, Northamptonshire and Lincolnshire, oolites were extensively employed, giving the characteristic honey colour, or darker brown, to the buildings' external appearance. Sandstones and gritstones further north would again have changed the visual aspect; some half-timbering or plastered cob walls could be expected anywhere.

Some of the more specialized craftsmen probably maintained permanent workshops, but we can envisage most building work actually being carried out on the site, starting, of course, with the digging of foundation trenches. The material so derived, which, in the case of a large building could be considerable, was normally used to level the site. Lime would have to be burnt and slaked, clay puddled, mortar and plaster mixed, stone cut and finished. At Verulamium, a plaster-mixing pit had been lined first with a wickerwork basket, while plank and joist impressions, on the under surface of a concrete floor in the Cirencester basilica, may indicate a lost mortarboard sealed beneath the floor. At Fishbourne the masons' yard, where stone for fine wall and floor surfaces was prepared, was identified beneath the palace buildings. Not only were there many waste pieces, but also quantities of silver sand, indicating the way in which the slabs were cut. A metal wire or thin bar was strung horizontally between two pivoted, vertical iron bars. The wire was then swung back and forth over the surface of the stone, on which wet silver sand had been placed, so in time cutting through it. Similar waste material, related to the Temple of Claudius at Colchester, was also found. A house at Cirencester had a neat stack of sandstone roofing slates (fig. 69) set upright against an external wall and ready for repairs.

Of the building workers themselves we know very little. A sculptor, Sulinus, set up altars at both Cirencester and Bath, and may have had a workshop in the former town. Certainly, a group of sculpture found there might be attributed to him, while other pieces from the same town indicate that he was not the only sculptor in the field, the standard of execution sometimes being remarkably high. Priscus, a native of Gaul, was a mason employed at Bath; his presence indicates that craftsmen from other provinces were attracted by, or imported to, work in Britain, and there must also have been a monumental mason at South Shields who was familiar with eastern art styles, for an elaborately carved tombstone was set up there to Regina, British wife of a native of Palmyra (Syria), called Barates. In an altogether more specialized class was a man at Bath who carved semi-precious gemstones with mythological and religious scenes for setting in signet rings.

It seems that mosaicists also came to Britain from time to time as work was required, and that by the fourth century, if not before, provincial workshops had been set up in a number of places. Of these, four have so far been identified at Cirencester, Dorchester, Water Newton and possibly Brough-on-Humber, but they are not necessarily all contemporary; indeed, there is sound evidence to suggest that the Cirencester firm had gone out of business before the Dorchester workshop was set up, while a fifth firm, in the Colchester–Verulamium region, is suspected of operating in the second century.

The first of the fourth-century firms to start work was that at Cirencester, and they developed a highly characteristic design incorporating Orpheus with his animals, birds and trees, which was not only used in Cirencester itself but also in several villas in the neighbourhood, such as Woodchester (fig. 60b). Interestingly also, a similarly patterned pavement, clearly originating from the same designer, is known from the imperial capital at Trier in Germany, suggesting perhaps that the master-craftsman had himself emigrated. The Brough-on-Humber firm seems to echo some of the Cirencester patterns, if in slightly cruder forms, and this perhaps points to an employee of the Cirencester workshop setting up on his own in another part of the country after the firm had ceased to trade. Some fifty mosaics have now been attributed to the Cirencester factory, and something approaching saturation of the area with its products must have been reached, a state of affairs only to be resolved by movement elsewhere.

It is sometimes possible to work out the manner in which mosaics were laid by observing the guidelines that were often inscribed on the underlying concrete surface. It is also possible that some of the more intricate panels were made up in the workshop and laid in a piece, with the intervening areas being filled in on the spot by standard geometric and floral patterns or plain tessellation. The four seasons mosaic in Cirencester is perhaps the best example of what could happen when an apprentice, or less skilled craftsman, was given the opportunity to try his hand at figure work. Summer and Autumn are set in braided roundels and are well up to standard; Spring is not and was clearly produced by a junior member of the firm.

In a number of places, the debris of mosaic floor layers has been identified, usually in the form of rough cut tesserae, which could be either chopped or sawn. A particular type of fine-grained oolite, found not far from Cirencester, breaks naturally into small, rough cubes, and was exploited. Other materials used were brick – both yellow and red – sandstones, ironstones, slates, and even coloured glass and chips of samian, according to the colours required in the pattern. Considerable quantities were found in the forum at Cirencester and also in another house near the town walls. At the villa at Rudston, noted for its primitive mosaic of Venus, heaps of tesserae of different sizes and colours were found in an outbuilding.

Plasterers were also highly skilled, and the white lime finish they produced on wall surfaces was fine enough to have paint applied directly to it. If the colour was applied when the surface was still wet, the process was called fresco and the pigment became bonded more firmly with the lime. Further colours could then be painted on, using white of egg, or milk, as size, a process known as tempera. Plasterers were also called upon occasionally to execute decorative stucco work, examples coming from the Fishbourne and London palaces and from the villa at Gorhambury, near Verulamium, where human figures seem to have been part of the design.

The wall-painters of Britain must have relied to a great extent on pattern books for their designs, as did their colleagues, the mosaic floor-layers, although many of the themes were freely adopted to suit individual tastes or skills. The laying-out lines can sometimes be detected on the plaster surfaces, and, although the standard of execution was normally quite high, frequent faults in perspective can be seen, of a type that so often occur in classical wall-paintings. The pigments employed were of mineral origin, some, such as bright blue, being prepared artificially from a copper frit. Occasionally, small lumps of pigment are found on excavation, together with the flat stone palettes used for grinding them to a fine powder.

Other technical processes, which would have required permanent premises, were those connected with tanning and cloth manufacture. Unfortunately no civilian tanneries have been positively identified in Britain although there are some suggestive details. A deep pit in a timber-framed building at Alcester may have been so used, while a dump of ox jaws beneath a later building at Silchester could represent the refuse dump of another factory, since it was customary to leave the heads on the skins, for identification, but to remove the jaws before steeping. A similar dump of cows' heads lying on the floor of a derelict house in Leicester might similarly be interpreted, although another possibility is a horn factory.

Shoemakers' or leatherworkers' shops are equally difficult to identify, although a simple rectangular building, lying between the Bath Gate and the amphitheatre at Cirencester, had many hobnails lying about the floor and may represent a boot and shoe factory. As in the military areas, leather is not an uncommon find from waterlogged deposits on civilian sites, but mainly turns up in rubbish deposits and not in the relevant shops. Nevertheless there is ample evidence to illustrate the leatherworkers' skills both in the boot and shoe trade and in the manufacture of other products. The former were normally made with openwork uppers of calfskin or other supple leather and were sometimes ornamented with embossed patterns; they laced up round the ankles. The soles were usually made of multiple layers of oxhide, sometimes giving a thickness of up to 6 mm, and waterproofed with a mixture of iron salts and soot. If hobnails were used, they were occasionally applied in the form of a pattern. Leather was used for garments, and the bikini pants from a well in London are a good example. It was also the covering for many pieces of upholstery and a fragment of cushion, once embossed in gold, came from London.

The textile industries involved a number of different processes, each of which probably had its own practitioners: spinning, weaving, fulling, dyeing. The first two operations seem mainly to have been carried on as a home industry, with spindle-whorls, distaffs and sometimes loom-weights from vertical looms being found on domestic sites; but at least one government clothing factory is known to have been situated in Britain, according to the Notitia Dignitatum, and is thought to have been at Winchester. Fulling and dyeing, however, required more specialized equipment, but, as with tanning, it is almost impossible correctly to interpret the pits, troughs, tanks and ovens which must have been used, in the absence of the materials themselves. Consequently, although a dyer's shop is suggested at Silchester, and, periodically, fulleries have been claimed to exist in certain villas, such as Darenth, on the evidence of small concrete-lined tanks, nothing can be proved, since the organic materials associated with the processes have, in every case, failed to survive.

The process of fulling, which was used to remove grease from new woollen cloth, involved its treatment with stale urine, so saponifying the fat and enabling it to be washed out. Fullers, therefore, usually operated the jars placed at street corners for the convenience of passers-by and, moreover, from the time of Vespasian, paid a tax for the privilege. Since the process also required large quantities of water, their workshops were usually placed close to an aqueduct, so that they could make use of the surplus flow. After the cloth had been treated and washed, it was dried and roughened with teazles, then bleached with sulphur fumes and finally clipped to give an even nap. The huge cropping-shears from Great Chesterford, 1.34 m long, must have come from a fuller's workshop. Since much the same process removed dirt from soiled clothing, fullers also acted as launderers.

Dyers made use of various vegetable and animal pigments, and as far as we know, most specialized in only one colour. Some of the plants needed have already been mentioned (p. 157), and it is likely that quite large quantities had to be grown or collected to satisfy requirements. Madder, wild lotus, meadow saffron, and dyers' bugloss among many others were all used.

Woollen cloth must have been by far the commonest in circulation, although there is evidence for the use of linen for shrouds at York and for containing cremated ashes at Caerleon, and flax may well have been grown in Britain, despite the fact that Spain was the chief supplier.

Agricultural and horticultural workers must also be included among those engaged in the productive industries, although much of the work which they did has already been detailed in Chapter 4. As today, their occupation will have depended on the seasons; ploughing and seeding, along with herding, will have alternated with hedging and ditching, wood cutting, reaping, threshing and parching grain, tree pruning, or wool clipping according to the time of year and to the nature of the farm on which they worked. Herdsmen and shepherds, for instance, probably lived with their animals on the hills during the summer grazing period, only returning to the farm in winter.

From the productive industries we can turn to the so-called service trades, remembering that many manufacturers also repaired goods. Among these trades, also, must be included such people as municipal and provincial slaves. We know of one of the latter at London, although his duties are obscure. The former, however, will have been responsible, under the appropriate officers, for maintaining public utilities, such as the aqueduct, and for cleaning out sewers and probably roadside ditches; the great sewers at Lincoln were equipped with manholes for this purpose. They probably also ran the public baths, stoking the boilers, clearing the flues and hypocausts, and cleaning out the accumulated scum in the baths themselves. Sweeping up litter in the markets would have been another task, during which they may have been able to enrich themselves by picking up lost coins, and the cleansing of the forum at Cirencester continued long after the floor had worn away. Although we have no evidence for individuals among such people in Britain, as a class they must have existed, since these jobs were presumably done by someone.

But by far the biggest group of service trades will have been the suppliers of food and drink. Ale must have been brewed in considerable quantities, although, as with all trades dealing in organic materials, the evidence is very slight. Who is to say, now, what a large oven, capable of supporting a vat of considerable size, was used for in the absence of more specific information? It could have been for baking, brewing, or dyeing, or steeping flax, or cooking, but Gallic beer is listed in Diocletian's edict and was probably not dissimilar to the British product.

Wine was imported in quantity and must have been available in most towns. A wine shop has been inferred on a corner site near the forum at Verulamium from the number of broken flagons and amphoras which it contained. After the emperor Probus relaxed the laws relating to the growing of grapes in the provinces during the third century, vines were grown and wine made in Britain. However, the increasingly wetter climate of the third and fourth centuries will not have favoured it.

Fruit and vegetables must have been marketed in large amounts and grape pips, fig seeds and the stones of various fruits indicate what was available, perhaps, in the case of imported fruits, in the dried state. Vegetables used in Britain have been mentioned elsewhere (see Chapter 4).

Butcher's shops, fortunately, leave better evidence in the form of bones, cut and sawn during the preparation of carcasses. At

Cirencester, two pits close to the market, filled with such bones, imply the presence of butchers, and it is possible that part was used as a meat market. In the row of shops opposite, almost every one had an oven, perhaps suggesting that they were providing cooked meats. Another butcher's shop, or sausage factory, has been suggested at Verulamium, not far from the London Gate. The by-products of these shops, chiefly bones, were not wasted and bone implements of many types, ranging from hairpins to inlays for wooden boxes, were commonly used. Shops dealing with these materials have been found at Catterick and Wroxeter, while an elaborate burial, possibly of a child from Colchester contained parts of a funerary couch covered with heavily-ornamented bone inlays.

Fish shops, especially those selling oysters or other shellfish, can likewise be more readily identified, in particular where the product was consumed on the premises, and a merchant appears to have occupied one of the shops leased out by the town in the forum at Caerwent, where numerous oyster shells were found. Oysters, judging from the ubiquity of their shells on almost all sites, must have been one of the commonest items of diet.

Flour was normally ground in the home for immediate use, on a pair of hand millstones. But commercial bakeries also existed, where the bakers probably ground their flour on a larger scale. Big hour-glass shaped millstones, driven by donkeys, have been found at London and Canterbury, and military, water-driven mills have been identified on Hadrian's Wall. Other mechanically-powered mills existed at Lincoln, Great Chesterford and Wanborough, but we cannot be sure that flour was the product. An iron slice for removing loaves from the oven has come from Verulamium and a stamp for impressing a pattern on a cake, or loaf of bread, was discovered at Silchester, but, since the design shows a religious scene, it may have been used for a special occasion.

Moneylenders and bankers also figured among the population, and a room in the forum at Silchester, where many coins were found, has been suggested as the office of one of them. Moneylending operations, however, briefly figured in the early years of the Roman period, when some senators were said to have advanced large sums to Britons struggling with the expenses of romanization.

There must also have been various inns and restaurants, separate from those provided for imperial officials, but again, in the absence of detailed evidence, they are hard to identify and even more difficult to distinguish from shops only selling food.

The transport industry was divided between road, river and sea-going traffic. Harness fittings from draught animals and also metal parts of carts and wagons illustrate the first category. Horses, mules and donkeys undoubtedly drew light vehicles, used primarily for passengers, and examples can be seen depicted on masonry reliefs in Gaul and the Rhineland. Horses also provided the motive power for larger wagons in many cases, although oxen may also have been employed. If British vehicles were anything like those used in Germany and Gaul, there was probably a basic, four-wheeled wagon with low sides, drawn by three or four beasts, in addition to a much wider variety of two- and four-wheeled carts, gigs and chaises. Packhorses would have provided extra carrying capacity.

The rivers of Britain were no doubt plied by numerous barges, usually with flat bottoms. In the almost complete absence of native evidence, it is again possible to look at examples from across the North Sea, where, in the Netherlands, barges of this type are known from the Roman period. Some were as much as 35–40 m long, but medium-sized craft of about 20 m would have been more suited to British rivers. In most cases these boats were probably drawn by animal or human power along the banks, and evidence for mast-steps in some of the surviving examples should not necessarily be taken to mean the existence of sails, since towing-masts are known to have been common features. By so raising the towing rope, bankside obstructions and other vessels could be more easily cleared.

Sea-going vessels are, however, known from Britain. A small, carvel-built ship, found beneath County Hall, London, can be dated to the later third century. The method of construction shows that the builder was acquainted with Mediterranean types of vessels, although the ship can only have been built in northern Europe. Another sea-going craft found at Blackfriars, London, sank, presumably in dock, while about to unload a cargo of building stone from Kent.

Harbours and docks are known in many places, one of the most impressive being the quay which flanked the waterfront of London on the north bank of the Thames. In fact, there was a succession of quays brought about by the fall in sea level during the first half of the Roman occupation, in consequence of which the waterfront was gradually pushed forward, altogether by about 40 m. The earliest, built in the late first century, consisted of a massive box-framed, timber structure backed by open-fronted warehouses, which must within a short time have been left high and dry by the retreating tide. Two successive quays of slighter construction and each on different lines replaced it in the following years, the latest dating to the middle of the third century. An ancillary to any harbour is a lighthouse, and at Dover there still stands on the Castle Cliff most of the tower (fig. 100) of one of a pair which once marked the entrance to the harbour below between the two bluffs of the cliff. But Dover was more probably a naval base, and it is not known if civilian ports in Britain were similarly equipped. Ancillary also to any dock were the derricks and cranes used for lifting heavy cargoes, and a large stone foundation on a quay just outside the legionary fortress at York has been interpreted as the base for a crane. A baling hook of Roman date from London, in addition, reminds us of the dockers who unloaded the ships, and who on several occasions carelessly dropped goods overboard including crates of samian pottery and another of cucumbers.

Fig. 100. The Roman lighthouse, or pharos, on the east cliff beside Dover Castle. Another is known to have matched it on the west cliff. A vessel approaching at night would therefore have navigated between the lights to reach harbour safely. The upper part of the masonry is medieval.

We may also look with profit at the domestic duties of housewives, and their servants and slaves, if they were fortunate enough to possess them, since the duties of cleaning and cooking will then have passed to them. Floors must have been swept, scrubbed and even polished, and one mosaic in a house at Dorchester had limber-holes left in the walls at floor level to allow washing water to escape. Lamps had to be cleaned and filled and wicks provided; fuel had to be supplied for braziers or hypocausts and the fires had to be stoked. Shale furniture must also have been kept polished with oils or waxes, since it is liable to split and flake unless this is done. Wooden furniture was also subject to attacks by wood-boring beetles, and fleas, bedbugs and probably clothes moths had to be combatted; a bedbug has been found at Alcester, fleas at York, while a carbonized wooden object attacked by furniture beetle comes from Brough-on-Humber.

Cooking was carried out mainly on gridirons, such as that from Silchester, or on tripods over open fires, although various types of closed oven are also indicated. Most of the utensils were of pottery, but in the richer households, bronze and iron pots, frying pans or skillets were additionally used. Kitchen knives, ladles and flesh-hooks, two or three pronged hooks for pulling boiling meat away from the bone, are comparatively common finds. The wide variety of food available has already been discussed above and in many cases may have been supplemented by hunting. The food itself, if we are to judge by contemporary authors, contained many items where the combination of flavours and textures would seem strange to most modern palates; sweet-and-sour dishes appear to have been great favourites.

While all these household duties were being undertaken, the lady of the house, if she was not herself engaged, was able to spend hours over her toilette, helped probably by a slave girl. Personal trinkets, depilatory tweezers, perfume flasks, mirrors and combs have all been found in Britain, illustrating this side of daily life, and a head of hair surviving from a York burial shows not only the careful braiding which was kept in place with jet pins, but also the artificial reddish tint which had been applied. Neither must we forget that the master of the house, in the days before Hadrian when beards once more became fashionable, had to be shaved with fine bronze or iron razors and his hair, and later, beard trimmed with small shears. It is not unlikely, also, that men of fashion had their hair waved and set, following the manner of Nero, as is so obvious from representations on his coins.

In these days of job comparability and inflation-related wages, it is informative to look back to another occasion when an attempt was made to regulate not only wages but also prices: Diocletian's Edict of maximum prices, published early in AD 301, by which he sought to fix ceilings on prices and wages throughout the empire. The attempt was a failure and, despite invoking the death sentence for breach of the code, had ultimately to be repealed, mainly due to the difficulty of enforcement. But at least the lists provide some comparative values.

The basic agricultural wage for a day labourer was 25 denarii, but he also received the fringe benefit of food. Four days' wages, therefore, were required to buy 9 litres of wheat, if it was being sold at the maximum price. A shepherd received marginally less, but a carpenter and baker twice as much. Shipwrights earned the same as a carpenter if aboard an inland vessel, but slightly more if sea-going. A barber could charge 2 denarii per customer, but since shaving was a lengthy process, he would be hard put to make a fortune. This compares with the charge of 6 denarii per animal which a veterinary surgeon could make for hoof trimming. Teachers were graded according to the level of tuition, an elementary teacher being allowed to charge up to 50 denarii per boy per month, so requiring some fourteen pupils to equal the income of an agricultural labourer, whereas a teacher of rhetoric could charge five times as much; a jurist pleading in court could, by contrast, command a fee four times as much again. A tailor could charge up to 60 denarii for a first-quality cloak, but only 20 for a pair of breeches, and this seems to compare unfavourably with the cobbler's price of 120 denarii for a pair of farmworker's boots (hobnails extra). From this it can be seen that the farmworker had to labour for five days before he could buy a pair of boots. Somewhat surprisingly also, a pair of patrician's shoes cost only 150 denarii.

The figures must, of course, be viewed with some caution, since it is possible that the charges actually made were less than the maximum. But, if it is also remembered that business opposition was largely responsible for the edict's repeal, it is likely that the figures given were more often than not being exceeded. Moreover, all but one of the inscriptions which carry information on the edict come from the eastern empire, and we cannot know how the figures applied to the west, although there was probably a close similarity. Nevertheless, they allow us to put the value of work in perspective, and equate them approximately to the cost of living.

CHAPTER 7

Superstitions and Beliefs

Men and women have always been superstitious creatures. The more they are at odds with their environment and the less control they feel they have over it, the greater their belief in unseen powers, and it is when these basic superstitions are channelled into recognizable forms that they become religious convictions.

In antiquity, their fears and hopes were expressed in a variety of ways. An altar erected in Roman Britain to the *Genius Loci* (fig. 101) – the spirit of the place – simply means that on some occasion a person coming home one night, slightly drunk from the pub, was frightened out of his wits by a barn owl or other natural phenomenon; consequently the place attracted a reputation for being haunted and subsequently an altar or altars were erected to placate the ghost, since it was recognized that the spirit of a dead person was helpful if propitiated, but spitefully destructive if neglected, and could, in extreme cases, even take possession of the living. Similarly, a promise made for the erection of an altar to a favourite deity might inspire a hope for a successful journey or business venture. There was therefore a strong contractual element in most early religions.

British religion before the arrival of the Romans was highly fragmented, consisting of little more than a collection of local superstitions, which might, though different in place or name, bear strong resemblances to one another according to their attributions. However, some of the more advanced Iron Age tribes appear to have had patron deities who watched over the welfare of the people, their crops and animals. The only indication of a more truly corporate religion was that provided by the Druids, who, from their centre in Anglesey, held some sway over almost all the tribes in the midlands and south-east. They were implacably anti-Roman in outlook, having, by their political interference in Gaul, already been outlawed by the edicts of several emperors. Consequently, we may imagine that the hard core of Druidism fled to Britain as refugees and provided a stiffening to resistance in AD 43.

Roman attitudes to the Druids were governed by two main factors: apparent dislike of the Druids' human sacrifices and disapproval of their involvement in political and educational affairs. We may indeed wonder about the relative importance of these two reasons, since some modern writers tend to favour the first as the real cause for the Roman hounding of the Druids. It might be thought surprising, in view of the numerous instances we are given of Roman attitudes towards 'blood' sports of a human kind, that they would have any such objections; they were not a noticeably queasy race. Neither must we forget that an aggressor will often invent purely cultural reasons to excuse his actions against the aggressed. Even now, religious bigotry is still one of the commonest forms of pretext for making unprovoked attacks in order to achieve seemingly desirable political objectives. We can also remember the unmentionable acts attributed by certain pagan writers to early Christians in Rome, and so accept that the Romans' expressed dislike of Druidic sacrificial practices was the excuse, partly to salve the Roman conscience, partly for external consumption, for the violent suppression of a sect which acted as a focus for disloyalty and a foment for disobedience. This view is even more acceptable, if the general Roman tolerance towards foreign religions is compared with it. The Romans themselves were just as superstitious as other people in the ancient world, and they were far too cautious to risk running foul of nameless deities in remote areas; so cautious, indeed, that a specific temple, the Pantheon, was erected in Rome, just in case some such nameless deity had been left out of the official reckoning. Only if religious practices became mixed with politics did the state intervene, and, although disgust might from time to time be expressed about the rites of some of the more esoteric cults, little action was taken against them, providing they stayed within the law. But Druidism and Christianity, and on occasion Judaism, owing to their political involvements, were seen as enemies of the state and treated accordingly. A Roman, accused of religious intolerance in such a context, would have roundly protested his innocence, claiming the purely civil nature of the crime of the early Christians, the refusal to take the oath of loyalty to the emperor.

Fig. 101. Altar to a *genius loci* from Cirencester. The inscription above the crowned and draped figure reads: 'to the holy Genius of this place' (*Corinium Museum*).

Apart from Druidism, the areas of Britain in the south-east which were subjected to Belgic influence before the conquest were probably affected by other superstitious beliefs. It may be that the concept of a central tribal deity then arose, and there is certainly a marked similarity between certain classes of temple in these parts of Roman Britain and those in parts of north-west Gaul. Indeed, the prototype for these temples in Britain has been claimed to lie in the even earlier Iron Age, at Heathrow, and was excavated when London Airport was constructed.

Tribal intercourse may also have led indirectly to the establishment of other religious centres, albeit probably of a more local nature. It is possible to point to many sites which appear to coincide with tribal boundaries and which, during the Roman period, developed as combined religious and trade centres, so probably continuing earlier usage. There took place fairs and markets, as the late Sir Ian Richmond so admirably described them: ' . . . associated with ancient sanctuaries whose deity hallowed the transaction and gave to the market or fairground a sacred peace which folk no less superstitious than quarrelsome would not violate by quarrels and brawls'. If commercial enterprise was to continue in times of inter-tribal unrest, such centres would have been essential.

Apart therefore from the suppression of Druidism, the religious beliefs of the British were at first untouched by the Roman invasion. But, even though the empire was polytheistic in outlook, the cult of the imperial house had been grafted on to the basic cults of the classical world, ostensibly to act as a unifying force in an otherwise religiously heterogeneous community. Consequently, one of the first acts of the new government in Britain was to introduce the imperial cult. As far as is known, this first took the form of an altar, a massive temple and a provincial centre at Colchester (figs. 102–3). Much has been written about the original dedication of the temple, since emperors were not normally deified until after death, and Claudius is known to have discouraged an attempt in Egypt to proclaim him a god; most other emperors acted likewise. So that it would have been unusual, not to say bad form, for the Colchester temple to have been dedicated to Claudius in his lifetime. There are reasons, however, for not so believing, and it is now considered more likely that the temple itself was not completed until after Claudius' death. That being so, the dedication to *Divus Claudius* would have been perfectly correct.

Fig. 102. Model of the Temple of Claudius at Colchester. In front at the centre stands the main altar, flanked, according to Tacitus, by Statues of Victory on pedestals. If compared with the plan (fig. 103) it can be seen that they are not in the right position (*Colchester and Essex Museum*).

Although the temple was destroyed in the Boudiccan rebellion, it must have been rebuilt, since we cannot envisage the ruins being left as a lasting monument to Boudicca. The temple was large and imposing, so much so that it excited interest even in Rome, and was surrounded by a colonnaded court. It was constructed in the best classical manner on an elevated podium and with an octastyle portico approached by a flight of steps. In front of the steps in the courtyard was the main sacrificial altar, surrounded by a screen and flanked by statues. Here would have been conducted all public ceremonies, since the temple itself was simply the repository for the cult statue of Claudius, probably well above life size.

In the provinces the imperial cult was served by a council elected, or appointed, by the native peoples, and in Gaul and Britain it represented the tribal groups or civitates. This provincial council nominated annually the chief priest, whose task it was to reside in

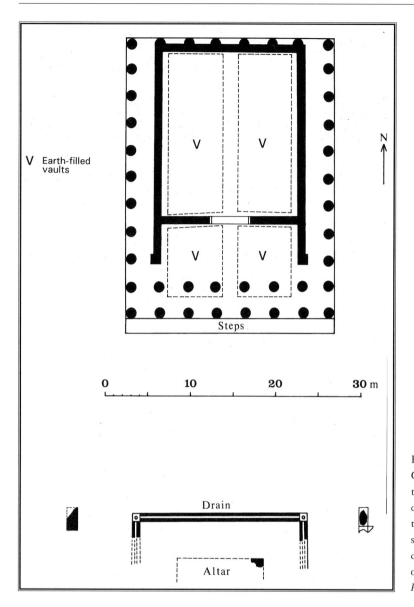

V Earth-filled
   vaults

Fig. 103. Plan of the Temple of Claudius at Colchester. Here the altar and statues are correctly placed with respect to the Temple. The altar was surrounded on three sides by a drain and possibly an ornamental screen (*after R. Niblett*).

the cult centre and arrange all ceremonies and festivities connected with it. The cost was considerable and had to be met by the office-holders, so it is not surprising that Tacitus mentions various complaints in the period before the Boudiccan rebellion, when civitates were few and the costs therefore fell across only a narrow sector of the British people. But the provincial council also had the power to communicate directly with the emperor and to some extent, therefore, represented a safeguard against an over-zealous governor or procurator, even if that power was seldom used.

There seem to have been buildings in Colchester associated with the temple, and therefore presumably acting as the administrative headquarters of the provincial council, but it has often been claimed that the cult centre was transferred to London by the end of the first century, by which time London had also become the administrative capital of the province. A fragmentary inscription from London, now lost, invokes the *numen*, or spiritual power of an emperor, on behalf of the province of Britain. Even if such an inscription had come from a temple, it is not, in itself, sufficient evidence to show that the principal temple of the cult was then in London. Indeed, it would be surprising, cult centre or not, if there were no dedications to the emperors by the province in its capital. The fact, provided by a tombstone, that the wife of a provincial slave was buried in London, at best shows the presence of the council in the capital, and need not relate to the cult, for it is not unknown in the empire for the two to be separated. There is no reason to believe, therefore, that Colchester ever ceased to possess the principal temple in Britain devoted to the imperial cult.

Despite the initial resistance to the cult, which played its part in the background to the Boudiccan rebellion, it came ultimately to be accepted in a variety of manifestations. In the chartered towns, other than Colchester, temples to the cult will almost certainly have existed, although only at Lincoln is the site of one possibly suspected. Nevertheless, M. Aurelius Lunaris, *sevir Augustalis* of both York and Lincoln, is testimony to its practice in both places. At Chichester, the *domus divinae* – the deified dynasties of the emperors – is invoked in one dedication of a temple of Neptune and Minerva (fig. 15) and in another is coupled with Jupiter. At Brough-on-Humber a similar formula was used in the dedication of a new *proscaenium* for the theatre, and illustrates what may be appropriately called the secular side of the imperial cult, which called for expressions of loyalty in many everyday matters. Hence the frequent references in building dedications to deified members of an emperor's household. Such expressions were also forthcoming in another way. In order to circumvent the difficulty of worshipping a living emperor who had refused divine honours, provincials frequently invoked his spiritual power, the *numen Augusti*, and altars and inscriptions which include this formula, either on its own, or coupled with another deity, are comparatively common, suggesting that in time the cult became reasonably popular, even extending to the countryside. In the area around the Fens and the east Midlands some small bronze busts, usually identified with certain second-century emperors, have been found. They are of a size to fit a staff or ceremonial sceptre, and may have been part of the regalia of priests whose country temples included the imperial cult. An example of the latter is recorded on an inscription from Nettleham, a few kilometres north of Lincoln; it couples the numina Augustorum with Mars Rigonemetos, itself a conjunction of classical and Celtic deities.

Along with the imperial cult came the other official observances of the Roman empire, enshrined in the deities of the whole classical Pantheon: Jupiter, Neptune, Pluto, Juno, Minerva, Mercury, Venus, Mars, Apollo, Diana, together with immortals such as Hercules. Abstract concepts such as Fortune, Fate or Victory were also personified in the form of deities. In classical theology, a temple was considered the residence of the deity to which it was dedicated, but the ceremonies celebrated at different temples might in time grow apart, giving rise to recognizably separate forms of the cult. So we find Jupiter Capitolinus, named after the temple on the Capitoline Hill in Rome, Jupiter Dolichenus from Doliche in Commagene, and Jupiter Heliopolitanus from Baalbek (Heliopolis), both in Syria.

There is evidence, either in the form of inscriptions or of statuary, for the practice of almost all the main classical cults in Britain. Certainly the army, with its official observances to the Capitoline Triad – Jupiter, Juno and Minerva – as well as to other deities will have been primarily instrumental in their introduction, and secondarily, by a process of diffusion, to the higher centres of romanization, such as London, the chartered towns and civitas capitals. We have already noted the temple at Chichester jointly dedicated to Neptune and Minerva (p. 247), while at Lincoln, worshippers of both Apollo and Mercury were organized in guilds. Jupiter, in a north-western provincial guise, appears at Cirencester, Chichester and probably Wroxeter and Catterick as well. Minerva again appears in Bath and in London, but in both places linked with other deities, and, indeed, it is not common to find unadulterated classical cults in civilian centres of Britain.

It is therefore in the military versions that we find the best evidence for these cults. The army possessed a calendar of well-regulated, religious events which were observed corporately by each unit. These would include the annual oath of loyalty to the emperor and to other gods, notably Jupiter. It was the custom on such occasions to erect new altars to the deity on the edge of the parade ground, the discarded pieces being ceremoniously buried, and a cache of such altars dedicated to Jupiter was found at Maryport (Cumbria).

Each unit also maintained a shrine in its headquarters building in which would be placed the appropriate imperial statues and also the military standards when not in use. The obligations to carry out these observances to the letter were very real, in view of the contractual nature of the religion. Any backsliding or slovenly performance on the part of the celebrants might have been deemed to be breach of contract by the deities invoked and, so it was thought, might have threatened the whole safety and welfare of the empire and its rulers.

But the Roman army, containing men from many parts of the empire, all with their own beliefs, and certainly no less superstitious than resident Britons, not only introduced new cults to Britain, but also did not hesitate to make appropriate gestures to the local cults they found here. Consequently, there grew in time a broad spectrum of religious beliefs which incorporated both classical and native deities, in which gods and goddesses of one canon were often identified or equated with those of the other. So it can be seen that an almost infinite number of conjoint deities became possible and, in the process, Celtic beliefs received a classical veneer, while at the same time classical cults became acceptable to the Britons. Such a union would not have been possible unless both forms of religion had contained an underlying, common creed, and the people practising them a common basic spiritual need. It is interesting that, during the Roman period, the only religions which did not, or refused to, integrate with the general run, were those possessing a completely different theological approach, such as the monotheism of Christianity or Judaism.

Examples of the fusion of beliefs are many and occur in all contexts. At Bath, Minerva was equated with Sul, or Sulis, the local deity of the hot springs and commemorated in a great temple of classical proportions set within a precinct which also contained the bathing establishment (fig. 104). Much of the temple tympanum has been recovered and was decorated with winged victories and also, in the centre, with a hirsute face (fig. 105). The latter is often identified as the Medusa head, an attribute of Minerva, although its portrayal, even on a classical building, owes much to Celtic art. It seems far more likely, therefore, especially in view of the prominent position which it occupies, to be a representation of Sul, which, in Old Irish meant eye or sun, so accounting for the flame-like locks of hair and beard, looking not unlike the corolla of the sun. As the guardian of a hot spring it would be an appropriate representation. But a more recent interpretation is that it is a representation of the giant Typhoeus, who personified geothermal activity.

Fig. 104. The Great Bath in the bathing establishment situated adjacent to the temple precinct at Bath (*Bath City Council*).

In another guise Minerva is equated with the patron goddess Brigantia on a relief from Birrens, near Carlisle, where the latter deity is decked in the attributes of the former. Mars became a favourite deity in the Celtic field and was equated with many different native godlings, and surprisingly his field of influence, which in the classical religion was that of a war god, became greatly modified, sometimes appearing as a healing figure. Such an example is Mars Rigonemetos from near Lincoln, or Mars Medocius from a temple outside Colchester. Some of these mixed deities were themselves imports into Britain, such as Mars Lenus, or Ocelus, from near Trier, which occurs at Caerwent and Carlisle, or Mars Rigisamus from Aquitania who was worshipped at West Coker (Somerset). Mapon was equated with Apollo in the north-west and has left a legacy in the modern place-name Clochmabenstane on the north shore of the Solway. Silvanus, a classical god who ruled the wild, appears as Callirios at Colchester and Vernostonos at Ebchester, near Durham. Jupiter is sometimes depicted as Taranis, the wheel god.

Fig. 105. Central face on the tympanum of the temple at Bath. Originally interpreted as the snake-locked Medusa head – an attribute of Minerva – it was then identified as Sul and most recently as the giant Typhoeus who personified geothermal activity (*Bath City Council*).

The fused religions were recognized by Roman and native alike. To the former it was an essential part of the romanizing of provincials, being called the *interpretatio Romana*; to the latter it was but an extension of an already multitudinous system. Somewhat naturally, also, the further away from centres of romanization, the stronger remained the Celtic flavour, and in many remote country places in Britain, the old religious beliefs and superstitions continued virtually unchanged throughout the Roman period. Yet, fortunately for us, they were sometimes romanized to the extent that sculptures or inscriptions recorded the presence of a deity who would otherwise have remained nameless and without form. From time to time, some of these local deities achieved a wider popularity, probably on account of their supposed powers, and the large and splendid temple with its accompanying guesthouse and bath building at Lydney in Gloucestershire, was dedicated to Nodens, a god of healing and finding, whose fame had certainly spread across the Bristol Channel and perhaps even as far as Silchester.

One important Celtic manifestation was widespread over both Britain and Europe: the concept of the Mother Goddess, or Earth Mother, or in the classical canon, Ceres. It was essentially a fertility cult, and, since she was considered a most powerful deity, was sometimes portrayed in a triple or, more rarely, a quadruple form. In most religions, including Christianity, the number three had a mystical importance, which was sometimes used to denote the power of the deity and its all-embracing activities. In Britain, the cult of the Matres was widespread and some excellent sculptured reliefs have been found at London and Cirencester. At Cirencester, and again at Bath, the cult was of a form which took the title the Sulevian Mothers, and on one sculptured plaque they appear as three severe-looking matrons, sitting upright on a bench and nursing baskets of loaves and fruit (fig. 106).

Fig. 106. Sculptured relief of a triad of Mother Goddesses from Cirencester. They sit on a bench, upright and severe-featured. Each holds a tray containing loaves or fruit (*Corinium Museum*).

In the main, however, Celtic deities remained essentially local manifestations, such as the water-nymph Coventina at Carrawburgh on Hadrian's Wall. There, a small shrine was erected around the spring which gave rise to the myth and was decorated by sculptures picturing Coventina, sometimes singly, sometimes in triplicate. Into the basin, which collected the water from the spring, were thrown the offerings of suppliants to the deity; mostly these people were of humble origin and the small coins, bronze pins and brooches were the best oblations they could afford, and considerable numbers accumulated over the years. Another similar local god, Antenociticus, was worshipped at Benwell, also on the Wall; he was represented by a splendid head in stone of a handsome young male, which was nevertheless executed in a highly Celtic artistic style. A nameless but complicated deity, formed of the combination of an owl, a bull and a female bust, presided over a temple erected in the long-deserted hillfort of Maiden Castle during the late fourth century. In this context, it is interesting to record the returns frequently made to places with old associations during the fourth century, probably as a reaction to burgeoning Christianity. Maiden Castle was not the only hillfort reimbued with religious significance at that time and Lydney and Chanctonbury Ring (Sussex) are but two other examples. The association of cults with places, affectionately remembered in the imaginations, lore and legends of the native peoples, is hardly surprising.

Fig. 107. An altar erected to the three witches at Benwell on Hadrian's Wall (*photography by courtesy of the Museum of Antiquities, University of Newcastle and the Society of Antiquaries of Newcastle upon Tyne*).

Reference was made at the beginning of this chapter to the unspecified *genius loci* and the place which it probably occupied in the minds of the inhabitants. It can probably be connected with a somewhat similar manifestation, which is more normally depicted in a nameless form as a series of little hooded figures – the *genii cucullati* (*cucullus* = a hooded cloak). They are recorded in several parts of Britain and there is a fine relief from Housesteads, showing the three figures full face; it is not possible to determine their sex, and this is a common feature of these illustrated versions. Benwell, not so very far from Housesteads, has produced an altar to the three witches (fig. 107), and

Fig. 108. Sculptured relief of a triad of *genii cucullati* from Cirencester (*Corinium Museum*).

there is something remarkably witch-like about the portrayals at Housesteads. From Cirencester comes an even more remarkable piece of sculpture illustrating the same theme, on which the figures are represented with such severe simplicity and in such low relief that it is little more than a cartoon, but a cartoon endowed with all the verve and movement that such basic treatment can often impart to a subject. The trio this time are shown in side view, trotting to the right, and their faces and figures, but for the lower legs, are completely concealed by the all-enveloping cloaks, so introducing an element of anonymity and mystery; when looked at with half-closed eyes, they almost seem to move (fig. 108). The cult seems to have been popular in the country around Cirencester, and several similar, but less inspired, sculptures have been found, some of which contained four, or even five, figures.

They appear not only on sculptured reliefs, but also on pottery, and one of a number of interesting vessels, probably manufactured at

Colchester, displays a group of genii cucullati, some apparently floating through the air, and being chased by a hunchback (fig. 109); physical deformities such as this, or a squint, are often viewed with superstitious fear by primitive peoples. Another pot depicts several animal-headed men picking grapes.

It is when we arrive in a world peopled by witches and little hooded figures, by hunchbacks and animal-headed men that we approach the very roots of superstition in Roman Britain. Such creatures are the basic apparatus of all folklore and legend: the world of dwarfs and goblins, of fairies and the wee people, of witches and wizards and Herne the Hunter. There can be no doubt also that the fear engendered by an abstract concept takes on a less menacing appearance if it is endowed with a physical personality. Hence the very necessary invention of all these characters. Nowadays, they only inhabit children's stories, and their menace has supposedly been neutralized in civilized societies; only a residue of somewhat humorous superstition lingers on. But to the inhabitants of Roman Britain, they would have represented very real forces for good or evil, to be propitiated with gifts and libations and to be treated with respect.

Such feelings were indigenous to Britain and Rome alike and it was only in the outward expression that differences occur. We have looked at some of the native examples, and to them we can add an example of a purely classical method of averting the evil eye: the phallic symbol which was a good luck emblem of high potency. Such devices seldom occur in Celtic religious contexts, so that their introduction to Britain will have occurred after the Roman invasion. It was a device, however, which achieved considerable popularity and was rapidly absorbed into the general catalogue of mystical symbolism. Quite frequently the phallus was endowed with limbs, and appears so on pottery vessels from Colchester, while an extraordinary miniature sculpture from Wroxeter depicts a winged phallus drawing a chariot (fig. 110). Remembering the interest of Celtic religions in the human head, it is likely that, where a phallus is given a face or head a combination of classical and native concepts has taken place.

The worship of the more formalized deities took place at many different types of temples and shrines. Although classically styled temples are known in Britain, they tend to be rare and restricted to cities and towns, and, of course, include the great temples of Claudius at Colchester and Sulis and Minerva at Bath. A little has

Fig. 109. A colour-coated beaker from Colchester decorated in relief with figures of a hunchback, animals and hooded figures (*Colchester and Essex Museum*).

Fig. 110. Relief of a winged phallus drawing a chariot; found at Wroxeter (*Graham Webster*).

already been said of these two temples and their precincts, but it is from Bath that we obtain most information about a British example of a classical temple (fig. 111).

The temple at Bath lay in an enclosure, or precinct, formed by a double portico, with the hot spring rising in the south-east quarter, and with the baths, therefore, forming a separate wing which extended beyond the enclosure in that direction. The temple sat on its podium approximately in the centre of the precinct, and seems to have been of pseudo-peripteral form with engaged columns of the Corinthian order on back and side walls, and with a tetrastyle portico at the front. Fragments of the pediment with its portrayal of Sulis (or Typhoeus), held aloft within a wreath by winged Victories, in the centre of the tympanum, have already been mentioned above (p. 249). Within the precinct was another ornamental façade, making use of the Doric order and apparently incorporating the Four Seasons supported by attendant Cupids. The principal altar stood well before the flight of seven steps leading up to the temple and immediately north of the hot spring; it was decorated with figures of deities at the four corners among whom Bacchus, Hercules, Jupiter and Apollo have been

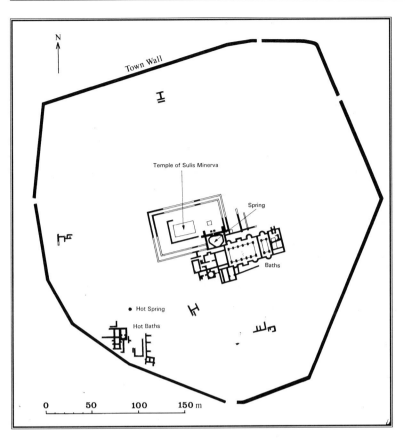

Fig. 111. Roman Bath. At the centre lies the temple of Sulis Minerva in its precinct, to which is attached the baths at the south-east corner. Other bathing establishments also existed in the town (*after B. Cunliffe*).

identified. In front of the altar stood at least two statues, one of which had been given by L. Marcius Memor, augurer of the temple.

The basin into which over a million litres of water flowed daily from the spring, at a temperature of between 40–50°C, interrupted the line of the precinct porticoes at the south-east angle. In 1978–9, a dangerous amoebic contamination of the water caused the spring to be temporarily diverted while the basin was cleaned out. This not only showed in detail its very careful construction, but also revealed the collapsed roofing vault and produced numerous votive offerings which had been thrown into the water during the Roman period. Over 6,000 coins as well as 40 curses inscribed on metal sheets (p. 269) were recovered. The level of water in the basin was originally maintained by a sluice and from it the flow was divided in two; one channel ran to the main outfall, while the other fed the Great Bath and its subsidiaries. In addition to the naturally-warmed waters, two other bathing-wings were included, heated by more conventional hypocausts, one at each end of the Great Bath.

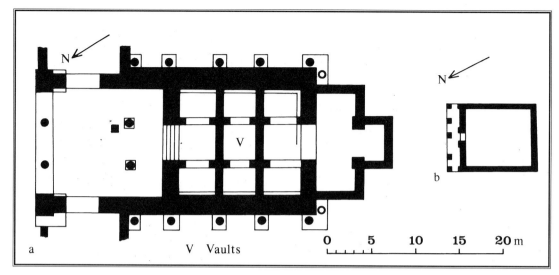

Fig. 112. Classical temples at: a) attached near the western corner of the forum at Verulamium (*after R.E.M. Wheeler*); b) Corbridge (*after M.J.T. Lewis*).

There can be no doubt that the water was endowed with magical, and, consequently, curative properties. It seems to have been used by Britons as well as by people from other provinces, and may, as already noted (p. 199), have acted as an official convalescent station for the Roman army, since several dedications by, or tombstones of, soldiers are known at Bath. But neither the waters nor the deities could cure old age and an unknown decurion from Gloucester died there, aged eighty. The spring which served the Great Bath of the Romans, now known as the King's Bath, was not the only source in the town and it is not often realized that there were at least two other hot springs in close proximity, both of which seem to have been invested with the same religio-medical function. Both the Cross Bath and the so-called Hot Baths seem to have been dedicated to the same deities, Sulis and Minerva, while the Hot Baths has additionally produced an altar to Diana.

Other classical style temples are known at Corbridge (fig. 112b), where a group of at least five cluster beside the north-east angle of one of the military arsenals, whose exterior wall was diverted to avoid the sacred sites. Temples were added, one on each side of the council chamber, to the south-west range of the forum at Verulamium during the middle of the second century, and seemingly appear classical in conception, since they were incorporated in the architecture of the forum colonnade (figs 39b and 112a). There was also an interesting small temple at Wroxeter in Insula VIII. It had been constructed in an area once occupied by shops which were burnt down in the mid-second-century fire, and may have been associated with a house constructed alongside it, perhaps as a residence for a priest. The dedications are not known, but masonry fragments found in the area included the chariot-pulling phallus referred to above (p. 253), and also pieces suggestive of horses, relating perhaps to the Celtic goddess Epona. Moreover, to the rear of the temple is an unusual enclosure surrounded by concentric walls some 4–5 m apart. It is possible that it was provided for displays or competitions of an equestrian nature, in which case it is the only building in Britain so far to resemble a rudimentary circus (p. 29).

By far the commonest type of temple in Britain, however, was one with a distribution roughly corresponding to the areas of pre-Roman, Belgic settlement, south of a line drawn from the Humber to mid-Wales. It matches a parallel distribution in north-west Gaul. They are usually called the Romano-Celtic type. In ground plan they have the appearance of one square within another, or, less commonly, of concentric circles or polygons (fig. 113). When restored to their original appearance on paper, it seems likely that the inner unit, no matter what its shape, rose as a tower above a surrounding portico, and acted as the repository for the cult figures; its interior would have been lighted by clerestory windows. Occasionally, also, additional wings or porticoes seem to have been added, as in one of the principal temples near the centre of Verulamium (fig. 113e), which was enclosed within its own precinct walls and later associated with the theatre. Sometimes also the inner chamber is provided with an apse which projects across the portico to the rear, as at Chelmsford, or at Caerwent, where a temple was situated across the road from the basilica, and where the precinct is provided with an entrance hall and possibly a priestly residence as well.

The positioning of temples, often eccentrically within their enclosures, shows that, in many cases, they were of secondary importance and that pride of place went to some totem which has since disappeared; it may have been a tree. Sometimes also there is evidence for continuity between Iron Age and Roman times, and both these factors can be demonstrated at the Trinovantian religious centre as Gosbecks Farm just south of Colchester (fig. 7). A massive ditch outlined an almost exactly square area in the pre-Roman period and was ultimately filled during the first century AD, when the enclosure was enlarged and marked anew by a double colonnade or portico. In the south-east corner of the original ditched enclosure, a Romano-Celtic temple was constructed, implying that whatever it was that had given the site its religious significance in the Iron Age, still survived into the Roman period. As at Verulamium, this temple was associated with a theatre (fig. 125c) and with two other big

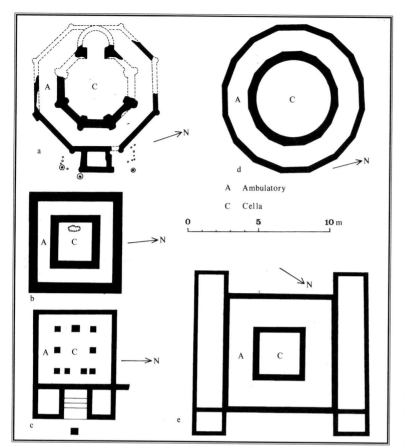

A   Ambulatory

C   Cella

0   5   10 m

Fig. 113. Romano-Celtic temples at: a) Chelmsford (*after P.J. Drury*); b) Caistor-by-Norwich (*after D. Atkinson*); c) Springhead (*after W.S. Penn and S.R. Harker*); d) Silchester (*after G.C. Boon*); e) Verulamium (*after M.J.T. Lewis*).

enclosures. Since, also, a fine bronze statue of Mercury was ploughed up in a nearby field, it seems probable that he was included in the dedications. Mercury was the god of trade, so the existence of a fairground combined with temple and theatre, as already suggested above (p. 244), was simply continuing a practice which certainly originated in the Iron Age, if not before.

In some towns and other settlements, temples were grouped together, such as at Caistor-by-Norwich, where two lay side by side, north of the forum, or at Springhead where there were four within a precinct. At Silchester, a sacred site of some importance lay just inside the east gate and was connected to the forum in the town centre by what could be interpreted as a processional way. At least two, and possibly more, temples occupied the precinct, in addition to some other buildings (fig. 36). Such arrangements are reminiscent of the large temple complex at Trier in Germany, where a considerable number of religious buildings were congregated, some within their own precincts.

Simpler forms of shrine and temple are also known in Britain. They were normally small, and could be rectangular, such as that at Springhead (fig. 114e), or the centurion's shrine dedicated to Silvanus on Scargill Moor, near Bowes. Sometimes, this type terminated in a semicircular apse, as in the temple of Antenociticus at Benwell, or the *nymphaea* at Chedworth or Housesteads (fig. 114c). Many were circular, such as those at Maiden Castle and Frilford; the latter was at one of the number of places where combined religious and commercial activities took place on the borders between one civitas and another. It was certainly preceded by a circular Iron Age building of probably similar function, as was the temple at Maiden Castle. In these cases the native antecedents of the type are not in doubt and clearly followed a different line of development from that which produced the Romano-Celtic temple.

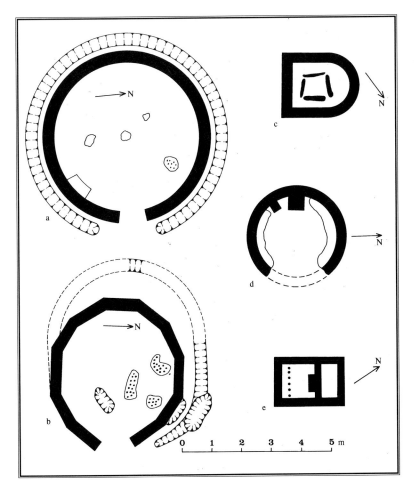

Fig. 114. Small shrines and temples at: a,b) Brigstock (*after G.M. Knocker*); c) Housesteads (*after I.A. Richmond*); d) Bowes (*after I.A. Richmond*); e) Springhead (*after W.S. Penn*).

Unrelated to them, therefore, is the circular shrine of the prefect of the first cohort of Thracians which was a companion to the centurion's shrine near Bowes (fig. 114d); both were dedicated to Silvanus or his local variant, Vinotonus. Polygonal forms are also known, such as those favoured by the Corieltavi at Brigstock (Northants) (fig. 114a, b) and Collyweston (Rutland). In both places they occur in conjunction with circular temples. Inside the hillfort at Chanctonbury, on the South Downs, there was, in addition to a Romano-Celtic temple of normal plan, a horseshoe-shaped building which may have been yet another shrine.

All these temples lacked the external portico of Romano-Celtic types and would then have been simple roofed edifices. It is usually more difficult to detect in them evidence for internal arrangements. The hexagonal temple at Collyweston appeared to have a bench running round three sides, while sundry pits and post-holes appear in others. The two shrines at Bowes were equipped with altars, but not apparently with statues of the deity.

There must have been many priests to serve these temples. Their ceremonial regalia is found from time to time, like the bronze coronets, with their attached silver plaques depicting deities, from Cavenham (Suffolk) and Hockwold (Norfolk), or the sceptres from a priestly burial at Brough-on-Humber.

Among the cults introduced to Britain were also those that originated in the eastern empire or beyond, an area noted for its exotic religions. As in Britain, where Celtic beliefs became infused with classical leanings, so in the eastern empire there was to some extent a similar fusion between classical and eastern cults.

In most cases the deities were introduced to Britain by soldiers or merchants. One of the most popular seems to have been the cult of Jupiter Dolichenus, and evidence for his worship appears on northern military sites such as Corbridge, where parts of a statue and architectural fragments from a temple or shrine have been identified. The temple of the Dolichene cult was planned on eastern house styles and required several rooms. An altar from Corbridge, erected by a centurion of Legio VI, joins Jupiter Dolichenus with Caelestis Brigantia. Since Juno Caelestis was the offical consort of Jupiter Dolichenus, it can only imply the equation of Juno with the patron deity of the Brigantes, and this admirably demonstrates the way in which widely differing cults became mixed up. We have already seen that, at Birrens, Brigantia was, in contrast, linked with Minerva. Juno Caelestis was also sometimes called the Syrian Goddess (*Dea*

Syria) under which guise she is mentioned on an altar and on a statue base at Carvoran; the latter contains a dedication in verse made up of ten iambic senarii, and in reality represents the apotheosis of Julia Domna, Syrian-born wife of the emperor Severus, who was sometimes accorded the honour. Both Jupiter Dolichenus and Jupiter Heliopolitanus are mentioned on other altars from the same place. Since the fort was for a time occupied by a regiment of Syrians, the association of the deities is not surprising.

Other deities from the same part of the empire are also found in Britain, such as the cult of Astarte and her consort Heracles (Syrian Hercules) practised at Corbridge, where two companion altars with dedications in Greek have been found; one was set up by a priestess of the cult, Diodora. But its orgiastic nature did not make for its popularity, and more widespread in Britain was the cult of Cybele, the Great Earth Mother, and her consort Attis, also of Syrian derivation; dedications or attributions to one or other are known from places as widely spaced as Chester, London, Carrawburgh and Gloucester, where an anthropomorphic altar carved to represent Attis playing pan-pipes has been found. No shrine has yet been positively identifed with the cult, but the triangular temple near the London Gate at Verulamium has been tentatively associated with it. It is an unusual building whose shape was more probably dictated by the available ground at a road intersection than by any theological requirements, but the occurence of imported Italian pine seeds, the cones of which were used for burnt offerings, having pleasant olfactory properties, caused the suggestion to be made.

Egypt was also a fruitful source of cults which reached Britain. A shrine to Serapis existed in the colonia at York and a fine dedication by a legate of Legio VI has survived. The building appears to have been apsidal, and situated not far from the postulated imperial palace; it may have been founded by the emperor Severus, when he was based at York, and who was enthusiastic about the cult. Heads of the god have been found at Silchester and at London, where it was associated with the temple of Mithras (see below). A shrine to Osiris may have existed at Rochester, where a small terracotta head of the god was found.

But of all eastern deities imported into Britain, the best attested is Mithras. As a religion, Mithraism was different from most ancient, contractual cults, since it demanded certain standards of conduct from its followers, who therefore had to undergo various processes of initiation, involving tests of physical and moral fortitude. Theologically, Mithras was a derivative of the Persian

Fig. 115. The temple of Mithras situated just south of the fort at Carrawburgh, on Hadrian's Wall. Facing the entrance are the three main altars dedicated to Mithras, above which would have been depicted the scene of Mithras slaying the bull.

worship of Ahuramazda, and was a cult in which the deity, depicted as the power of light, or good, was considered to be waging a constant battle against the power of darkness, or evil. In this he was aided by two torch-carrying acolytes Cautes and Cautopates, representing dawn and twilight. The mythology is complex and, since it was essentially a mystery religion, not always easy to grasp. The subduing of wild creation, in the form of a bull, was attributed to Mithras, who, by slaying the animal, released its blood and so gave rise to all useful plants. Consequently, the principal portrayals of the god illustrate the bull-slaying scene, but add also the serpent and scorpion, creatures of the powers of darkness, who attempted to defile the life-giving flow. Another apparition shows Mithras' birth from a rock, or, less commonly as at Housesteads, from an egg. He was also frequently invoked on altars in conjunction with his main ally, the Sun, so that inscriptions might record *Sol Invictus* as at Rudchester or *Deo Soli Mithrae* as at Castlesteads.

In view of its nature, it is not surprising that the cult appealed most to certain classes of society, such as soldiers and merchants, and

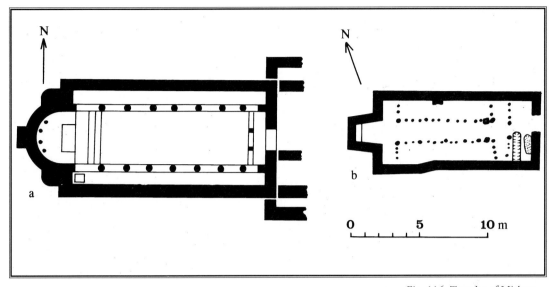

Fig. 116. Temples of Mithras at: a) London (*after W.F. Grimes*); b) Carrawburgh (*after I.A. Richmond*).

the Mithraea known in Britain were placed where they could draw their congregations from among such people. Membership was achieved by means of initiation into several different grades which were individually named, such as Lion, Raven, Bridegroom, Soldier or Father, and the ceremonies included ordeals by fire, water or fasting.

The principal Mithraea in Britain were those at London (fig. 116a), where no doubt merchants were among its devotees, Caernarvon, Housesteads, where the sanctuary was contained in a cave, Carrawburgh (figs 115–16b) and the three legionary fortresses; there are, however, indications of others in several places, and recent excavations have disclosed a possible temple at Leicester. In the main, the cult had more attraction for legionary than auxiliary soldiers and, at Housesteads, the primary dedicators, whose altars occupied the place of honour at the head of the temple, were respectively a centurion and an orderly on the governor's staff. Even in London, the donor of the bull-slaying panel was a veteran of Legio II Augusta.

The temples themselves were usually quite small, rectangular buildings, sometimes, as in the case of London, with an apse at one end, or, as at Carrawburgh, with a recess, in which the principal altars and other iconographic pieces could be placed (figs 115–16b). The main body of the temple was divided in three longitudinally, so that a central aisle was usually flanked by raised platforms on which the benches of the worshippers would be placed. A screen normally separated the temple proper from an antechamber, or narthex, which in the Mithraeum at Carrawburgh had been equipped, at one stage, with a hearth set beside a sunken, coffin-shaped 'ordeal' pit.

It is not surprising, also, that the character of Mithraism, with its belief in the powers of good and evil, its symbolism and the demands made upon its adherents, brought it into abrupt collision with Christianity. In Britain, it was late to develop so that it was at its most powerful at just the time when Christianity was also in the ascendant, and Christianity, like Mithraism, must be seen as an oriental import into the province.

The difference in the treatment that was at first accorded to both these religions in the Roman empire was conditioned by the refusal of early Christians to take the oath of loyalty to the emperor. Consequently Mithraism was permitted and tolerated whereas Christianity was banned and its followers persecuted. But it must be remembered that refusal to take the imperial oath was as much a secular as a religious offence, so it could be argued that persecution was not an act of religious intolerance, but punishment of a treasonable crime which struck at the very unity of the empire. Almost all stories of the early martyrs come from Christian literature and we may be sure were heavily coloured with propaganda; the desire for martyrdom on the part of the people concerned cannot either be overlooked, since the Christian ethic placed as much, if not more, emphasis on the afterlife as on life in this world. It is also important to remember that the Roman empire was always suspicious of people who banded together for whatever purpose, no matter how innocent, and regulated such associations closely. So what appeared to the government to be a secret society whose members, additionally, refused to take the loyal oath would, from the first, be marked down as extremely undesirable.

Naturally there is little evidence for early Christianity in Roman Britain since, before the Edict of Toleration in AD 313, any references would have been covert, with openly expressed convictions attracting punishment. But there is an interesting cryptogram from Cirencester in the form of a word-square:

R O T A S
O P E R A
T E N E T
A R E P O
S A T O R

Fig. 117. An acrostic scratched on second- or third-century wall plaster from Cirencester. It contains a hidden reference to Christianity (*Corinium Museum*).

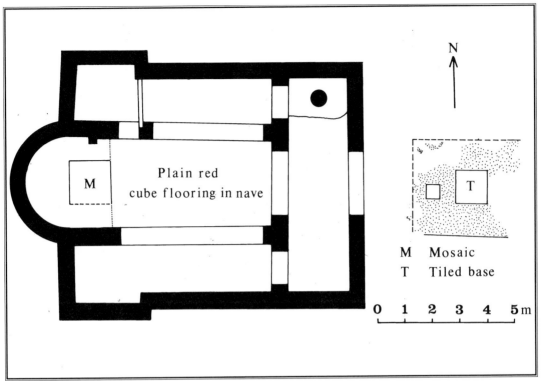

Fig. 118. A building situated near the south-east corner of the forum at Silchester, which has been interpreted as a Christian church with a separate baptistry to the east (*after I.A. Richmond and S.S. Frere*).

It had been carefully scratched on the painted surface of some wall-plaster, which stylistically belongs to the second or third century (fig. 117). For many years it was not thought to have any special meaning other than perhaps some magical significance. Translated it means: the sower Arepo guides the wheels carefully. Symbolically the wheel can be taken as a reference to eternal life, but it appears in both pagan and Christian mythologies. However, it has been shown that if all the letters are taken and rearranged they form a cross with a common N, each bar being made up of the word PATERNOSTER, the opening words of the Lord's Prayer, with two A's and two O's left over. In early Christian symbolism AO, or Greek AΩ, was adopted to represent the 'beginning and the end' of the Revelation of St John. We need not doubt, therefore, that Christianity was being practised in Cirencester at a time when open references might have attracted persecution. Apart from this and another similar acrostic found at Manchester, we cannot say where, or to what extent, it was followed in the years before it became a permitted religion.

Nevertheless, by AD 314, only a year after the Edict had been promulgated, no less than three British bishops, the metropolitans of three of the provinces, from London, York and Lincoln, together with the representatives of the fourth, probably from Cirencester, attended a council of the Church at Arles. So we might conclude that the British Church was well organized for some time before the Edict and wasted no time in coming into the open. For the fourth century, there is, however, more evidence, although much of it comes in the form of Christian symbols, such as the chi-rho (☧) monogram, on personal possessions; this monogram is made up in Greek of the first three letters of the word *Christos*.

One building with probable Christian significance is the so-called church at Silchester (fig. 118). It is a small, temple-like structure close to the south-east corner of the forum and it cannot have been constructed before the middle or later part of the third century. Consequently, if it is accepted as a church, for which, it must be admitted, there is no absolute proof, it is more likely to have been built during the early or mid-fourth century, after the Edict of Toleration.

The building possesses a nave, side aisles, a narthex, an apsidal west end and two transept-like rooms at the heads of the aisles. The floor of the nave was covered with plain brick tesserae with a black and white chequerboard mosaic panel in the apse. Outside to the east lay a base, perhaps for a basin, and a carefully constructed soak-away pit, which together have sometimes been considered as a detached baptistry. Despite the fact that, if a church, the orientation is reversed, such arrangements are not unknown in the empire, but there are difficulties in accepting this interpretation, not least of which is an apparent disuse before the end of the fourth century. Yet none of its features are entirely inconsistent with a Christian building.

More certain is the identification of a timber-framed church of late fourth or early fifth century date inside the Saxon Shore fort at Richborough. This too possessed an external baptistry, with the font sunk in the ground and lined with waterproof cement.

The most striking evidence for a building of Christian worship, however, is the domestic oratory constructed in a suite of rooms of the villa at Lullingstone. Their attribution is in no doubt since wall-plaster recovered from the rooms produced fragments of painted ☧ monograms surrounded by floral wreaths. Moreover the rear wall of the main chapel was decorated with a painted frieze containing praying figures each set in a columned niche. Various identifications have been given to the figures, since they are by no means identical, and the excavator considered them to represent the household.

Taken as a whole, there is probably more evidence for Christianity from villas than from urban sites. In addition to Lullingstone, there was the hallowing, by the sacred monogram, of the water basin at Chedworth. A mosaic incorporating the same device is known from a villa at Frampton, near Dorchester, where it was amalgamated with a rollicking pagan scene associated with Neptune. Most important perhaps is the mosaic from Hinton St Mary, on the borders of Dorset and Wiltshire, with its portrayal of Christ, together with, probably the four evangelists and animals gambolling in Paradise. Remarkably also, another part of this pavement depicts Bellerephon mounted on Pegasus slaying the mythical beast, the Chimera. The same scene is utilized in the main dining-room at Lullingstone and its apparent association with Christianity has led some authorities to suggest a symbolic significance, which enabled a pagan scene to be incorporated in Christian iconography. A number of villas such as Walesby (Lincs.), Icklingham (Suffolk) and Wiggonholt (Sussex) have produced sizable lead tanks bearing the Christian monogram. It is not certain what purpose they served, although it has been suggested that they acted as baptismal fonts.

The rise of Christianity engendered a reaction, confirmed by the emperor Julian in AD 355. In Britain it is to be seen in the number of late pagan temples which appear in rural places, such as Maiden Castle and Lydney, in contrast to the apparent strength of the Church among the gentry. Whether this, therefore, represents a social as well as a religious reaction on the part of the lower classes is a possibility, as we may read into it a desire to return to the old times. This re-emergence of paganism in the countryside can to some extent be contrasted, also, against apparent acts of Christian iconoclasm against temples situated in or near towns or forts. The Mithraeum at Carrawburgh seems to have been systematically levelled and used as a rubbish-dump, while at least one temple west of Colchester was similarly treated, with the walls being razed to ground level. But care must be exercised in making such assumptions, since not every derelict pagan temple need have been subject to the attentions of Christian vandals.

Britain also had its share of early Christian martyrs, of whom perhaps the most famous was St Alban, executed at Verulamium probably during the principate of Severus, although earlier arguments attributed his death wrongly to the long persecution under Diocletian in the early fourth century. A *martyrium* was reputedly built on the place where he was executed, on a hill-top overlooking the town, and legend would place it under St Alban's Abbey, although recent excavations there found no trace of it. Two other martyrs, Aaron and Julius, are also recorded from Britain, but less is known about where and when they met their deaths.

The early Christian Church was from time to time rent by schisms. One of these was the Gnostic sect which, while denying Christ, seized on the idea of a universal redeemer. The noted mosaic pavements in the villa at Brading in the Isle of Wight contain portrayals of various aspects of this cult. More serious, however, was Pelagianism, started by a Romano-Briton, Pelagius. It involved the doctrine of divine grace and seems to have been strongly supported in Britain even though its protagonist early left the province. It was particularly damaging in the fifth century after official Roman government had ceased, and it caused serious rifts which assumed political importance in the subsequent control of the country. The official Church was sufficiently aware of the damage being caused for St Germanus, Bishop of Auxerre, to be sent to combat the heresy in AD 429 and again some fifteen years later. While in Britain, he visited Verulamium and was also, on one occasion, able to lead an attack on a band of marauding Saxons, putting them to flight in the so-called Allelujah Victory. Indeed it has been argued that Pelagianism was one of the major contributory causes for the ultimate decline of Roman Britain.

Two further interesting aspects of superstitious beliefs may be considered; the use of magical amulets to protect the wearer from certain ills, and the wish to cause harm to one's adversaries by putting up an appropriate curse, inscribed on lead or bronze plates, in a prominent position near a shrine or temple. Even now, people wear lucky charms, but would probably be loth openly to ascribe any specific function to them, despite their private feelings. So much more force then would similar charms have had in antiquity, when people were a prey to more primitive superstition. It is certain that numerous small phallic objects, manufactured as pendants or brooches were worn as good luck charms, and even in some instances attached to horse harnesses. An infant burial at Catterick had six such objects accompanying it; they were so fashioned as to have formed a necklet on a leather strap. Small bronze swastikas, with the arms in the reverse position to the Nazi emblem, were likewise considered as protecting the wearer and sometimes appear as brooches. Occasionally, also, metal plaques are found bearing an almost meaningless jumble of letters, like a lead disc from Brough-on-Humber, which, in addition to the necessary 'spell' was also inscribed on one side with a crude representation of male, and on the other, female genitalia.

Some amulets, or tokens, were intended to be more specific. A particularly interesting one comes from the villa site at Lockleys (Herts.). It is an intaglio of a hard, haematitic material, probably originally mounted as a locket to hang round some part of the body, or else to be enclosed in a leather or fabric pouch. Both sides are carved, the obverse including portrayals of the Egyptian deities Isis and Bes, together with a representation of the human womb and a seven-toothed key, all enclosed within a border of a snake devouring its tail, which in Egyptian mythology was a symbol for Eternity. The reverse carries a representation of a sacred beetle, or scarab, while both sides have encircling legends in Greek letters, which in either magical or palindromic form make up invocations to Typhon, an elemental force, to Ororiouth, a spirit providing protection in cases of gynaecological disorders, and Iao, the equivalent of the Jewish Jehovah. Amulets of this type are referred to by classical authors and appear to have been used especially to shorten or relieve the pains of childbirth. The conflation of Egyptian, Semitic and Greek superstitions is clearly magical rather than religious.

Fig. 119. *Curse from London. It is inscribed on both sides of a roughly cut lead sheet; a nail hole in the centre indicates where it was presumably fixed to a wooden post or building. It reads:* 'T. Egnatius Tyrannus is cursed and P. Cicerius Felix is cursed' (*Museum of London*).

Another amulet which makes use of Hebrew words intermixed with Greek comes from Caernarvon and was inscribed on a rectangular piece of gold leaf. On it some deliberate religious invocations are mixed with magical alliterations and symbols and followed by a prayer: protect me Alphianos.

Curses were normally scratched on lead sheet, an easily impressed medium, and then probably nailed to a post (fig. 119) in a prominent position in a temple or a shrine, or thrown into the sacred waters of a spring or river. Quite a large number are known from Britain and cover a wide variety of circumstances. In order to increase the power the same inscription was sometimes scratched on both sides of the sheet. One from London reads: 'I curse Tretia Maria and her life and mind and memory and liver and lungs mixed up together, and her words, thoughts and memory; thus may she be unable to speak what things are concealed, nor be able . . . '. There the sheet is broken, but not before poor Tretia Maria has received some unpleasant prognostications as to her future, presumably for threatening to reveal secret information. Another from Old Harlow reads: 'To the god Mercury, I entrust to you my affair with Eterna and her own self, and may Timotheus feel no jealousy of me at the risk of his life-blood', an overt threat to Timotheus not to interfere in the abduction of his wife, girlfriend, daughter or sister.

Most curses, therefore, were appeals to a deity or supernatural force to inhibit physical or mental processes of the cursed, such as eating, sleeping, drinking or thinking; or they can invoke damage to some physical organ of the body. In the main they seem to fall into four classes: those which involved unfaithful consorts, or rivals in amatory affairs, those which might affect the performance of athletic rivals, or rivals at law, and those which condemned thieves. One of the most interesting in the last class is a curse from the temple of Nodens at Lydney, which should therefore date to the late fourth century. It reads: 'To the god Nodens, Silvianus has lost a ring, he promises half its value to Nodens. Let him not grant health among those of the name Senicianus, until he brings it back to the temple of Nodens', and then additionally, 'curse renewed'. It seems probable that both Silvianus and Senicianus had gone to Lydney, hoping that the deity would cure them of some disease or physical ailment. No doubt both stayed in the guesthouse, from which, no doubt also, the latter walked off with the former's ring. An appeal to the god by Silvianus to withhold the request for health by Senicianus would, in the circumstances, make excellent sense, until the ring was returned. Strangely enough a polygonal gold ring, bearing an intaglio labelled Venus, has been found at Silchester. Moreover, subsequently a legend had been scratched on the outside: 'May thou live in God, Senicianus', a form of words which is typically Christian. Was this the same Senicianus, who finding his journey to Lydney had done him no good, subsequently embraced the Christian faith? What then also of the curse being renewed? Such evidence, when it occurs, illuminates the personalities of Roman Britain with a sudden, bright light, revealing their hopes and fears, ambitions and failures, which were not so very different from people today. We shall never know the full story behind this curse and the ring, nor the circumstances in which the two protagonists passed their lives, but, for one short moment, they stand revealed in all their human weakness.

A deep-seated belief in some form of survival after death was common to both Classical and Celtic worlds, so that the introduction of Roman burial practices into Britain, as with classical religion, placed no great strain upon the recipients of the new ideas. In the Roman world, as represented by Vergil, Hades was recognized as a place, which not only punished evildoers in Hell but also rewarded others in Heaven. Nevertheless, this was perhaps a restricted view which not all people shared, even if they believed in the survival of the spirit, probably underground in the regions of their final interment. Burial rites, therefore, grew up to take account of these convictions, which were sometimes coupled with the idea of a resurrection into the vegetable kingdom. It is not surprising, also, that they were easily grafted onto indigenous customs, since fundamentally there was little difference in the beliefs.

In Britain at the time of the conquest, both inhumation and cremation were practised, with a greater predominance of the latter in the south-east, where large cremation cemeteries appear at such places as Swarling and Aylesford in Kent, or Welwyn in Hertfordshire. Within a particular rite, however, it is possible to detect evidence of social stratification from the quality and quantity of grave goods included with the burial. Some were extremely richly furnished with all the trappings of life being included for the life hereafter; they were clearly graves of the aristocracy and were in some instances surmounted by a barrow. But the very poorest graves seldom contained more than a cooking-pot for the ashes, and perhaps one other vessel, intended to hold food for the journey to the next world.

Both rites were likewise practised in the Roman world, but cremation seems to have been undoubtedly the most popular among immigrants to Britain after the conquest. From the middle of the second century, however, there was a gradual change to inhumation, which seems to have been brought about more by altering fashion than by any fundamental change in belief. It certainly cannot, as is sometimes done, be related to the rise of Christianity. Such changes are detectable in Britain before then and by the late third century, the rite of cremation was seldom being carried out.

The laws relating to the burial of the dead in the Roman empire were governed principally by the old republican statutes which forbade the interment of bodies or cremated ashes within the boundary of a town or fort, the only exception being children under ten days old, who had no legal existence. Consequently if burials other than those of infants are found apparently inside a town or fort they take on a special significance; either they represent foul play followed by secret and hasty interment, or they relate to earlier or later boundaries of the settlement concerned. That being so, it is sometimes possible to use the distribution of cemeteries as indicators for urban boundaries, perhaps in those times before they became crystallized by the construction of defences. For instance, at Canterbury, little is known of the boundary before the fortifications were built in the late third century. Yet we may conclude that it never greatly changed over the years, since, on most sides, earlier cemeteries run right up to the walls, but do not appear within them, with the possible exception of an area beyond the River Stour which may have been omitted from the town when the defences were built.

Major urban cemeteries are, therefore, to be found outside towns and most frequently lining main roads; in this respect they followed Roman practise, but whether by accident or design is not so easily determined. Given the legal requirements, graves and tombs would be most accessible if placed beside a road, and would interfere less with agricultural or other uses. Some well-attested examples occur outside many major cities and towns in Britain such as those which lined the main road to London outside Colchester, or the Tadcaster road leading out of York.

Individual cremation burials were often marked by an upright gravestone on which was usually inscribed a suitable reference to the dead person and, normally, either a pictorial representation taken from his life or the scene of his funerary banquet. Many are known from Britain of both civilian and military forms (figs 120–1). A much-favoured piece of iconography from the latter was the cavalryman's tombstone depicting an armed horseman riding down a fallen enemy, who lies, or crouches, at the hooves of the horse. The tombstone of Sextus Valerius Genialis from Cirencester (fig. 120) shows him in such an act. Below this representation is an inscription recording his name, his regiment of Thracian cavalry, his origin as a Frisian tribesman, his membership of the troop of Genialis, his age at death, forty years, and the fact that he had served twenty years in the army. Then follows the abbreviated form of *Hic Situs Est, HSE* to denote that he was buried at the spot where the stone was erected. This formula is usually restricted to the first century but had real meaning, since the *H* was omitted from a tombstone of a sailor from Chester, who was lost in a shipwreck; his body was presumably not recovered, so that the stone was more of a memorial than a tombstone. Finally the letters *EFC* are an abbreviation for *(h)eres faciendum curavit*, a reference to the erection of the stone by his heirs.

Civilian tombstones of this type often show a family group and are frequently accompanied by a more elaborate invocation. The stone to commemorate Flavia Augustina and her children at York shows the whole family, father, mother, a boy and a girl, while another, erected for a thirteen-year-old girl, Corellia Optata, contained an invocation to the spirits of the underworld in verse form, and was put up by her father.

The information to be gained by a study of these tombstones is considerable. Not only do we learn of the people themselves, the positions they occupied and the lengths of their lives, but also details of their clothing and furniture which is so often illustrated as well. It has, however, been argued that they do not form a sound basis for calculation of life expectancy, since tombstones are, by their nature, the product of a supposedly limited social class. Yet, it is perhaps not so strange that the one instance in Britain, at York, where statistical comparison can be made of age at death between the better off and the poor produces much the same result for both.

Other methods of marking cremation burials were either by the erection of an earth mound over them or by placing them in masonry mausolea, and, indeed, it may be that the former is the forerunner of the latter, since it is likely that some mausolea were topped off with a mound of earth. Certainly, both forms have much the same distribution in Britain, both lying south-east of a line running roughly from Dorset to the Wash. Roman barrows can normally be distinguished from those of other periods by their pronounced conic shape and sometimes also by a low bank ringing the mound within the ditch. Moreover, they usually occur in groups besides main roads such as that of Stevenage (Herts.). Occasionally, barrows are found in the neighbourhood of villas, such as those at Bartlow (Essex), or that at West Mersea (Essex), which was contained within a masonry circle, reinforced by internal radial walls and external buttresses, to retain the weight of the earth filling.

The full development from barrow to masonry tomb is perhaps best demonstrated by the mausoleum at Keston (Kent), where a buttressed wall enclosed a circular space about 9 m in diameter. A door led into the interior and it is probable that the latter had once been equipped with niches to contain cinerary urns. Sometimes several such tombs, or *columbaria*, were placed within a walled enclosure, like that at Lockham (Kent), which may have been the property of a rich family or of a burial club, the existence of which, in Britain, is attested by inscriptions.

Fig. 120. Tombstone of S. Valerius Genialis, trooper of a Thracian regiment of cavalry, from Cirencester (*Corinium Museum*).

The poorer classes, however, could probably only afford a post or some other means to mark the site of a burial, so that it could be visited to provide the necessary libations for the dead. It is likely, that, in some instances, the neck of the cremation vessel, left projecting above the ground, acted as a marker; by covering the top with a flat slab of stone or tile, adequate protection could be given and, at the same time, libations of wine or honey or other material could simply be poured in after the lid had been lifted.

The actual cremation of the body was carried out in special areas, sometimes, as at Riseholme (Lincs.) incorporated under the burial mound, or else, as at York, situated in the middle of a busy cemetery. The ashes would be collected in a container which varied according to the wealth of the person and which could range from a humble cooking-pot to a glass, pottery or lead vessel, or a combination of one or more. At Chichester, a wooden box was sometimes inverted over a burial, or, elsewhere, it might be contained in a stone or brick-lined cyst. Sometimes, also, special provision for making libations was incorporated in the form of a pipe running from the surface to the canister, as in the Caerleon pipe-burial.

The change from cremation to inhumation led to a corresponding alteration in methods of burial. The body, usually in an extended position, was sometimes contained in a wood, lead or stone coffin, or sometimes in a combination of wood and stone or lead and stone. Elaborate stone sarcophagi, sometimes ornamented and inscribed, replaced the earlier, upright tombstones. Ornamental examples were clearly not intended for burial, but rested above the ground or in a recess in a tomb. It is not surprising, therefore, that they are sometimes found to be occupied by a person who cannot be identified with the commemorative inscription. More often than not, however, no coffin was used, the remains being interred perhaps in a sack or shroud. Certainly in the cemeteries of the poorest people, such as that at Trentholme Drive, York, or near the amphitheatre at Cirencester, bodies seem to have been treated in a most unceremonious way, with later often interfering with earlier burials, even where decomposition was not complete. They must, therefore, have presented a somewhat gruesome and unhygienic appearance, with partly rotted and dismembered limbs lying around on the surface.

A custom, which grew in Britain with the increasingly-used rite of inhumation, was partial embalming by pouring liquid plaster of Paris around the body in the coffin, so that, on hardening, it

Fig. 121. Tombstone of M. Favonius Facilis, Centurion of Legio XX which served at Colchester immediately after the invasion. Unusually it does not give his age or length of service, but the portraiture is excellent. It was set up by his two freedmen and, as with fig. 120, carries the forumula *HSE* (*Colchester and Essex Museum*).

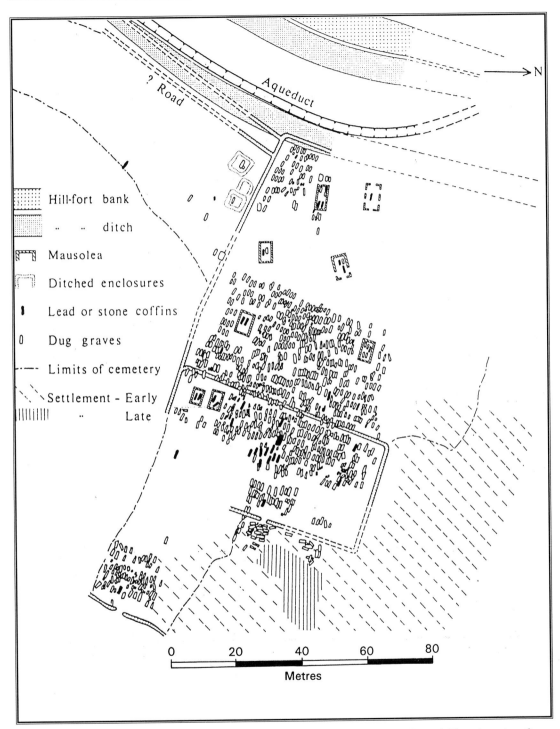

Hill-fort bank

" " ditch

Mausolea

Ditched enclosures

Lead or stone coffins

Dug graves

Limits of cemetery

Settlement – Early

" Late

? Road

Aqueduct

N

0   20   40   60   80
Metres

Fig. 122. The cemetery at Poundbury, just outside the north-west corner of Dorchester (Dorset). The orientation of most of its burials would indicate the practice of Christianity. Some family groups used small vaulted mausolea, decorated internally with painted plaster (*after C.J. Green*).

recorded impressions of the deceased, their shrouds and sometimes other perishable objects which had been included in the burial. Frequently, also, this process preserved heads of hair, as with that from York. The custom appears to have been mainly restricted to those areas where gypsum is found, such as York and Dorchester (Dorset), although it is not unknown elsewhere in the empire, having apparently originated in north Africa. In Britain, it has been claimed to represent a Christian burial rite.

Grave goods were, of course, included in both cremation and inhumation burials, the quantity and quality reflecting roughly the wealth and social class of the dead person. They will normally have included refreshments for the journey to the underworld and the person's most valued possessions. Flagons, amphoras, bowls and dishes commonly occur; occasionally something more valuable is included as at Winchester, where two joints of meat had been placed on a beautifully incised shale trencher. There was the probable army veteran's child at Colchester who was buried with the much-loved toys, that included not only many pottery and glass vessels, and terracotta animals, but also human figurines intended for giving dolls' dinner-parties, while the terracotta head and shoulders of a young child can only have come from a rag doll of a type which is still made today. Sometimes a coin was placed in the mouth of the corpse; it was the fee to Charon, the ferryman of the River Styx, to carry the person to the underworld. It was so placed because both hands would have been encumbered with cakes for two of the heads of the dog Cerberus, guardian of the underworld. Women's graves were frequently equipped with toilet articles, such as mirrors, depilatory tweezers, nail cleaners and parers, and bottles of scent or other cosmetics. Personal ornaments are commonplace, since they were probably left on the body at burial, and include a wide variety of pins, bangles, rings, bracelets, necklaces and brooches, some of which may, of course, have been used for fastening the shroud.

The rise of Christianity, however, brought about a decline in the use of grave goods, since the Christian ethic was concentrated on the more spiritual side of the life-hereafter. Christian cemeteries can usually be distinguished from other inhumations by the uniform east-west orientation of the graves. The Poundbury cemetery at Dorchester (Dorset) (fig. 122) and the Lankhills cemetery at Winchester are excellent examples. The former has been estimated to occupy some 2 ha with a density of some 2,000 graves per hectare. Most of the burials were contained in plain wooden coffins, with the head placed to the west, and with few grave goods. Some apparent family groups were distinguished which contained two adults and one or two children, with one of the interments in each group embalmed in plaster of Paris in a lead-lined, heavy wooden coffin. There were also a number of rectangular mausolea, at least two of which had handsomely painted walls and vaulted roofs; human figures are represented in the decorations and appear to be portraits of important and distinguished people taking part in some ceremonial, probably the burial of the deceased, who is depicted wearing white clothing. The burials in these mausolea were also grouped and were placed in more elaborate lead or stone sarcophagi, with the bodies again often being embalmed in plaster of Paris. They seem to represent, therefore, a development of the 'family group' burials, perhaps on the part of richer or more prominent people.

The Winchester cemetery, although possibly Christian, is interesting for the items of late Roman military equipment which it contained, and which must represent elements of the town garrison in the late fourth or even early fifth century. Another very probable Christian cemetery has recently been excavated at the small town of Ashton, near Oundle. It contained, within an enclosure, 178 identified burials aligned in moderately neat and regular rows and orientated east-west; some system of marking the graves must have been employed to prevent later disturbances. Grave goods were almost entirely absent.

Group cemeteries also occur in another form, where compartments, or *loculi*, for containing caskets or coffins, open out in rising tiers from a central corridor. A possible example of this mode of burial was found at Lincoln, where several stone coffins in close juxtaposition came to light north of the town; it was probably the property of a burial club.

One last type of monument has to be considered in this context: the war memorial, or, as it should more correctly be called, the triumphal monument. These were erected not so much to commemorate the dead, as today, but to record a major victory on the part of the Roman army. Several are known in Britain and the most famous is undoubtedly the great triumphal arch at Richborough, erected late in the first century, probably to commemorate the final and successful establishment of the British province. It was a four-way arch, placed on a massive foundation, over 10 m deep, to prevent the weight from carrying it into the soft, underlying sand. Unfortunately, it was almost entirely destroyed when the Saxon Shore fort was built in the late third century, but enough fragmentary pieces survived to show its plan and to demonstrate that the structure had once been clad in white marble, imported from Italy. The top of the monument would have been ornamented with trophies of victory, and inscriptions, probably in letters of bronze, would have recorded the circumstances of its erection.

Evidence for two further, similar monuments comes from the northern frontier region. Two fragments of an inscription, found in Jarrow Church, almost certainly once belonged to a prominent memorial erected on Tyneside to record the completion of the Hadrianic frontier. Its position is most likely to have been in advance of the termination of the Wall at Wallsend. It refers specifically to the frontier works as a consolidating feature and speaks of Hadrian's desire to keep the empire within its limits.

Another, in the form of a circular, domed shrine, once existed north of the Antonine Wall beyond Falkirk. Known as Arthur's O'on, it was dismantled in the eighteenth century and the stone used for a mill-dam, but it appears to have been associated with Winged Victories and legionary eagles. It is set in a prominent position and it would have been visible for many miles; it is, therefore, likely to be more than an ordinary shrine. Its position would suggest that it commemorated the successful completion of the Scottish war conducted by Lollius Urbicus which culminated in the construction of the Antonine frontier.

CHAPTER 8

Leisure

O ne of the most popular myths concerning Rome relates to the pleasure-loving habits of its inhabitants, which, if taken at its face value would lead us to believe that no one, not even the common people, except the slaves, ever did any work. The reverse was, of course, the case, and most people, throughout the empire, worked a seven-day week, which had been known from the time of Augustus, and which was relieved only by holidays granted on the occasion of various religious festivals. Each day, from dawn to dusk, was divided into twelve hours, so that the length of the 'hours' varied according to summer or winter. Work normally began at daybreak and continued until midday – the sixth hour – although many businessmen and shopkeepers probably continued until dark, or even later. Consequently, if a man or woman was fortunate in his employment, it is probable that he had a certain amount of free time. In contrast, retirement was an admired, but seldom achieved concept, and most people probably continued work, either till they dropped, or were prevented from doing so by some incapacity.

The amount of time available for recreation for most people was, therefore, not unduly small and could be spent in a number of ways.

One of the commonest ways of relaxation, and in towns probably also the most universal, was a visit to the public baths. Most bath-houses in the Roman world were equipped with an open space, the *palaestra*, as at Silchester (fig. 42c), or, more appropriately for the British climate, a covered hall, as at Wroxeter or Leicester (figs 42a, b), in which a variety of ball-games could be played or very strenuous exercise indulged in, such as running, wrestling and boxing. After this exercise a bath would be taken in the normal manner, or, if the weather was clement, a dip in an open-air swimming-bath, as at Wroxeter, although these were not on the whole popular in Britain. Certainly, if the size of most urban public baths in Britain is taken as a guide, there was accommodation for a considerable number of bathers at any one time. It is probable, also, that itinerant food sellers would have displayed their wares in and around the palaestra, so that it would have been possible to take a snack or a drink, in much the same way that ice cream or hot dog vendors now frequent places of public recreation and entertainment. Some towns appear to have had smaller, probably privately-run bath-houses, as at Canterbury, but in the main these were probably little better than the 'massage parlours' of today.

Another, more polite way of enjoyment among the wealthier classes was the fashionable dinner-party, given at the ninth hour, in the afternoon. Tacitus refers to sumptuous banquets and, given the readily identifiable dining-rooms in houses, it is inconceivable that this form of entertainment did not take place in Britain. It was customary in the better circles for readings or recitations to take place during dinner, or for dancers, jugglers or acrobats to perform afterwards. The child's toys from the Colchester burial (see p. 276) included figures made to recline at a dining-table, while others read from scrolls. The questioning mind of a child would have undoubtedly asked what they were doing, and it is to be assumed the answer was readily forthcoming. It was also customary after a dinner-party to spend the evening drinking, either at the same house or at the home of one of the guests. Since, however, dinner was the only real repast of the day, and was usually restricted to no more than three courses, the popular idea of orgiastic gluttony, often attributed to the Roman world, is largely the product of modern imagination battening on the views of one or two ancient satirists, as in the story of Trimalchio's feast by Petronius.

The apparatus of the dinner-party is well known in Britain and includes pottery vessels graded in size accordingly for drinking wine or beer and sometimes decorated with an appropriate motto such as 'long life', or, 'give me neat wine'; normal practice was to dilute wine with water, and to drink it unmixed was considered the action of the intemperate. We might, therefore, wonder about the bibulous habits of the man who owned that particular beaker at Verulamium. Glass, pewter, and even silver, drinking vessels are also known. Samian ware, and later pewter, was undoubtedly used for dinner-parties, but exceptionally the very rich could afford silver dishes and plates, like those which were found at Mildenhall (Suffolk) and which were probably imported from an eastern province.

There is little doubt, also, that conversation pieces were provided in dining-rooms, in the form of a mosaic or wall-painting, since the best mosaics were usually placed so as not to be covered by table or couches. Vergilian references occur in one medium or the other in several villas, as well as at Silchester, indicating at least some degree of familiarity with classical literature on the part of the owners. The cultured man was therefore expected to show an interest in the arts, which he might encourage by commissioning a sculpture, mosaic or painting.

For the less well-to-do, who could not afford, or did not belong to the social class that gave dinner-parties, there was almost certainly an abundance of cafés, wine and ale shops and brothels to suit all pockets in most towns and lesser settlements. But in this respect the countryman was at a distinct disadvantage when compared with urban inhabitants, apart from the fact that he may well have had to work longer hours.

Various games of skill or chance were also played extensively among, seemingly, all classes of society. Many northern British sites produce quantities of flat, round discs, cut from stone, pottery or brick. Considerable variations occur in size, and the large majority are unmarked, and it is just conceivable that they were stoppers for flagons or amphoras, kept in place by a seal of pitch or resin. On the other hand, they could equally have been used as the pieces in some quite elaborate game, whose rules and form of play have long since disappeared. Board games of various types certainly existed, and, at Silchester, a tile inscribed before firing with chequerboard patterns, was probably manufactured as the result of idle moments in the brickworks; although, of course, they could have been made deliberately for sale as gaming boards. Gaming pieces of glass, pottery, stone, bone and lead occur widely and usually in quite large numbers, although such objects could also have been used as aids in arithmetical calculations. Sometimes the pieces are inscribed with numerals or letters and three from Silchester bear the letters FVR (thief), MAR (abbreviation for *martialis* – warlike) and PRIMVS (first). It is difficult to visualize the game played with them but several possibilities can be imagined, the most probable being some sort of battle-game. Sometimes, also, different coloured glass was used to denote opposing factions and these can be marked, on occasion with spots to give the numbers. A fine glass set occurred with a rich burial at the Lullingstone villa, together with bronze angle pieces indicating the one-time presence of the gaming board 48.3 cm square. There were fifteen white and fifteen brown pieces (fig. 123), but no dice; although the pieces each had a different number, or colour, of dots on the upper surfaces, it was concluded that they were only decorative. The game represented may have been *ludus latruncularum*, similar to chess or draughts, which would account for the absence of dice. Another set, denoting perhaps an even more intricate pattern of play, was found in Bermondsey, London. There were twelve pieces carved from bone combining the word SEXTIII with other varying devices.

Fig. 123. Glass gaming pieces from the temple-mausoleum at the villa at Lullingstone (Kent). There were fifteen white and fifteen brown pieces, each decorated with a different number, or colour, of dots. Also found were the remains of a wooden games-board (*Fox Photos Ltd, by courtesy of G.W. Meates*).

But such games were not restricted to the Roman world and a fine set, together with indications of a board, came from an Iron Age burial at Welwyn Garden City (Herts.). It included twenty-four glass counters, arranged in colour groups of six pieces each – white, blue, yellow and light green – and also six fragments of glass beads or bracelets. Experiments with the latter showed that, if thrown like dice, they could only fall with a flat or rounded surface uppermost, and therefore, they were probably used in their place. That being so, it is likely that the whole set represented a race-game for four players, perhaps not unlike backgammon.

Dice, usually carved from bone, and sometimes of slightly eccentric shape, are similarly common finds, and indeed the sport became so popular in the empire that edicts were promulgated against it; loaded dice are not unknown. Bone counters from Leicester were worn in such a way as to suggest tiddleywinks.

Music must also have played its part in leisure hours. Bone pipes have been found in London, and mouthpieces from bronze trumpet- or horn-like instruments also turn up from time to time in Britain, although they may have come from military sources. A small bronze statuette from Silchester shows a girl playing a simple pipe, although double-pipes are sometimes displayed in other contexts, as, indeed, are multiple pan-pipes. Stringed instruments were also known, and a thin fragment of ivory from Cirencester may have come from a *cithara*, a lyre-like instrument. But it is probable that, in Britain, apart from the army, most musical activities would have been restricted to religious ceremonies or theatrical performances.

Hunting and fishing appear to have been popular sports, but again it is difficult to gauge the extent of their followings in Britain. The Celtic peoples were great hunters on horseback. Moreover Britain was famed for its hunting dogs, of which there were probably several kinds, before the Roman invasion, and small bronze statuettes or

Fig. 124. Altar to Silvanus from Bollihope Common (Co. Durham). It refers to a prefect of a cavalry regiment, perhaps on a visit from his own fort at Lancaster, killing a wild boar of remarkable fineness, which none of his predecessors had been able to bag (*photo by courtesy of Dr Roger Tomlin*).

depictions on sculpture show breeds ranging from mastiff and greyhound-like animals to Scotch terriers. Hunting scenes were commonly illustrated on certain types of decorated pottery vessels, notably those produced around Colchester and Water Newton during the late second century, to which the name Hunt Cup has been given. Hounds chasing deer are the most familiar representations.

Apart from deer, wild boar was almost certainly hunted in Britain, providing excellent, if somewhat dangerous, sport. A splendid altar dedicated to Silvanus and set up far out in the country on Bollihope Common (Co. Durham) (fig. 124) records the death of a 'boar of remarkable fineness which many of my predecessors had been unable to bag'. It was dedicated by G. Tetius Veturius Micianus, prefect of a cavalry regiment, stationed at Lancaster. The nearest fort to Bollihope Common is at Binchester, and it has been suggested that Veturius was visiting, perhaps while on leave, the prefect there, and was invited to take part in a hunting expedition. It also attests the antiquity of the dangerous sport of pig-sticking.

It is likely that bears were also hunted in Britain, both as game and also for capture for use in the amphitheatre. But coursing for hares was probably commoner, and a sculptured relief from Bath illustrates the moment when the hare has just been put up and the dog is about to be unleashed. Game birds were also shot with bows and arrows or trapped with nets or bird lime, and the pheasant was probably a Roman introduction to Britain. Finally, it should not be forgotten that most weapons found on civilian sites in Britain would have been for hunting, since, by law, it was one of the few occupations in which a man might appear armed.

Fishing was probably practised more for a livelihood than for a recreation; nevertheless it is mentioned as a sport in contemporary Roman literature, and barbed fish-hooks of bronze have sometimes been found on British sites. Weighted nets were also used, as were three-pronged fish spears, or tridents.

The principal entertainments of the Roman world were, however, provided by the theatre, amphitheatre and circus and they have been introduced in Chapter 3. In Britain the theatre seems to have been a rare diversion which was, in most cases, connected with a temple. The juxtaposition of temple and theatre was common in the Graeco-Roman world, and usually indicates the presence of a deity popular enough to attract large crowds on festival days. Consequently, theatres are not only to be found on urban sites, but can exist just as easily in a rural setting, as the one at Gosbecks Farm, south of

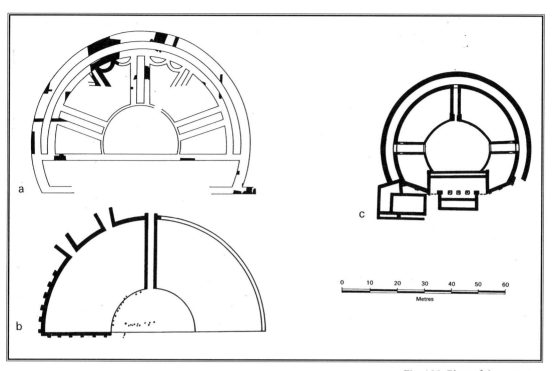

a

b

c

Fig. 125. Plans of theatres at:
a) Canterbury, early third
century (*after S.S. Frere*);
b) Gosbecks Farm, Colchester,
second century (*after R.
Niblett*); c) Verulamium, fourth
century (*after K.M. Kenyon*).

Colchester (fig. 125b). The theatre there represents the romanization of a site of ancient native sanctity, which may at one time have been the prime religious centre of the Trinovantes. At first it was built with wooden walls retaining raking banks of earth, on which the seating would have been placed, the banks being arranged in a near semicircle around a similarly shaped central space, or orchestra, across the diameter of which was placed the stage, also built of wood. An entrance into the orchestra led through the banks on the opposite side to the stage. Although the main walls were rebuilt in buttressed masonry by the middle of the second century, the stage seems to have remained entirely of timber. The orchestra was used for the seats of important people.

Another, very much smaller, 'theatre', of similar nature to that at Gosbecks Farm, has been discovered at Catterick, on the north bank of the River Swale, where it was situated beside a trapezoidally-shaped temple. A theatrical mask, made of pottery, and probably manufactured in the Nene Valley, was found with the buildings and may have been used in the performances.

Despite the existence of a temple-theatre at Gosbecks, the colonia at Colchester possessed its own urban theatre according to Tacitus, who refers to it in the events he describes as leading up to the Boudiccan rebellion. Parts of a masonry theatre have recently been discovered in the insula immediately north-west of the precinct containing the Temple of Claudius (fig. 33); enough was recovered to show that its diameter was about 70m. However it dates to the post-Boudiccan period, so that the theatre mentioned by Tacitus probably lies beneath it and may have been built of timber. More theatres may yet be found; one is suspected at Cirencester and certainly others would be expected at least in London and the coloniae, if not in the civitas capitals. An inscription from Brough-on-Humber mentions the gift of a new stage building, but a theatre in such an out-of-the-way place must almost certainly have been, once more, related to a temple.

The theatre at Canterbury, on the other hand, is a much more imposing building, although marginally smaller, than that at Gosbecks Farm, and again seems to have been related to a religious enclosure. The first structure was erected towards the end of the first century and appears to have been of Romano-Gallic form. It was, however, replaced by a much more substantial building of more classical plan in the early third century (fig. 125a).

The best-known theatre in Roman Britain is probably that at Verulamium. As at Canterbury, this had first been built in Romano-Gallic form. Consequently the orchestra, instead of being semicircular in shape, was almost a full circle, with the stage buildings forming a chord across it between the curving arms of the seating banks. But also, as at Canterbury, later alterations tended to give it a more classical profile (fig. 125c). At Verulamium, however, we are left in no doubt of the association of the theatre with one of the principal temples in the town. Indeed, before it was built, towards the middle of the second century, an open space, presumably for religious gatherings, occupied the same area in front of the temple. The provision of a theatre can, therefore, be seen as an attempt to accommodate the spectators in greater comfort, as well as enabling better crowd control to be practised.

It is exceedingly difficult to visualize what was performed in those theatres connected specifically with temples. The rituals will, presumably, have varied from deity to deity, but would normally have included scenes depicting the particular functional attributes of the god or goddess concerned, and will have been composed of part thanksgiving and part invocation. Attendances at such festivities were obviously considerable, since a theatre as large as that at Gosbecks Farm would have accommodated perhaps up to 5,000 or more people.

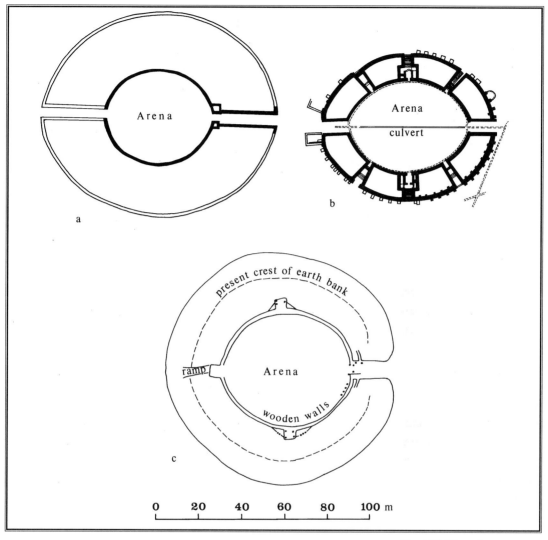

Fig. 126. Plans of amphitheatres at: a) Cirencester (*after A.D. McWhirr*); b) Caerleon (*after R.E.M. Wheeler*); c) Dorchester (*after R. Bradley*).

The requirements of the crowd would have been catered for in other ways as well, with stalls, and booths selling food and drink, or small commemorative trinkets relating to the deity, such as the bronze votive figures and miniature sacrificial axes from the rural temple site at Woodeaton (Oxon.). The further association of such places with fairs and markets has already been mentioned (p. 244), and the overall effect will probably have been not unlike some modern places of religious pilgrimage.

In urban theatres, however, performances will normally have consisted of pantomimes, mimes or recitations. The former employed actors who, by changing their clothes and face-masks, were able to represent different characters, who performed with a chorus and instrumental accompaniment to an audience that was probably familiar with most of the themes. Mime, from which the modern pantomime is descended, employed stock characters who performed highly topical sketches, more often than not of a ribald and coarse nature.

In Britain, as in other provinces with large garrisons, the amphitheatres tended to fall into two types. The military amphitheatre, or *ludus*, was used, not only for entertainments, but also for training exercises, drills and parades. Since the size of the audience was known from the first, they did not have to be constructed to contain more than the necessary number of seats, and, at Caerleon, the central arena therefore occupies a larger percentage of the total area of the building. In contrast, in civilian amphitheatres, a much higher proportion had to be devoted to seating. This can easily be appreciated by comparing the civilian amphitheatre at Cirencester with that at Caerleon (fig. 126).

In general, both types consisted of a central, elliptical arena entirely surrounded by raked earth banks for the seating, normally retained between masonry walls. The entrances to the arena penetrated the seating banks at both ends of the long axis; it is probable that they were, for part of their length, vaulted so that the seating could be carried over the top, as at Cirencester. In many cases, the masonry walls were preceded by timber, as at the legionary ludus at Chester, although occasionally as at Dorchester (Dorset) (fig. 126c), such wooden walls were not replaced. There, a Neolithic henge monument on the southern edge of the town was pressed into service as an amphitheatre. Consequently it did not follow the standard pattern, and possessed only one arena entrance; the retaining walls of the arena, which included perimeter passageways, were never replaced by masonry.

Access to the seats was probably, in most cases, from external staircases. Quite often, also, there appears to have been provision made, in the form of special boxes, for eminent people. They were normally situated immediately on a level with the top of the arena wall at either, or both, ends of the short axis, and sometimes, as at Caerleon, were placed over shrines to various deities, such as Nemesis or Fortune. Shrines, alternatively, could be placed in small chambers on each side of the arena entrance, as at Chester and Cirencester. A shrine at Chester had an altar to Nemesis still standing in it when excavated, while a lead curse (see p. 269) found at Caerleon read: 'Lady Nemesis, I give thee a cloak and a pair of boots; let him who wore them not redeem them except with his life's blood.'

It is unlikely that the seating of amphitheatres in Britain was often protected from the elements, although both theatres and amphitheatres in the Mediterranean region often had canvas awnings hoisted to ward off the sun rather than the rain. There is, however, a suggestion that Caerleon may have been so equipped.

Both legionary fortresses at Caerleon and Chester had their amphitheatres, but that at York has yet to be identified. Neither, for that matter, has any amphitheatre been discovered at fortresses of an earlier date, such as Exeter, Gloucester or Wroxeter. Nevertheless, some forts, such as Tomen-y-Mur were provided with them, although of smaller and more appropriate size for an auxiliary regiment. In the civilian sphere, almost all chartered towns and civitas capitals will have possessed them, although, as yet, none are known at the former sites although one has now been discovered at London under the Guildhall. Among the civitas capitals, amphitheatres still stand, as grass-covered mounds, at Cirencester, Dorchester, Carmarthen and Silchester; others are known at Chichester and Caerwent; a recent aerial photograph of Caistor-by-Norwich shows what may be an amphitheatre some little distance south of the town, but it is very small and is perhaps more likely to be a Romano-Gallic theatre. Normally they were constructed on the outskirts of a town, since they required large areas of ground; consequently they were often excluded when fortifications were built. That at London, which was within the defences and at Caerwent, which was constructed inside the walls, are the only exceptions in Britain. Other amphitheatres are known at the minor settlements of Charterhouse (Somerset) and Richborough. Another possibility, at Leicester, is suggested by a sherd of pottery found there with a graffito carved on it and reading: 'Verecunda actress; Lucius gladiator'. It may have been dropped by a member of a company of travelling players.

The types of displays performed in amphitheatres will have varied enormously, ranging from gladiatorial combats to cock-fighting or bear-baiting. The former were expensive, since the fighters had to be hired from a contractor, who trained and kept them. No training establishment has ever been identified in Britain, but a heavy, bronze helmet of typical gladiatorial pattern has been found at Hawkedon in Suffolk. It may well have been part of the loot taken from Colchester during the Boudiccan rebellion. In Britain, commoner shows probably involved wild animals fighting together, and the province could produce bulls, wild boars, bears, wolves and dogs. Occasionally, wild-beast hunts may have been simulated, but it is doubtful if more exotic animals such as lions or tigers often figured, since the price would have been exorbitant; certainly no instance of the recovery, on excavations, of the bones from such animals has been recorded. Sometimes, also, animals may have been tamed to perform circus acts, and it should not be forgotten that public executions were often carried out in the arena. Boxers, wrestlers, jugglers and acrobats may all have taken part, and a colour-coated piece of pottery from Water Newton depicts a female acrobat performing her feats on top of animals with two gladiators fighting nearby.

Apart from the existence of the buildings themselves, an interest in theatrical and amphitheatrical performances was displayed in many other ways. One theatrical mask from Catterick has already been mentioned (p. 285) although it could have been an *oscillum*, hung outside a door to ward off evil spirits. Parts of another, of tragic mien, have been found at Baldock, while another miniature mask, carved of ivory, was discovered near the legionary bath-house at Caerleon. There is a marked contrast between the styles of the latter and the Catterick mask, as might be expected. Caerleon, with its strong citizen body, would have required performances measuring up to the true Roman standards; consequently the mask shows all the classic features to be expected. The Catterick mask, on the other hand, with its lentoid, rather than round, holes for the eyes, its straight nose, and narrow slit of a mouth, comes largely from a Celtic world.

A further interest in theatricals might be implied from the Leicester wall-paintings, where at least two tragic masks were included, together with a simplified architectural illustration resembling a proscaenium. Another face-mask was depicted on a wall fresco from Cirencester.

Scenes from the arena were used to decorate pottery and glass vessels. Although the latter were almost certainly imported, the former were frequently made in Britain and therefore imply a first-hand knowledge of the shows on the part of the potters. The colour-coated Colchester vase shows a fight between a heavily armed gladiator (*mirmillo*) and a man armed only with net and trident (*retiarius*), and names them as Secundus Memnon and Salvenus

Valentinus respectively. There is also a reference to the thirtieth legion, stationed at Xanten on the Rhine. It is possible that the vase, which probably dates to the second century, was made as a souvenir or commemoration piece to record the visit to Colchester of a troupe from Xanten, but, since the legionary reference has been scratched on after firing, presumably by the owner, we cannot be certain.

One of the mosaics from the Bignor villa illustrates a scene of nine winged cupids dressed as gladiators and undergoing training with three instructors standing by. It is a lively scene, depicting different types of combat; in one, a retiarius lies wounded on the ground. Another scene of a gladiatorial battle is shown on one of the mosaics from the villa at Brading (I.O.W.).

Small portable articles, such as the ivory handle of a pocket-knife, carved to represent a gladiator, from South Shields, or the bronze statuette of another from London, may represent souvenirs sold by itinerant traders during the course of the games. A bronze statuette of an athlete, found in a bath-house at York, may on the other hand have been used to decorate the palaestra, and so be more symbolic of exercise there, than of an arena scene.

The last of the three principal forms of amusement in the Roman world, the circus, is not well attested in Britain, and no building related to this entertainment has yet been positively identified. Normally, they were long, but comparatively narrow buildings with a central spine set lengthwise down the middle, round which the races would be run; seats were provided on the perimeter and stables were usually situated at one end. Nevertheless, horse- and chariot-racing, the sports carried on in them, could also take place wherever there was a large enough area of level ground. Remembering the Celtic love for hunting on horseback and both Roman and Celtic love of gambling, it would be surprising if racing had not become an accepted sport in Britain. At the villa at Chedworth, an inscription had been roughly scratched on a wall, referring to a 'green company'. In Rome, the four racing colours, each belonging to a different faction, were red, white, blue and green, so that the Chedworth inscription may be an allusion to horse- or chariot-racing, perhaps at nearby Cirencester. Two more references come from Lincolnshire, one from the colonia itself, in the form of a fragmentary stone carving showing a boy charioteer, the other from the villa at Horkstow, where a mosaic graphically depicts a combined horse and chariot race in progress. One chariot, in turning the corner at the end of the straight has hit the central wall and lost a wheel, so tipping out the charioteer, who is being helped by a dismounted horseman. It may be, however, that the latter scene is not so much topical as allegorical, since it is combined with an Orpheus mosaic. Glass beakers were also imported to Britain showing circus scenes, presumably as companions for those on which gladiators fight. A small bone plaque, found in a burial at York, was inscribed with a phrase, the language of which is appropriate to gladiators or charioteers.

In the context of horse-racing, there is the interesting building which appears to belong to a temple at Wroxeter (p. 254 and 256). Among the deities venerated in the temple was certainly a god or goddess associated with horses, since fragments of a life-size stone head of a horse were found in it; a small cast bronze horse's head, and parts of a bronze headstall may also have come from it, although there is the possibility that they originated in the earlier, military layers. In Celtic mythology, the principal horse goddess was Epona, although it is probable that others like her also existed. To the rear of the temple was a large and unusual enclosure, which has not yet been fully excavated; it was approximately rectangular with rounded corners and may well have extended for over a hundred metres and as far as the town fortifications. There was a large central space surrounded by twin parallel walls, some 4 m apart, on which, it has been suggested, wooden seating could be erected, and opinion so far seems to favour its interpretation as a primitive amphitheatre. But if the principal deity of the temple was connected with horses, it seems far more likely that races or other forms of equestrian activity were practised on festival days, and the building would have been more appropriate for this purpose.

Leisure implies more than just time spent in pleasurable pursuits; it can also imply idleness and the unseemly acts which sometimes spring from it. Consequently, it is of interest to note the first recorded act of senseless, urban vandalism of a deserted building in Britain, at Leicester. The house which contained the fine painted wall-plaster appears to have been unoccupied and possibly roofless in the late second century. Parts were taken over by various manufacturers, and a deposit of cows' heads was found on the floor of a room, after it had been stripped of its mosaic floor. But, apart from the industrial workers, other less desirable people seem to have visited it from time to time and scrawled upon the walls; one such graffito mentioned a mare's arse, another had a clear

Fig. 127. Painted wall-plaster from the portico of a house in Leicester. The scene includes a central architectural perspective, flanked on either side by groups of figures, with another architectural scene beginning on the right-hand side. The vandals have attacked the principal areas of decoration, so leaving the gaps (*photo: F.M.B. Cooke*).

reference to sodomy. When the building was ultimately demolished, the clay walls were tumbled to the ground, carrying much of their painted plaster with them, which was then recovered in the course of excavations. After one of the main panels had been restored, it was found to have four gaps in it, which started at ground level and rose no higher than the height of an average man. These gaps coincided with the four main decorative features of the panel: two groups of human figures on either side of an architectural perspective. We must assume, therefore, that the plaster from these gaps had been deliberately destroyed before the building had been demolished, otherwise the fragments would have been found, as with the rest. But a vandal, intent on destruction, is most likely to pick the centrepieces of an ornamental display for immediate attention, and we may conclude that this had happened at Leicester (fig. 127).

Other acts of wanton damage, as opposed to religious, or official, vandalism which was more commonplace, are difficult to identify, and appear mostly as minor incidents, such as the graffiti which were scratched on the walls of the council chamber in the basilica at Caerwent, presumably after law and order had broken down. Indeed, graffiti written on plastered walls are not uncommon, and in many cases were probably scrawled by children while the houses were still occupied. The word EQVVS, together with a 'pin' chicken emerging from a highly distorted egg, from a house at Verulamium were probably so caused by a child in an idle moment.

Taken as a whole, therefore, there is no lack of evidence of the way in which spare time was spent in Roman Britain, although it is not as plentiful as that from some other provinces.

CHAPTER 9

And After the Romans?

We saw in Chapter 1 how the Roman invasion of Britain came about as the result of the coincidence of a number of events. So in the end, many factors contributed to the decline of Roman Britain, not all of which are yet fully understood, as, from the end of the fourth century onwards, if not before, the evidence becomes less, and much more difficult to interpret. The forces at work were partly internal, partly external, and appear at times almost as a death wish on the part of the empire. It has been said that every great institution carries within it the seeds of its own destruction, and this is probably true of the Roman empire.

It is extremely difficult, if not entirely impossible, to point to a particular stage in the decline of fourth-century Britain (fig. 31), and say that at that moment the rot started. The peak of general prosperity, which had started early in that century, was probably reached within the reign of Constantine I. After that it is possible to trace at first a very gradual decline, relieved by minor recoveries from time to time and place to place, until the worsening military situation culminated in the barbarian conspiracy (see p. 53) of AD 367. Even then all was by no means lost, and given different people and different circumstances thereafter, a totally different outcome might have resulted.

Then came, in AD 383, the British revolt led by Magnus Maximus against the central authority. As has so often been the case in history, the ambition and greed, the success or failure of only one man can alter the whole course of subsequent events. So it was then, and from AD 383, the rate of decline in Britain became more precipitous, partly because a considerable reduction in garrison strength caused less money to circulate, partly because repressive measures implemented after the rebellion probably removed permanently from the scene many of the most able people in the provinces. Further events, ending with the military reorganizations of AD 395–401, accelerated the process, by which time the garrison strength had again been severely reduced. Growing dissatisfaction with the officials of the central government in Britain, who could no longer fully control events, also brought its repercussions, and between AD 405–7, the diocese threw up, in turn, three usurper emperors. The last of these, Constantine III, responded to the confidence expressed in him by the Britons by taking almost all remaining army units to Gaul in order to expand his own sphere of influence and to expel marauders; once more, personal ambition had intervened. In disgust, the British leaders threw out Constantine's remaining officers and also the last officials of the central government.

The hiatus in government which followed, during which the Britons were presumably managing their own affairs, culminated in official instructions being issued by the emperor Honorious, probably as the result of a request for help, that they must conduct their own defence. The letter was sent to the civitates of Britain, and it is to be assumed, therefore, that the decurions had assumed ultimate responsibility. But it is not surprising that, in such circumstances, strong men would come into their own, and among them one called Vortigern appeared upon the scene; his name, in fact, means 'high king'. It would appear that he was devoted to Pelagianism, the Christian heresy which was strongly represented in Britain (see p. 268), particularly among the ruling class. It is interesting that he adopted a purely British name, and it has been suggested that he was the leader of the anti-Roman party, intent on maintaining the independence of Britain. To do so, he appears to have traded land, especially in Kent, but possibly also elsewhere, with the Saxons in return for armed protection.

The most dangerous enemies of Britain at the time were the Picts and secondly the Irish, and settlements of Saxon federate soldiers seem to have been placed by Vortigern at strategic places on the east coast and also inland, such as at Dorchester-on-Thames.

But the orthodox Church also had a strong following, and eventually Vortigern was outmanoeuvred, partly by the visit of St Germanus to combat the heresy in AD 429 and, later, partly by a serious rebellion of his Saxon troops. After this, he appears to have been displaced by Ambrosius, a member of the orthodox party, and it is probable that it was he and his supporters who, appalled by the progress being made by the Saxons and others, directed the final appeal for help to Rome, the so-called Groans of the Britons: 'To

Aetius, thrice consul, come the groans of the Britons . . . the barbarians drive us into the sea, the sea drives us back to the barbarians; between these two means of death we are either killed or drowned.' Dated to between AD 446 and 454, most probably to the former year, it is the last firm date which we have in the dissolution of Roman Britain. The appeal, however, went unanswered; Rome no longer had time for an erstwhile, remote province.

Perhaps surprisingly, in the period under discussion, no great and immediate decline occurred in the Romano-British way of life, beyond that which had already come about in the late fourth century. Almost all the evidence now being produced tends to show that, in most areas, life continued much as before. Indeed Bede, admittedly writing two centuries later, refers to it as a time of peace and prosperity, after the Britons had ejected the Roman officials. There were changes, certainly, but they were caused more by abandonment and decay than by warfare, and many of the buildings which were left to fall down were those which were now superfluous to contemporary requirements. The first sufferers, as already indicated in Chapter 4, were the isolated farms and villas, bereft of their markets in towns because the highways were no longer safe or kept repaired. But it is important to distinguish individual cases, as some places were seemingly more resilient than others. Yet many towns appear to have survived in full operation even when deprived of their chief sources of supply. It is probable that they relied, in the end, on local produce, and the corn-drying oven, inserted into a farmers' house at Verulamium (fig. 44d), is eloquent evidence of what was happening. But despite the restrictions on food supply, Verulamium still had a functioning aqueduct and water distribution system, and moreover, new masonry buildings were still being erected, while the forum at Cirencester seems to have been used as a market-place until at least AD 440. But, by that time, it is necessary to draw distinctions between one area and another. For instance, the areas of east Kent, east Anglia and the middle Thames Valley were probably most affected by the rebellion of Saxon federates, and it is likely that by the mid-fifth century those areas had disappeared under Saxon subjugation. There is evidence from Canterbury, and at some other towns, of Saxon mercenaries being given an insula in the town for their own dwellings, presumably in return for military service, while at Caistor-by-Norwich there is a cremation cemetery which was used mainly by federate soldiers of like kind.

Although slow decay rather than violence at the hands of enemy raiders seems to have been the main cause of destruction, there were, nevertheless, places where the end came with fire and slaughter. Probably early in the fifth century two of the signal stations on the Yorkshire coast so suffered. Isolated villas, such as North Wraxall (Wilts.) or Lullingstone (Kent) went up in flames and at the former, two bodies were thrown down a well. No doubt they had attracted the attentions of a raiding party, or even of a rebellious peasantry, and the apparent presence of troops at the former may well have provided the reason. On the whole, however, Britain does not seem to have suffered, as did parts of Gaul, from social upheavals which led to open rebellion of slaves and labourers.

In such circumstances, it is probable that villa-owners abandoned their homes to their fate and, at first, sought sanctuary in the nearest walled town or settlement. But as the pressure of Anglo-Saxon settlement increased, so whole areas may have been evacuated by the upper classes, who fled westwards. What then happened to the slaves and peasants is not known; some, like their masters, may have fled also, but those remaining would probably have fared no worse under Saxon than under Romano-British domination. There is, for instance, a record of Celtic-speaking Britons remaining in the Fens as late as the eighth century.

So long as towns could provide enough inhabitants to man their defences and had enough food, they were largely safe from Saxon assault. The Saxons had neither the equipment for breaching fortfications nor the tenacity to mount a siege; nevertheless they could destroy all standing crops, so that periodic famines may have resulted. It is somewhat surprising, therefore, to find some towns being deserted for no very obvious reason, often, as in Wales and the west country, in favour of a nearby Iron Age hillfort, as at South Cadbury or possibly Dinorben (fig. 74). Alternatively, it seems that, at Cirencester, the nearby amphitheatre was fortified as a stronghold. But by this time, each place has to be considered on its own merits. With communications unsafe, or cut altogether, as seems to have happened to the main road from Silchester to Dorchester-on-Thames, each town and village tended to become a small isolated enclave of surviving Romano-British customs and institutions. What happened at one, therefore, was not necessarily common to all.

But the end when it came, if not violent, could still be abrupt. At Cirencester, for instance, a new ditch dug beside a main road in the town centre remained unfilled with road silt, an indication that traffic had ceased; instead it collected decaying leaves and grass – and two unburied corpses. At Silchester, attempts seem to have been made to protect, or delimit, an area round the town by means of large dykes. These appear mostly on the side facing towards the Thames valley. Since one of the earliest rebellions, and consequent takeover of an area, on the part of Saxon federate troops, seems to have centred on the garrison town of Dorchester-on-Thames, the dykes probably represent an attempt by the townspeople of Silchester to restrict the rebels.

What then led the inhabitants of towns apparently to abandon their safe refuges ultimately in favour of less desirable places? A combination of factors was almost certainly responsible and together caused a depopulation so serious as to render the defence of most large towns an impossible task; hence the removal by the survivors to smaller, more easily fortified sites. Among the reasons, we might include flight to more distant places of safety, famine, rebellion and ultimately a major pestilential epidemic.

By the middle of the fifth century, therefore, parts of eastern and central Britain had been taken over by the rebel Saxon federate troops, reinforced probably by other migrants from across the North Sea. But other movements had also taken place. In Wales and the west, the first half of the fifth century was marked by raids from across the Irish Sea, and to help combat them Cunedda, a chieftain from the Votadini whose tribal area was situated south of the Firth of Forth, was transferred with a body of supporters to north Wales. Ultimately the trouble was settled by a fortuitous marriage between the opposing factions and the increasing strength of Christianity in the Celtic parts of the British islands.

It would seem, therefore, that until troubled by the totality of events in the middle of the century, some form of central control had been successfully retained. Thereafter, the disintegration became faster, and may be seen as being linked with the final collapse of overall authority and the eclipse of almost all surviving traces of Romano-British culture and institutions.

Vortigern was replaced by Ambrosius, and he sometime after by the even more shadowy figure of Arthur. But it did not all go the way of the Saxons, despite some local success on their part. Towards the end of the century, the Britons, who still could command cavalry, rallied and inflicted a major defeat on the Saxons at the unidentified site of Mount Badon. After it there ensued another period of peace and stability which is reputed to have lasted for two generations. Into such a stage of equilibrium might best be fitted the Silchester Dykes.

By the middle of the sixth century, the Saxon advance had been resumed, perhaps with the added impetus caused by the arrival in Britain of an epidemic of bubonic plague which was affecting most of the Mediterranean world. By the end of the century most remaining areas of Britain, excluding the Celtic regions of the south-west, Wales and Scotland, had been overrun. In those regions there sometimes survived a legacy of Roman Britain, such as the Latin loanwords taken into early Welsh, and possible systems of land tenure. Elsewhere, the institutions which had nourished Britain for nearly four centuries were extinguished. If Roman towns became English towns, it was largely the accident of geography which so decreed it, and apart from possible continuity of settlement in them, they were completely changed. Villas sometimes coincide with English villages, but again it is probable that the ideal situations which they normally enjoyed were those which equally suited villages. Yet, sometimes in those later years there comes an echo of a vanished era, such as the Anglian *praefectus Lindocolinae civitatis* who governed Lincoln in the seventh century. But it is only an echo, with no substance in it; Roman Britain had passed into history.

Further Reading

General

There is now a very large literature on the subject of Roman Britain, which continues to grow every year. Consequently only a selection of further reading material can be listed here. The list includes not only the most recent material, but also some of the classics from past decades, so that readers can see for themselves how the subject has developed. Foremost among the latter should be included R.G. Collingwood (ed. I.A. Richmond), *The Archaeology of Roman Britain* (London, 1969) and R.G. Collingwood and J.N.L. Myres, *Roman Britain and the English Settlements* (Oxford, 1937), which should be read in conjunction with its later replacement in the Oxford History of England series: P. Salway, *Roman Britain* (Oxford, 1981). Two other early publications are still valuable: I.A. Richmond, *Roman Britain* (Harmondsworth, 1963) and A.L.F. Rivet, *Town and Country in Roman Britain* (London, 1963).

The current standard work on Roman Britain is still, and is likely to remain for some time to come, S.S. Frere, *Britannia: A History of Roman Britain* (now in its third, revised edition, London, 1987). Other general treatments of the subject are M. Todd, *Roman Britain, 55BC–AD400* (Fontana, 1981); T.W. Potter and C. Johns, *Roman Britain* (London 1992); M. Millett, *Roman Britain* (London, 1995). Also important for the study is the Ordnance Survey, *Map of Roman Britain* (Southampton, 1978). More specialized but containing much useful information are A.L.F. Rivet and C. Smith, *The Place-Names of Roman Britain* (London, 1979) and A. Birley, *The People of Roman Britain* (London 1979). Behind the latter lie the two great volumes of R.G. Collingwood and R.P. Wright, *The Roman Inscriptions of Britain, Vol. I* (Oxford 1965); *Vol. II, Fascicules 1–8* (ed. S.S. Frere and R.S.O. Tomlin, 1990–95), with the indexes to Vol. I (ed. R. Goodburn and H. Waugh, 1983) and Vol. II (ed. S.S. Frere, 1995). Recent discoveries in all aspects of Roman Britain are collected in a series of articles, M. Todd (ed.) *Research on Roman Britain, 1960–89* (London, 1989). Annual archaeological discoveries, as well as inscriptions, since 1970, are reported briefly in *Britannia*, which also contains many useful articles on Iron Age, Roman and Dark Age Britain. Before 1970, they are to be found in successive volumes of the *Journal of Roman Studies*. From time to time papers relating to the subject are published in the *Journal of Roman Archaeology, Antiquaries Journal, Archaeological Journal, Antiquity, Archaeologia* and in the transactions or journals of the many county archaeological societies. For those wishing to visit sites, useful gazetteers are P. Somerset Fry, *Roman Britain: History and Sites* (Newton Abbot, 1984) and R.J.A. Wilson, *Roman Remains in Britain* (London, 1988). The former, although less comprehensive, is easier to use; the latter is more like a travelogue.

Chapter 1

The standard work on the British Iron Age is undoubtedly B. Cunliffe, *Iron Age Communities in Britain* (London, 3rd ed. 1991) which covers the period from the seventh century BC to the Roman conquest. The opening chapters of Frere's *Britannia* (see above) are a more condensed summary of the later part of that period. An excellent translation of Caesar has now been provided by Anne and Peter Wiseman, *Julius Caesar: The Battle for Gaul* (London, 1980), together with a short commentary. A stimulating account of European oppida is J. Collis, *Oppida: Earliest Towns North of the Alps* (Sheffield, 1984), and M. Jesson and D. Hill (eds), *The Iron Age and its Hill-Forts* (Southampton, 1971) is still useful, especially for the article by P. Fowler on the reuse of hillforts in the late and sub-Roman periods. As with the Roman period, the Ordnance Survey, *Map of Southern Britain in the Iron Age* (Chessington, 1967) is also, despite its age, still valuable.

Chapter 2

The invasion of Britain has been the subject of several specialized books from which can be picked the trilogy by G. Webster, *The Roman Invasion of Britain* (London, 1980), *Rome against Caratacus* (London, 1981) and *Boudica: the Revolt against Rome* (London, 1978) which also cover the first decades of the occupation. The later first century is, of course, the subject of the biography of Agricola by his son-in-law, Tacitus; translations are provided by the Penguin classics and the Loeb Classical Library. An excellent commentary has been compiled by R.M. Ogilvie and I.A. Richmond, *Cornelii Taciti: de Vita Agricola* (Oxford, 1967). A more modern survey of the period has been undertaken by W.S. Hanson, *Agricola and the Conquest of the North* (London, 1987), while the whole history of the northern frontier area has been the subject of several recent books: D.J. Breeze, *The Northern Frontiers of Roman Britain* (London, 1982); W.S. Hanson and G.S. Maxwell, *Rome's North-West Frontier: The Antonine Wall* (Edinburgh, 1983); D.J. Breeze and B. Dobson, *Hadrian's Wall* (Harmondsworth, 1978). The definitive, topographical survey of Hadrian's Wall is still J. Collingwood Bruce, *Handbook to the Roman Wall*, now in its 13th edition (ed. C. Daniels, Newcastle, 1978). The Ordnance Survey has likewise produced maps of each frontier: *Map of Hadrian's Wall* (Chessington, 1964) and *The Antonine Wall* (Southampton, 1969).

The comprehensive topography of Roman Wales is still best sought in V.E. Nash-Williams, *The Roman Frontier in Wales* (Cardiff; 2nd revised edition by M.G. Jarrett, 1969), now partly updated by J.L. Davies, 'Roman Military Deployment in Wales and the Marches from Claudius to the Antonines' in W.S. Hanson and L.J.F. Keppie (eds), *Roman Frontier Studies, Part I* (Oxford, 1980), pp. 255–77.

The third and fourth century coastal defences of the Saxon Shore are covered in some detail in S. Johnson, *The Roman Forts of the Saxon Shore* (London, 1976) and V. Maxfield (ed.), *The Saxon Shore: A Handbook* (Exeter, 1989). Also of interest is a collection of relevant articles in D.E. Johnston (ed.), *The Saxon Shore* (London, 1977), which, as with the previous reference, contains a good deal of evidence from the companion forts across the Channel.

Chapter 3

All categories of urban settlements are covered by two books: J. Wacher, *The Towns of Roman Britain* (London, 1995) and B.C. Burnham and J. Wacher, *The Small Towns* of *Roman Britain* (London, 1990). Of a smaller compass is G. de la Bédoyère, *Roman Towns in Britain* (London, 1992), but it has some excellent reconstruction drawings. A collection of papers from a conference held in 1992 was edited by A.E. Brown, *Roman Small Towns in Eastern England and Beyond* (Oxford, 1995) and covers more than the title suggests. The early development of a selection of six major towns which began as legionary fortresses is considered in G. Webster (ed.), *Fortress into City* (London, 1988). There are also a number of volumes, covering individual towns from which might be selected A. Down, *Roman Chichester* (Chichester, 1988); P. Ottaway, *Roman York* (London, 1993); P. Marsden, *Roman London* (London, 1980); the stimulating book by D. Perring, *Roman London* (London, 1991), and G.C. Boon, *Silchester: the Roman Town of Calleva* (Newton Abbot, 1974). The last decades have also seen the growth of a massive series of excavation reports from Canterbury, Exeter, Lincoln, London, Verulamium and York, among others.

Chapter 4

There is an equally large mass of literature on villas and the countryside: J. Percival, *The Roman Villa* (London, 1976) is a useful introduction, although not confined to Britain. A good general survey of country matters is still S. Applebaum in H.P.R. Finberg (ed.), *The Agrarian History of England and Wales*, Vol. I, ii (Cambridge, 1972). K. Branigan, *The Roman Villa in South-West England* (Bradford-on-Avon, 1977) and K. Branigan and D. Miles, *The Economies of Romano-British Villas* (Sheffield, 1988) are also to be recommended. Edited collections of papers are contained in A.L.F. Rivet (ed.), *The Roman Villa in Britain* (London, 1969); M. Todd (ed.) *Studies in the Romano-British Villa* (Leicester, 1978). As with towns, there is a number of excavation reports of individual villas such as Gorhambury, Gadebridge Park, Fishbourne, Gatcombe and Lullingstone. The peripheral areas of the south-west, Wales and the north are covered by several titles: A. Fox, *South-West England* (London, 1964); J.L.P. Foster and G. Daniel (eds), *Prehistoric and Early Wales* (London, 1963); A.C. Thomas (ed.), *Rural Settlement in Roman Britain* (London, 1966) and P. Clark and S. Haselgrove (eds), *Rural Settlement in the Roman North* (Durham, 1981).

H.C. Bowen and P.J. Fowler (eds), *Early Land Allotment* (Oxford, 1978), while not restricted to the Roman period, contains many articles relating to fields and their associated settlements. An exhaustive survey of farm implements is contained in S.E. Rees, *Agricultural Implements in Prehistoric and Roman Britain, parts i and ii* (Oxford, 1979). General husbandry is well described in K.D. White, *Roman Farming* (London, 1970) and there is an excellent account of a Roman garden in B. Cunliffe, *Fishbourne: A Roman Palace and its Garden* (London, 1971).

Chapter 5

A collection of articles edited by D. Braund, *The Administration of the Roman Empire, 214BC–AD193* (Exeter, 1988) is a good introduction to the subject, more fully developed in J.S. Richardson, *Roman Provincial Administration* (Bristol, 1984). In addition, there is D. Braund, *Rome and the Friendly King* (Exeter, 1984) on the subject of client rulers. More specific is F.F. Abbott and A.C. Johnson, *Municipal Administration in the Roman Empire* (New York, 1926).

The best introduction to the highly technical subject of Roman coinage is probably H. Mattingly, *Roman Coins* (London, 1960), with the historical contexts of coins being discussed by M. Grant, *Roman History from Coins* (Cambridge, 1968).

Specific to Roman Britain are R. Reece, *Roman Coinage in Britain* (London, 1987) and G. Askew, *The Coinage of Roman Britain* (London, 1951). A good account of the principles of Roman law is to be found in H. Jolowicz, *Historical Introduction to the Study of Roman Law* (Cambridge, 1972), supplemented by F. Schulz, *Classical Roman Law* (Oxford, 1951). The interaction of military and civilian areas of government, especially in the later empire, has been considered by R. MacMullen, *Soldier and Civilian in the Roman Empire* (Harvard, 1963). A wealth of examples, quoted from the original sources, with commentaries, and covering a very wide range of legal and administrative matters is contained in N. Lewis and M. Reinhold (eds), *Roman Civilization. Sourcebook II: the Empire* (New York, 1966).

Much of the organization and work of the Roman army is digested by G. Webster, *The Roman Imperial Army* (London, 1979), with the daily life of the soldier, among other matters, being described by G.W. Watson, *The Roman Soldier* (London, 1969). Much information about the workings of the army has been derived from studies of Trajan's Column: I.A. Richmond, *Trajan's Army or Trajan's Column* (Rome, 1982), and F. Lepper and S. Frere, *Trajan's Column* (Gloucester, 1988). The origins of the auxiliary regiments are dealt with in P.A. Holder, *The Auxilia from Augustus to Trajan* (Oxford, 1980). A recent book on the cavalry, covering almost every aspect from recruitment, units, equipment, training, supply and welfare is K.R. Dixon and P. Southern, *The Roman Cavalry* (London, 1992). Unfortunately, little has yet been published on the logistics of the army, although it is a subject that is now receiving more attention. Of interest is an article by R.W. Davies, 'The Roman Military Diet' in *Britannia* 2 (1971), 122–42. The information cited for Inchtuthil can be found in L.F. Pitts and J.K. St. Joseph, *Inchtuthil: The Roman Legionary Fortress* (London, 1985) combined with E.A.M. Shirley, 'The building of the legionary fortress at Inchtuthil' in *Britannia* 27 (1996), 111–28. The latter volume also contains an article by R. Kendal, 'Transport logistics associated with the building of Hadrian's Wall'.

Chapter 6

Some references mentioned in the preceding section are equally applicable here, particularly those relating to the army. A good general introduction to economic matters is K. Greene, *The Archaeology of the Roman Economy* (London, 1986), to which can be added the now somewhat dated, but magisterial surveys of M. Rostovtzeff, *The Social and Economic History of Ancient Rome. Vols 1 and 2* (Oxford, 1957) and I. Tenny Frank (ed.), *An Economic Survey of Ancient Rome* in 5 vols. (USA, 1933–40): the British section occurs in Vol. 3. Interesting information on the costs and payments for public works are contained in R.P. Duncan-Jones, *The Economy of the Roman Empire* (Cambridge, 1982) and *Structure and Scale in the Roman Economy* (Cambridge, 1990). Also useful are S. McGrail (ed.), *Woodworking Techniques before AD1500* (Oxford, 1982) and J.P. Adams, *Roman Building Materials and Techniques* (London, 1994); also I.M. Barton (ed.), *Roman Public Buildings* (Exeter, 1989).

The standard work on roads in Roman Britain remains the monumental classic I.D. Margary, *Roman Roads in Britain* (London, 1967), while the more recent book D.E. Johnston, *An Illustrated History of Roman Roads in Britain* (Bourne End, 1979) is also worth studying. A more general treatment, covering most of the empire, is R. Chevalier, *Roman Roads* (London, 1976). The essential tool of surveying which lay behind road and building construction is considered by O.A.W. Dilke, *The Roman Land Surveyors* (Newton Abbot, 1971). Roads, bridges, aqueducts and all manner of other structural processes needed some knowledge of rule-of-thumb engineering: J.G. Landels, *Engineering in the Ancient World* (California UP, 1978).

The extent of literacy in Roman Britain has long been a subject of contention; central to the problem is K.H. Jackson, *Language and History in Early Britain* (Edinburgh, 1953). Also of interest is a short article by J.C. Mann, 'Spoken Latin in Britain as evidenced in the inscriptions', *Britannia* 2 (1971), 218–24. The practice of medicine is well recorded in R. Jackson, *Doctors and Diseases in the Roman Empire* (London, 1988).

Metal extraction and working has received a great deal of attention, and in consequence there are numerous publications, from which might be selected J.F. Healy, *Mining and Metallurgy in the Greek and Roman World* (London, 1978) and R.F. Tylecote, *Metallurgy and Archaeology* (London, 1962). Treatment of specific metals can be found in H. Cleere and D.W. Crossley, *The Iron Industry of the Weald* (Leicester, 1985); G.D.B. Jones and P.R. Lewis, 'The Dolaucothi Gold Mines', *Antiquaries Journ.* 49 (1969), 244–72; W. Gowland, 'Remains of a Roman silver refinery at Silchester', *Archaeologia* 57, i (1900), 113–24.

As with metals, the manufacture of brick, tile and pottery has an extensive literature. A.D. McWhirr, *Roman Brick and Tile: Studies in Manufacture, Distribution and Use in the Western Empire* (Oxford, 1979) is a collection of articles covering a wide-ranging treatment of the first two categories, and V.G. Swan, *The Pottery Kilns of Roman Britain* (London, 1984) deals with the last. A general review of Roman glass is contained in D.B. Harden, 'Ancient Glass II: Roman' in *Archaeological Journ.* 126 (1969), 44–77.

Two books gather information on nearly all the aspects reviewed in this chapter. A brief, but comprehensive, survey is contained in A.D. McWhirr, *Roman Crafts and Industries* (Aylesbury, 1982), while fuller treatment is accorded in D.E. Strong and D. Brown (eds), *Roman Crafts* (London, 1976).

Chapter 7

The background to religion in Britain before the Romans is covered very adequately in A. Ross, *Pagan Celtic Britain* (London, 1974), while the specific subject of the Druids is admirably dealt with by S. Piggott, *The Druids* (Harmondsworth, 1974) and M.J. Green, *Exploring the World of the Druids* (London, 1997). For the Roman period M. Henig, *Religion in Roman Britain* (London, 1984) is to be recommended. A shorter, but quite comprehensive, survey is by M. Green, *The Gods of Roman Britain* (Aylesbury, 1983). More abstruse aspects can be found in E. and J.R. Harris, *The Oriental Cults of Roman Britain* (Leiden, 1965). An almost complete corpus of temples in Britain is contained in W. Rodwell, *Temples, Churches and Religion in Roman Britain, Vols I and II* (Oxford, 1980), to which can still usefully be added M.J.T. Lewis, *Temples in Roman Britain* (Cambridge, 1966).

The essential book for the study of Christianity is now C. Thomas, *Christianity in Roman Britain to AD 500* (London, 1981), which can be supplemented by a collection of papers in M.W. Barley and R.P.C. Hanson, (eds), *Christianity in Roman Britain, 300–700* (Leicester, 1968); also of interest is D. Watts, *Christians and Pagans in Roman Britain* (London, 1991). Still worth reading is an earlier article by J.M.C. Toynbee, 'Christianity in Roman Britain', *Journ. British Archaeological Association* (3rd Series), 16 (1953), 1–124.

A general account of burial customs is contained in a collection of papers R. Reece (ed.), *Burial in the Roman World* (Oxford, 1977), together with an earlier treatment by J.M.C. Toynbee, *Death and Burial in the Roman World* (London, 1971). A book which covers the Roman period through to the late medieval and which contains an interesting article on disease is S. Bassett (ed.), *Death in Towns* (Leicester, 1992). More recent evidence has also been collected in R. Philpott, *Burial Practices in Roman Britain* (Oxford, 1991).

Chapter 8

A monumental work, which contains everything one wants to know about baths and bathing in the empire is I. Nielson, *Thermae et Balnea, Vols I and II* (Aarhus, 1990). Chariot- and horse-racing are now well covered in J.H. Humphrey, *Roman Circuses: Arenas for Chariot Racing* (London, 1986), while gladiatorial matters are dealt with in M. Grant, *Gladiators* (London, 1967). Still useful also is the chapter on recreations (Chapter 13) in J. Liversidge, *Britain in the Roman Empire* (London, 1968). Functions of the theatre are contained in W. Beare, *The Roman Stage* (London, 1950). The comprehensive survey of all manner of buildings in A. Boethius and J.B. Ward-Perkins, *Etruscan and Roman Architecture* (Harmondsworth, 1970) naturally covers those used for recreational purposes. M. Henig, *Art in Roman Britain* (London, 1995) is a worthy successor to the two books by J.M.C. Toynbee, *Art in Britain under the Romans* (London, 1964) and *Art in Roman Britain* (London, 1962). Also of interest in this context are J.M.C. Toynbee, *Animals in Roman Life and Art* (London, 1973) and H.J.R. Murray, *A History of Board Games other than Chess* (London, 1952). Finally, no account of leisure activities would be complete without a reference to Roman cookery: B. Flower and E. Rosenbaum (eds), *Apicius: the Roman Cookery Book* (London, 1958).

Chapter 9

The contentious subject of the end of Roman Britain has produced much literature. Among the earlier versions are: J.N.L. Myres, *Anglo-Saxon Pottery and the Settlement of England* (Oxford, 1969); L. Alcock, *Arthur's Britain* (London, 1971); E.A. Thompson, *The Early Germans* (Oxford, 1965). More recently M. Todd, *The Northern Barbarians* (London, 1975); S. Johnson, *Later Roman Britain* (London, 1989) have fleshed out the arguments. A slighter book of equal interest is C.J. Arnold, *Roman Britain to Saxon England* (Beckenham, 1984). Most provocative and not always credible is R. Reece, 'Town and Country; the end of Roman Britain' in *World Archaeology* 12, i (1980), 77–92. A monumental treatment of the period – not always easy to comprehend – is J. Morris, *The Age of Arthur* (London, 1973), while a collection of papers by P.J. Casey (ed.), *The End of Roman Britain* (Oxford, 1979) looks more closely at a variety of associated topics.

Index